Capitalist Goals,
Socialist Past

Capitalist Goals, Socialist Past

The Rise of the Private Sector in Command Economies

EDITED BY

Perry L. Patterson

Westview Press

BOULDER • SAN FRANCISCO • OXFORD

This Westview softcover edition is printed on acid-free paper and bound in library-quality, coated covers that carry the highest rating of the National Association of State Textbook Administrators, in consultation with the Association of American Publishers and the Book Manufacturers' Institute.

Published in 1993 in the United States of America by Westview Press, Inc., 5500 Central Avenue, Boulder, Colorado 80301-2877, and in the United Kingdom by Westview Press, 36 Lonsdale Road, Summertown, Oxford OX2 7EW

Library of Congress Cataloging-in-Publication Data
Capitalist goals, socialist past : the rise of the private sector in
   command economies / edited by Perry L. Patterson.
      p.   cm.
   Includes index.
   ISBN 0-8133-8402-8
   1. Privatization—Europe, Eastern.   2. Privatization—Former
Soviet republics.   I. Patterson, Perry L.
HD4140.7.C37   1993
338.947—dc20   93-20305
                                                                                            CIP

Printed and bound in the United States of America

The paper used in this publication meets the requirements
of the American National Standard for Permanence of Paper
for Printed Library Materials Z39.48-1984.

10   9   8   7   6   5   4   3   2   1

Contents

Acknowledgments

This book grew out of a panel (suggested by Herbert Levine) on the rise of private entrepreneurship presented at the 1989 meetings of the American Association for the Advancement of Slavic Studies. Since then, the nature of the Central and East European regimes discussed, the group of authors, and the outlines of the book itself have changed dramatically in a process of natural evolution. I am grateful to all who played a role in the project at an earlier stage, whether or not their names appear in this final product.

Along the way, I have accumulated debts to the following individuals, who have read various portions of this manuscript or who have identified potential contributors: Janet Mitchell, Erik Whitlock, Kristin Onofrio, Mike Marrese, Milan Vodopivec, Stuart Brown, Joel Leander, Doug Fordham, Amber Corbin, and Faye Kisel. Their (so far) unrequited help has been most appreciated. In addition, I wish to thank Rebecca Ritke, our editor at Westview Press, for her early and unflagging support for this project.

Perry L. Patterson

1

Overview: The Return of the Private and Cooperative Sectors in Eastern Europe and the Soviet Union

Perry L. Patterson

The nations of Eastern Europe and the former Soviet Union have all embarked in recent years on a dramatic course for turning their state-owned economies into economies where a private sector will grow and perhaps predominate. Yet, as dramatic as reform intentions may be, it has now become clear that the road to reform is strewn with landmines capable of delaying or subverting even the best-laid plans. Throughout the former Communist nations, plans for reform have been repeatedly proposed—some have even been implemented—yet the region as a whole remains in political and economic crisis. Private sectors have grown in all of the nations, yet the nature of those private sectors has received much deserved criticism, as we shall see.

Much also remains from the Communist years. This includes everything from firms still owned (or heavily influenced) by the state, to long-ingrained cultural and bureaucratic attitudes toward private entrepreneurship and markets. Thus this book begins with a survey of the role of the private sector (including semi-private cooperative forms) during the years of traditional socialism.

The nations of Eastern Europe and the Soviet Union have frequently shared similar attitudes toward private and cooperative enterprise in the years since World War II. In the pre-Gorbachev years, the official ideology tended to rank state–owned-and-operated enterprise as the most "pure" form of socialism, followed by cooperative (or collectively-managed) enterprise, and with truly private forms considered largely a regrettable relic of the capitalist past.[1] In more recent times, however, a widespread trend of redefining "socialism" to include private enterprise emerged, and cooperative enterprise has often been praised as both more effective and more truly "socialist" in outcome than state-run forms.

Despite similar official ideologies regarding the private and cooperative sectors, however, considerable differences in actual policy toward
such enterprises existed both well before *perestroika* and as reforms began
in the 1980s. Thus, a major goal of this book is to acquaint the reader with
both the shared features and the diversity of the private and cooperative
experience in the nations of the (formerly) Communist bloc of Europe.
In addition, we hope to provide an understanding of the challenges
now being faced as the former socialist nations seek to create economies
driven largely by prospering private entrepreneurs.

Why the Private Sector Is Needed

Theoretical Issues

While the advantages of a privately-owned market economy may
seem obvious to many in the developed nations of the West, such advantages were long denied in the Soviet bloc, or were at the very least held to
be less decisive than the virtues of central ownership and planning. Thus,
a review of major points in this debate seems in order.

The capitalist argument for a privately-based market economy has
often begun by considering the efficiency associated with small-scale, privately-owned, "perfectly competitive" firms. As any Western micro-
economics textbook will demonstrate, "perfect competition"—consisting
of markets with many small privately-owned firms and with ease of
entry and exit to and from each industry—should lead to outcomes
where firms produce output at minimal cost and are unable to gain excessive profits. Thus, consumers pay the minimum possible price for the
goods they want. Furthermore, freely fluctuating prices, influenced by
consumer demand, lead the firms to produce (at least approximately) the
mix of goods desired by the public.

Socialist arguments for central ownership and planning might start by
noting the seeming dominance of very large firms, or "monopolies," in
capitalist economies. If, indeed, "monopolies" predominate, then little
effective competition may ensue among capitalist enterprises, and the
large firms may choose to operate at above-minimum cost, to tack on
large profit margins, and to engage in advertising practices designed to
lead, rather than follow, consumer demand. Thus, the private, capitalist
economy seems to be one where consumers both pay more for goods
than necessary, and also consume plenty of goods that they would avoid
in the absence of advertising pressures. In the meantime, capitalist
owners get rich through excessively high profits. This, in turn, may lead
to a subversion of political democracy.

While both of the above arguments are open to criticism, the important point is that the Communist parties of Eastern Europe and the Soviet Union were long firmly convinced that an economy could be run more successfully via socialist planning than by capitalist markets. Interestingly, and despite the socialist critique of monopoly under capitalism, practical socialist planning meant creating a network of state monopoly firms (on the basis of possibly lower average costs associated with large production runs), but then carefully controlling most operating decisions via central governmental institutions and ministries. In this model, one could allege that the state, knowing the consumption desires of the populace, could force firms to produce what was desired, and at lowest possible prices. Moreover, the state would reap any excess profits, applying them to various social needs (including investment for long-run growth), and preventing wide discrepancies among the standards of living of various social groups.[2]

Economic Performance of the Nations of Eastern Europe

The issue of who was right in the above debate was never tested under ideal circumstances. Economic socialism in the East was combined with political totalitarianism of a sort which seemed destined to sap the strength of long-run creativity in the Soviet bloc, regardless of potential strengths of a democratically-controlled socialism. The very strong association of socialism with totalitarianism in many minds led, in addition, to the seeming decision at the end of the 1980s to throw out much of socialism along with the Communist parties which had instituted socialism by force.

As the nations of Eastern Europe and the former Soviet Union have increasingly opted for a transition to privately-owned market economies, the available data on the performance of the socialist economies seem largely to support the transition. That is, socialism as it existed ultimately failed to deliver on many of its promises. In particular, after apparent early growth spurts, all of the most developed socialist economies showed noticeable signs of slowing down in the 1970s and clearly began to fall behind much of the developed West in the 1980s. For economies which had long restricted private consumption in favor of massive capital investment initiatives, the failure of socialism to grow faster than capitalism in later years was particularly damaging. As the peoples of the Soviet bloc began to realize the failures of the system, morale suffered as well; the period of the late 70s and early 80s in the Soviet Union came to be called the "period of stagnation." The appellation would have applied well throughout the region.

Table 1.1 shows some of the details of the decline in growth rates experienced in Eastern Europe and the Soviet Union.[3] Table 1.2 gives per

Table 1.1
Real per Capita Income
Average Annual Growth Rates (percent)

	1970-75	1975-80	1980-86	1980-86 compared to 1970-75	
	(1)	(2)	(3)	(4)[a] (3)/(1)	(5)[b] (3)-(1)
Bulgaria	5.7	2.6	3.5	.61	2.2
Hungary	4.6	1.7	1.9	.41	2.7
GDR	5.7	4.2	4.4	.77	1.3
Poland	8.7	3.0	-1.3	--	10.0
Romania	11.1	6.9	4.0[d]	.36[d]	7.1[d]
USSR	4.4	3.3	2.3	.52	2.1
Czechoslovakia[c]	4.6	3.3	1.4	.30	3.2

[a]Comparison via ratio of 1980-86 growth rates to those of 1970-75.
[b]Comparison via difference between 1980-86 growth rates and those of 1970-75.
[c]Produced national income per worker in material production sector.
[d]Data through 1985 only.
Source: Patterson, "Domestic Economic Reform," 28; and *Statisticheskii ezhegodnik stran-chlenov soveta ekonomicheskoi vzaimopomoshchi* (Moscow: Finansy i statistika, 1987), 17, 18, 20, 23-26.

capita income levels as well. These tables reveal that, among the nations surveyed here, East Germany and Czechoslovakia had managed to produce the highest income levels in the bloc, and that their rate of slowdown had been comparatively mild. Thus, it was possible for Czech and East German leaders to argue for a time in 1987–88 that their nations did not need the radical reforms seemingly underway elsewhere. However, by 1990–91, reform had come to all parts of the bloc, and even the East German showcase of socialist successes came to look very pale in comparison with the West Germany with which it merged.

Table 1.2
Per Capita GNP in 1985
(in 1985 $US, at purchasing power parity)

United States	$16700
USSR	7400
Bulgaria	6420
Czechoslovakia	8750
East Germany	10440
Hungary	7560
Poland	6470
Romania	5450

Source: CIA, *Handbook of Economic Statistics, 1986* (Washington, DC: USGPO, 1986).

Private Market Activity Under Socialism

Despite repeated and often brutal attempts, the communist parties of the Soviet Union and Eastern Europe never quite succeeded in eliminating the private sector. Despite ideological fears that the private sector represented a class enemy whose main aim was to destroy the "workers' states," the governments of the East frequently had to recognize that private activity was both inevitable, and, often, actually beneficial from the point of view of the state. Thus, as early as 1921, Lenin was forced to allow the reintroduction of private retail trade and small-scale production in the Soviet Union. It is true that this was eliminated by 1930, but private agricultural output remained an important source of food throughout the Soviet period. In Eastern Europe, East Germany never fully eliminated private retail outlets and cafes; Poland kept an extensive small-scale independent farm sector; Hungary ended forced collectivization of agriculture in the second half of the 1950s; Yugoslavia embarked on a system of generalized collective "workers' management," if not full ownership, in the late 1940s.

Table 1.3 shows that the legal private sectors of the socialist states often made noticeable contributions to output and consumption levels. Thus, for example, in 1970, the non-socialized (private) sector in Poland officially made up 25.1 percent of national income (socialist definition), and constituted 84.6 percent of gross agricultural output. In the same year, 14.1 percent of East German income, 15.9 percent of industrial output, and 19.3 percent of retail trade and restaurant sales came from the non-socialized sector (although each of these figures declined noticeably in subsequent years). Only the Soviet Union, Bulgaria, and Czechoslovakia reported consistently negligible impact of non-socialist output over the period 1970–88. In these cases, ideology seems to have played a role both in reducing private output and in minimizing the official reporting of any such output. In the Soviet case (and probably those of Bulgaria and Czechoslovakia, as well), output not sold directly to the state was simply not reported in national income statistics.

An additional contribution to national well-being which could not have been included in official statistics came from the illegal and semi-legal private sector. Though such output is hard to measure in any nation, and almost certainly varied in its impact across the socialist states of Europe, we know that illegality did not prevent a substantial amount of private activity in sectors which were either wholly illegal or were deemed state monopolies. Thus, for example, private automobiles were frequently turned into taxis despite state transportation monopolies; doctors frequently brought home the bulk of their income (unreported for tax purposes) from private consultations; private

Table 1.3
The Share of the Non-Socialist Sector
in the Economies of the Soviet Union and Eastern Europe[a]
(percent)

	1970	1980	1985	1986	1987	1988
National Income						
Bulgaria	0.3	--	--	--	--	--
Hungary	2.6	3.5	6.3	6.5	6.8	7.1
GDR	14.1	3.5	3.4	3.5	3.5	3.6
Poland	25.1	15.6	19.8	19.0	17.8	18.8
Romania	3.3	4.5	--	--	--	--
USSR	0.0	0.0	0.0	0.0	0.0	0.0
Czechoslovakia	0.8	0.5	0.6	0.7	0.8	0.7
Productive Capital Stock						
Bulgaria	0.1	0.0	0.0	0.0	0.0	0.0
Hungary	1.2	0.9	0.9	1.0	0.7	0.1
GDR	5.0	0.7	0.5	0.5	0.5	0.5
Poland	20.5	21.1	20.7	21.1	20.8	20.8
Romania	1.5	1.5	--	--	--	--
USSR	0.0	0.0	0.0	0.0	0.0	0.0
Czechoslovakia	1.3	0.7	0.7	0.6	0.5	0.5
Gross Industrial Output						
Bulgaria	0.4	0.2	0.1	0.1	0.1	0.2
Hungary	1.0	0.7	1.4	1.5	1.6	2.1
GDR	15.9	2.5	2.1	1.7	1.7	1.8
Poland	1.7	1.5	3.0	3.4	3.4	3.9
Romania	0.4	0.3	--	--	--	--
USSR	0.0	0.0	0.0	0.0	0.0	0.0
Czechoslovakia	0.0	0.0	0.0	0.0	0.0	0.0
Gross Agricultural Output						
Bulgaria	0.1	0.1	0.1	0.1	0.1	0.1
Hungary	1.5	1.1	0.7	0.7	0.7	0.7
GDR	6.7	4.7	5.5	5.2	5.1	5.0
Poland	84.6	77.3	78.6	78.5	78.4	78.8
Romania	19.8	15.0	--	--	--	--
USSR	0.0	0.0	0.0	0.0	0.0	0.0
Czechoslovakia	4.9	2.6	2.7	3.5	3.3	3.3

(Table continued on next page)

Table 1.3 (continued)

	1970	1980	1985	1986	1987	1988
Agricultural Acreage						
Bulgaria	3.4	0.0	0.1	0.1	0.1	0.1
Hungary	2.9	1.6	1.3	1.3	1.3	1.4
GDR	5.8	5.1	5.0	4.8	4.6	4.6
Poland	81.0	74.5	76.6	76.5	76.5	76.3
Romania	9.2	9.4	--	--	--	--
USSR	0.0	0.0	0.0	0.0	0.0	0.0
Czechoslovakia	10.0	4.3	4.1	4.0	4.0	3.9
Retail Trade and Restaurants						
Bulgaria	0.1	0.0	0.0	0.0	0.0	0.0
Hungary	0.8	0.8	1.8	2.2	2.3	2.7
GDR	19.3	11.6	11.3	11.2	11.2	11.3
Poland	1.2	1.5	2.4	2.3	2.4	2.7
Romania	0.0	0.0	0.0	0.0	0.0	0.0
USSR	0.0	0.0	0.0	0.0	0.0	0.0
Czechoslovakia	0.0	0.0	0.0	0.0	0.0	0.0

[a]Calculated in prices of varying years for some countries, with occasional rounding. See source.
Source: *Statisticheskii ezhegodnik stran-chlenov sovieta ekonomicheskoi vzaimopomoshchi* (Moscow: Finansy i statistika, 1989), 49–50.

plumbers could be hired to fix state-owned pipes, but only in exchange for vodka.

If the state often turned a blind eye to private production of the above consumer services, it remained much more concerned about private trading or "speculative" activities throughout the socialist era. Much of the illegal private sector devoted itself to the lucrative business of buying up underpriced state supplies of goods, and reselling them at higher prices under the table. Some of this activity involved outright theft from the workplace or via breaking and entering. However, a substantial part probably occurred with the full knowledge of well-placed and often-bribed bureaucrats. Thus, the profitability of illegal private distribution and redistribution led not only to high and illegal private incomes, but also to the corruption of large parts of the party and government elites. Redistributive activity therefore seemed to produce no new goods (even though it may have improved their distribution) and simultaneously weakened the resolve of the state sector. As such, "speculation," whether in meat, automobiles or hard currencies, remained an object of severe government sanction, but the natural profitability (arbitrage possibilities made possible by fixed prices) of this industry ensured its continuation. As the Communist parties lost power in recent years and government enforcement weakened, "speculative" behavior rapidly became so widespread that further battles against it seemed hopeless, except through the end of price controls and of government restrictions on wholesale and retail trade.[4]

Reform and the Reemergence of the Private and Cooperative Sectors

Beginnings of Reform, 1953–1985[5]

With the death of Stalin in 1953, pressures to reform the economic systems of Eastern Europe and the Soviet Union which had long been suppressed now came to be openly expressed. Thus, by 1956 both Hungary and Poland seemed ready to embark on significant reforms with substantial market and private-sector elements. Such reforms were postponed in the face of the Soviet invasion of Hungary in that year, but by 1965 liberalizing talk in the USSR led Hungary, Poland and Czechoslovakia to engage in a second round of reform discussions which went far beyond the intent of decentralizers in Moscow. This time, even the Soviet invasion of Czechoslovakia in 1968 failed to prevent implementation of significant reform in Hungary, in the form of the New Economic Mechanism.[6] This Hungarian reform, along with Yugoslav worker-managed socialism, produced an extended social experiment to which economic decisionmakers across the Soviet bloc would refer (often enviously) throughout the years prior to Gorbachev's rise to power in Moscow. Indeed, even in the difficult years of Polish martial law in the early 1980s, Poland adopted a series of measures leading toward an enhancement of the private sector and of worker democracy.[7]

Perestroika, Gorbachev and the Advent of Radical Change[8]

Despite repeated reform efforts in the years following Stalin's death, such measures—if implemented at all—remained highly limited until Mikhail Gorbachev became the General Secretary of the Communist Party of the Soviet Union in March 1985.[9] Even then, it was not until approximately 1987 that Gorbachev's reform rhetoric began to be taken seriously, and substantial changes commenced in the USSR.

Indeed, it is not clear that the Soviet Communist Party, or Gorbachev himself, expected anything like the *perestroika* which had developed by the end of the decade. Initial pronouncements from Moscow leaned in the direction of giving more democratic freedoms to individuals, and more economic flexibility to *state* enterprise management, but there was little initial push for the wholesale abandonment of state property. Thus it was not until the dramatic ouster of communist governments throughout the socialist bloc in 1989 that truly radical reform could be freely pursued. In the meantime, however, interesting experiments with new private, quasi-private, and collective enterprise forms began; initial legislation for regulating a new private sector was debated; and some of the difficulties associated with creating the new private economy began to be felt in the states which had gone the furthest, i.e., Poland, Hungary, and Yugoslavia.

The Cooperative Sector

Due largely to the influence of Yugoslavia's "worker management" (though perhaps also supported by Lenin himself and by examples from nations such as Japan), a major thrust of changes sought by the governments of Hungary, Poland, Bulgaria and the Soviet Union during 1987–88 was a strengthening of the cooperative sector. Each of these governments passed new laws allowing for state factory space to be leased out to cooperatives, strengthening the position of workers in electing and controlling management, and allowing a degree of participation in profits, all with the idea of turning around worker apathy on the job. Degrees of success in promoting "cooperative" schemes varied, however. Often, such organizational forms were readily turned into *de facto* private enterprises run for the profit of socialist bosses. Furthermore, as workers became more motivated to work overtime in the "cooperative" sector, they lost motivation to work hard at their state-sector jobs, thus contributing to the decline of state industry.[10] By 1992, most of the nations discussed here had come to see the "cooperative" movement largely as a rear guard attempt to preserve vestiges of the socialist past, and the newly-legal private sectors and private property as the wave of the future.[11]

Difficulties in the Restoration of the Private Sector

The reasons for the failure of the private sector to bring immediate prosperity are numerous. Social attitudes have not always encouraged entrepreneurial behavior; government policies have often both reflected and fostered such attitudes; credit and other institutions have not arisen quickly enough to meet the needs of new producers; and finally, the new entrepreneurs themselves have often not been fully prepared for their new roles. Let us now turn to evaluating each of these hindrances in more detail.

Social Attitudes

Social acceptance of the new private sector has varied considerably among the peoples of Eastern Europe and the former USSR. In the nations where Soviet power had been imposed only in the 1940s, some portions of the population remembered how the private sector had

worked prior to World War II. In some nations, such as Hungary, a gradual longer-term increase of the prevalence of private shops and cafes
probably contributed to a relative lack of controversy over such new
forms of business. However, in Russia, where private retail outlets had
been strictly illegal since 1930, passions flared. Conservative-thinking
thugs robbed and burned out many of the early cafes. Owners of such
establishments found they had to resort to private security guards to protect themselves, as the state police themselves often were unfriendly to
the new institutions, seeing them as the source of unfair profits. A belief
that many of the new establishments were being run by members of non-
Russian ethnic groups often further helped to encourage thoughtless
attacks on new private firms.

Legal Barriers

The socialist governments which remained in power throughout
Eastern Europe and the Soviet Union through approximately 1990 were
only grudgingly supportive of the new private sectors, and often made
the establishment and operation of private enterprise extremely problematic. Numerous hurdles could be established. Lengthy paperwork for
registration of a new enterprise, or bureaucratic complaints about the
"appropriateness" of private enterprise in a given industry (often one
dominated by poorly run state concerns) could easily prevent would-be
entrepreneurs from even getting started. Failure of the bureaucracy to
lease out space to private business could also make production impossible. Requirements for import and export licenses and restrictions on the
availability of hard currencies could severely limit the sort of enterprises
that could be established. Taxes could reach confiscatory levels. And
while the overall legal and regulatory climate seemed to improve somewhat during 1991 and 1992, remnants of such policies have continued to
restrict private initiative throughout the former Eastern bloc.

Institutional Gaps

Even in the absence of laws directly antithetical to private sector output, other institutional and structural problems seemed likely to conspire
against the rapid rise of a successful small-scale private sector. Banks remained largely in state hands or controlled by large-scale still-socialized
industry, and remained reluctant to lend to an unknown, untested private
sector (especially one possessing little collateral or accumulated wealth
to offer in security for a loan). The use of stock- and bond-like instruments for raising funds seemed likely to proceed slowly where populations were unfamiliar with such instruments, and where accounting
professions had no experience in auditing the necessary financial state-

ments. Even in the cases where necessary financial capital could be amassed, prospective entrepreneurs would often discover that state-owned industry refused to produce necessary inputs (or at least was slow to recognize private-sector needs). Thus, the millions of Polish small-scale farmers for many years could not get state industry to produce suitable mini-tractors. Cooperative cafes in Moscow found they had to make most food purchases through expensive private sources, whereas state restaurants retained access to cheap state supplies. In sum, a set of unavoidable institutional barriers conspired to limit the possible productivity of the new private producer.

"Human Capital" Deficiencies

Even if the above social, legal, and institutional barriers to entrepreneurial success and general prosperity had disappeared overnight, it is likely that progress would still have been slow (and will remain so) due to "human capital" deficiencies in the new private entrepreneurs themselves. Forty-plus years of socialism in Eastern Europe and seventy-plus years in the Soviet Union have had considerable consequences for the successful operation of private enterprises. "Socialism" in most cases had meant no advertising, no organized capital markets, little contact with the demands of foreign markets, and the suppression of independent economic research. The consequences of such policies are that the new entrepreneurs are not well prepared to think about marketing issues or about difficult financial questions. Most of the new entrepreneurs are probably unfamiliar with such basic ideas as supply and demand charts and compound interest, and unfortunately, so are many of their potential teachers. Standard economics, financial, marketing, and legal texts from the West have only begun to make their presence felt. It seems certain that it will take a generation to produce the accountants, lawyers, MBAs and other professionals needed for direct competition with the capitalists whose skills have not atrophied.

Two Paths Toward a Private-Sector Economy

As the nations of Central and Eastern Europe came to the realization that the private and cooperative sectors were likely to increase their roles over time, two separate, but related demands have arisen: (1) the need to privatize (or cooperatize) existing state-owned enterprise; and (2) the need to promote new private and cooperative enterprises operating with new capital (from personal savings or foreign investment).

The privatization of existing state assets has so far received the greatest attention in the literature, and deserves attention here as well, as we survey the economic transitions underway in many of the nations of the former socialist bloc. However, the main focus here is on the growth of genuinely new (often small-scale) enterprises, defined as those operating with newly-created capital or producing heretofore non-existent products. Thus, we ask:

- What industries have been conducive to private and cooperative sector growth and why?
- What state regulations have helped and/or hindered the formation and operation of such new enterprises?
- What is the relation of large-scale privatization of current state-owned enterprise to the formation of new entities?

Difficulties in the Reemergence of the Non-State Sectors

As the former East-bloc nations have sought to create new private sectors for themselves, they have quickly discovered a host of reasons that this is much easier said than done. A sort of Murphy's Law ("if it can go wrong, it will") has often seemed to apply, where vitally needed and well-intended reforms have foundered on the rocks of a reality left over from the command-economy past. Examples of this are numerous. Remnants of a fixed-price system lead to all sorts of opportunities to steal goods at low prices from the state and resell them on private markets at a huge profit. "Old-boy" networks have remained in place (despite the abolition of communist parties), with considerable opportunities to gain access to property and new markets (notably hard currency) via payment of appropriate bribes. Price reforms have not always generated overnight improvements in goods availabilities, due to continued lack of distribution infrastructure and other production inputs. The new private and cooperative entrepreneurs have often engaged more in servicing foreigners and state-sector industry than in producing goods of immediate interest to consumers. The results of opening new markets have thus turned out to be disappointing to economists who made recommendations for privatization and for the populations who may have believed overly optimistic claims of reformist politicians.

Policy Dilemmas in the Transition Phase[12]

Unfortunately, it now appears that there are no easy solutions to the above-mentioned problems of transition. The chapters in this volume testify to the defects of plans put forth by numerous governments and by international organizations such as the International Monetary Fund, all of which turned to respected economists (both domestic and foreign) for advice on how to engineer the transition.

There seems to be little consensus on a whole range of important issues. For example, should the former socialist nations first devote efforts to promoting the small-scale indigenous private sector or should they first privatize existing large state firms? On the one hand, a fledgling small-scale capitalist will often find it hard to get supplies from and make sales to an ongoing state sector. Thus, the indigenous sector may fail to blossom. On the other hand, the privatization of state-owned firms in the absence of pre-existing (and competitive) private markets for related materials and firms may founder on the rocks of the "valuation question," i.e., of deciding what the state firm is worth.

Similar dilemmas plague the arena of regulation and taxation of the new private firms. Goals of preventing huge income and wealth disparities during the transition are easily translated into tax rates or operating restrictions which can make the new private sector a very unattractive proposition. The desperate need for balanced government budgets also places pressure for high taxes on the new entrepreneurs at both the firm and the individual level, especially since the privatization of existing state firms deprives the state of automatic revenues in the form of those firms' profits. Additional pressures arise from the need to fund (previously unnecessary) unemployment insurance.

The question of when to allow freely-determined market prices also interacts with questions of the transition to a private sector in very complicated ways. Suppose that a private firm sees that a state firm will sell goods at half the price which can be obtained through private channels (due to partially continuing price controls). Then, an obvious way for the private firm to prosper is to buy the state firm's goods (perhaps with the lubrication of a bribe), and re-sell them. Unfortunately, there is no obvious social benefit to such a transaction,[13] and the owners of the state firm (the nation's taxpayers) lose out while the owners of the private firm become rapidly more wealthy at the expense of the former.

The alternative to the above scenario—free up prices first, then begin privatization—may not be much better. Since the existing state industries are often dominated by single monopoly sellers, there will be a natural inclination to raise price above costs of production (and to reduce output). Moreover, as long as the banking system is willing to passively make loans to buyer firms regardless of their credit records, the buyer firms face no real incentives to bargain on price. Demand is, in a sense, unlimited. The likely result is skyrocketing prices with little increase in output levels.

There is a quick, but probably naive, answer to all of the above "sequencing dilemmas": "Do everything at once!" But this, too, is probably impossible, due to the very real legislative constraints of reforming an entire economy, while simultaneously reforming the political decisionmaking process in ways designed to enhance democracy, and hence, the right for all sides of economic debates to make their voices heard. Furthermore, social and cultural habits and biases seem unlikely to change fundamentally and quickly, even with the best of new policies. The reality is that no painless transition path or velocity seems likely to be found, and that the policy dilemmas discussed in this book are likely to remain unresolved for many years.

The Role of the Private Sector in the Transition Process

The fledgling private sectors of formerly communist Eastern and Central Europe interact in complex ways with the rest of the economic, social, and political institutions of those nations. On the one hand, a successful private sector might reinforce social and political change. On the other hand, the private sector is itself dependent on the continuing reform of supporting institutions such as regulatory agencies, banks, educational facilities and remaining state-owned firms.

This broad range of mutual dependencies is reflected throughout the chapters which follow. Thus, Ben Slay (Chapters 2 and 9), John Tedstrom (Chapter 3), and Evan Kraft (Chapter 6) focus on why the private sector is needed in the formerly socialist nations, and what particular contributions might be expected from that sector. The two chapters by Slay ask what sectors of the Polish economy seem most conducive to development of private firms, and what methods seem best suited to rapidly producing a functioning private sector. Tedstrom focuses on the need for a form of privatizing in Russia which would best create a "middle class," and the political and economic mindset which might accompany that class. Kraft investigates the size distribution of Yugoslav enterprises, with the aim of understanding what sort of firms have traditionally been lacking under socialism, and what sort are therefore most needed.

Other contributors to this volume ask what the new East European private sector will need in order to function well. Thus Michael Murphy (Chapter 7) investigates exit and entry incentives affecting the quasi private cooperative firms of the Soviet *perestroika* era, and asks what regulatory changes need to be considered to promote a reasonable degree of competitiveness and long-run thinking on the part of the new entrepreneurs, both cooperative and private. Dennis Rondinelli (Chapter 5) discusses the management and business development needs of Czech and Slovak private firms. David Bartlett (Chapter 8) examines the Hungarian experience with creating the sort of commercial banking structure needed by a growing private sector. Catherine Sokil-Milnikiewicz (Chapter 4) also focuses on Hungary in a search for lessons to be drawn from twenty years of attempting to promote a private sector in a challenging and ever-changing political environment.

The overwhelming sense of the chapters which follow is that a well-functioning East European private sector is both crucially important and terribly difficult to produce from scratch. It is our hope that the reader will seek and find here a better understanding of the dilemmas facing those nations whose socialist pasts are now receding, and whose futures seem to promise ever-greater attention to the goals of a prosperous, private-sector capitalism.

Notes

1. Initially, many co-ops were self-governing labor groups with little of their own capital. These groups would provide their services while utilizing state-owned facilities or equipment. Yugoslav adherence to collective "worker-management" principles was an exception to the preference for state control stated in the text.

2. For an introductory discussion of the mechanisms and rationales of the planned, or "command" economy, see Paul R. Gregory and Robert C. Stuart, *Soviet Economic Structure and Performance*, 4th ed. (New York: Harper & Row, 1990).

3. This section and accompanying tables are based on Perry L. Patterson, "Domestic Economic Reform in the Soviet Union and Eastern Europe: Causes and Interdependence," *Jahrbuch der Wirtschaft Osteuropas* 13, no. 2 (1989): 7–40.

4. An excellent source of detailed information on the Soviet second economy is *Berkeley-Duke Occasional Papers on the Second Economy in the USSR* (Duke University, 1985–1992).

5. This section is based largely on Patterson, "Domestic Economic Reform."

6. For a description of the New Economic Mechanism, see Sokil-Milnikiewicz, Chapter 4, this volume.

7. See Slay, Chapter 2, this volume.

8. For a thorough review of the plans put forth in the early years of Soviet *perestroika*, see Ed A. Hewett, *Reforming the Soviet Economy* (Washington, D.C.: The Brookings Institution, 1988).

9. Ben Slay (Chapter 2) and Evan Kraft (Chapter 6) both refer to a pattern of allowing growth of the private sector only within the limits necessary to ameliorate some of the major problems associated with state-sector production.

10. See Chapter 2.

11. See Murphy, Chapter 7, for a description of some of the regulatory reasons the cooperative sector may have failed to live up to expectations in the Soviet Union. For a description of the initial wave of cooperative formation in the Soviet Union, see Anthony Jones and William Moskoff, *Ko-ops: the Rebirth of Entrepreneurship in the Soviet Union* (Bloomington, IN: Indiana University Press, 1991).

12. A detailed and careful discussion of the possible macroeconomic consequences of privatization is contained in Hans Blommestein and Michael Marrese, eds., *Transformation of Planned Economies: Property Rights Reform and Macroeconomic Stability* (Paris: Organisation for Economic Co-operation and Development, 1991).

13. See, however, Murphy, Chapter 7, for suggestions that such redistributions may, in fact, be beneficial.

PART ONE

The Development
of Small-Scale Enterprise
in Former Command Economies

2

The Indigenous Private Sector in Poland

*Ben Slay**

The relatively large size of Poland's private sector, and the priority assigned to the growth of private enterprise since the unseating of the Polish United Workers' Party (PUWP) in August 1989, make the Polish case particularly important in the study of ownership transformation in the post-communist economies. As of early 1992, according to official statistics, the private sector employed over half of Poland's labor force[1] and, unofficially, probably accounted for close to 50 percent of Polish GNP.

The creation of a new private-sector economy in Poland is proceeding via two routes: (1) privatization, understood as the transfer of state property to private actors; and (2) the creation of new, or indigenous, private firms, usually of small size. Despite the attention which has been focused on privatization, growth in private enterprise since 1989 has occurred largely as a result of the formation and expansion of private firms that had not previously belonged to the state. This indigenous private sector has thus far been the driving force behind ownership transformation in Poland. (For a discussion of the privatization of state property, see Chapter 9.)

The indigenous private sector was an important feature of the Polish economy even prior to the collapse of state socialism in 1989. Because of the burdens under which it labored during the communist era (1949–1989), the private sector has traditionally suffered from serious cases of market failure, including firm sizes too small to capture economies of scale and scope, imperfect competition, corruption and regulatory abuse. While the liberalization of the private sector's legal and economic

* The author would like to thank the Radio Free Europe/Radio Liberty Research Institute for the research materials upon which this chapter is based, as well as the Social Science Research Council and American Council of Learned Societies for research funding.

environment that began in the late 1980s may solve some of these problems, it is unclear how much progress has been made since 1989.

The Private Sector in Poland: Historical Background

As occurred throughout Eastern Europe, the mixed economy of 1945–
1948 was replaced in Poland after 1949 with the Soviet model, based
upon the virtually complete nationalization of private industry and services and the collectivization of agriculture. Although agriculture was
decollectivized after the anti-Stalinist uprising of October 1956, the 1960s
and 1970s saw attempts at "voluntary" collectivization through economic
pressures. Prices for farm products were set at low levels relative to the
cost of agricultural inputs, and land was gradually socialized through
private sales to the state land fund.[2] Attempts at mollifying private farmers after the unrest of 1970–1971 were followed by retrenchment later in
the decade. The legal private sector's share of the non-agricultural labor
force displayed a downward trend during 1949–1972, with the exceptions
of 1955–1958 and 1964–1968 (see Figure 2.1).

The initial Stalinist assault on private enterprise confined the legal

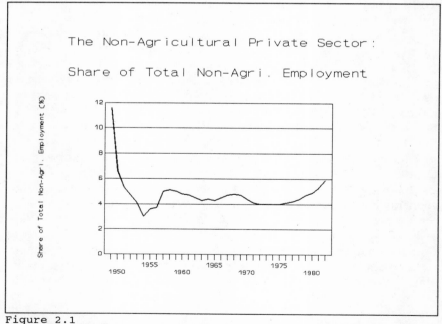

Figure 2.1
Source: Adapted from Anders Aaslund, *Private Enterprise in
Eastern Europe* (London: Macmillan, 1985), 230–231.

private sector to a small margin of the Polish economy, while driving many other private activities underground. However, because the "socialized" sector (consisting of state-owned firms and large cooperatives) was unable to effectively satisfy consumer demands, the communist political leadership would "uncork" private enterprise during periods of political tensions, in order to increase the quantity and quality of goods available to the population. The private sector would enjoy a short period of liberalization, and private activities would temporarily flourish. Once the tensions had abated, however, the antipathy towards the private sector reasserted itself, the screws upon the private sector were retightened, and the private sector's role in the economy again declined.

As Aaslund points out, these swings in the private sector's prospects under socialism in Poland can be correlated with changes in political stability.[3] (This correlation is sometimes referred to as "Aaslund's Law.") These swings are apparent in Figure 2.1 and Table 2.1, showing that the private sector's share of the labor force increased during times of political instability. The political crisis of 1956, brought on by the collapse of Polish Stalinism during 1953–1956, was the first example. The popular uprising in 1956 and Wladyslaw Gomulka's dramatic rise to power that just averted Soviet military action in Poland correspond to the expansion of the private sector's share of the labor force during 1955–1958 (Figure 2.1). Official policy towards the private sector during this time was less

Table 2.1
Private Sector Employment, 1980-1990

Year	Private Share of Total Employment	Private Share of Non-Agricultural Employment
1980	28.0%	3.5%
1981	29.1	3.8
1982	30.8	4.1
1983	30.7	4.6
1984	30.5	5.1
1985	30.5	5.3
1986	30.1	5.6
1987	30.1	6.2
1988	30.4	7.0
1989	33.3[a]	8.8[a]
	47.2[b]	21.7[b]
1990	38.9[a]	12.1[a]
	50.0[b]	22.6[b]

[a]1984 (old) prices.
[b]1989 (new) prices.
Source: *Rocznik Statystyczny* (Warsaw: Glowny Urzad Statystyczny, 1985), 55; *Rocznik Statystyczny* (1990), 93; and *Rocznik Statystyczny* (1991), xiv-xv.

rapacious than it had been during the previous five years, and in some cases even encouraged the private sector's expansion. The spontaneous decollectivization of agriculture that occurred during 1956 was officially recognized by the Gomulka leadership, and the urban private sector enjoyed a brief period of liberalization during 1956–1958. Credits were offered to private artisans, and entrepreneurs were permitted to make limited use of state production facilities. Gomulka turned to more conservative economic and political policies after 1957, however. Media censorship was tightened, the workers' councils established during 1956 were swallowed up in "self-management" confederations dominated by the PUWP, and the economic reforms elaborated by Oskar Lange, Michal Kalecki and other members of the Economic Council during 1956–1958 were not introduced. These developments correspond to the post-1958 decline in the private sector's share of the labor force (Figure 2.1).

The political and economic crisis of 1979–1982 produced another period of expansion for the private sector, as its share of the labor force increased from 4.4 to 5.9 percent (Figure 2.1). In addition to a 24-percent decline in national income produced,[4] triple-digit inflation (in 1982), and Poland's request to reschedule its foreign debt (1981), the 1979–1982 period was characterized by the political turbulence of Solidarity's initial challenge to the PUWP (1980–1981) and the subsequent period of martial law (1981–1983). The Jaruzelski regime's attempts at political "normalization" during 1982–1986 were accompanied by a small decline in the private sector's share of the labor force (Table 2.1), while heightening economic and political tensions after 1987—leading ultimately to the collapse of Poland's communist regime in 1989—saw the private share increase again.

These swings had important behavioral implications for private entrepreneurs. The initial assault on the private sector implemented during 1948–1953 effectively restricted it to market niches about which the captains of socialist industry were generally unconcerned, such as small-scale services and handicrafts. These niches afforded private producers a certain sanctuary, since the absence of state firms and large cooperatives meant little competition and relatively unsatiated consumer demands. Sanctuary was not stability, however. Harassment of the private sector took the form of legal restrictions, confiscatory and unstable tax policies,[5] and propaganda campaigns against "speculators" and "bloodsuckers."[6]

Because of the PUWP's legal, fiscal and political hostility, as well as constantly changing regulations, few private activities could be carried out without violating at least some laws. Since all private enterprise came to involve some degree of illegality, the distinction between "legal" and "illegal" activities became less clear. Otherwise honest entrepreneurs had no choice but to live on the edge of the law. This sometimes predatory and always uncertain regulatory environment produced widespread tax evasion and other forms of corruption within the private sector. (See Chapter 3 for a discussion of links between the private sector and corruption in the Soviet case). Bribery and corruption of regulatory agents also became the inevitable companions of private enterprise in People's Poland. In addition to higher costs associated with small-scale production, premiums for corruption and risk caused private-sector prices to be even higher than would otherwise have been the case. And since private firms in this system often had to pay for political "protection" to function, regulatory agents acquired a vested interest in preserving the status quo. Regulatory obstacles served as barriers to entry for other private entrepreneurs, allowing existing firms to enjoy monopoly positions within their niches and providing regulatory agents with a "take" of their monopoly rents. While elements of the public may have resented the private sector's high prices, "speculative" behavior and illegal activities, consumers also valued the respite private enterprise offered from the vagaries of the official economy.

Entrepreneurs in such an environment had few incentives to make long-term investments in their firms, or to be especially concerned about product quality or service. Rather, they were encouraged to adopt low-volume, high mark-up business strategies in order to make a quick killing and get out before things went sour. As one observer noted about Polish entrepreneurs:

"In the absence of stability they tended to invest grudgingly, looking for quick and easy profit. . . . Little wonder, then that the 'lower turnover, less trouble' attitude took root in the community of private entrepreneurs."[7]

In more formal terms, the private sector's weaknesses manifested themselves in problems associated with small-scale production, imperfect competition and informational asymmetries. According to official data, the average domestically-owned private firm in 1987 only employed two individuals.[8] These small private firms tended to use technologies that were obsolete even in comparison to state firms, and had a relatively low propensity to absorb innovation. According to one estimate, 90 percent of privately-owned workshops in the late 1980s were "equipped with outdated machinery, many times repaired in the past."[9] Imperfect competition refers to the lack of competition among sellers in their monopolized niches, the barriers to entry created by the regulatory environment, and the weak role of such dynamic-competition elements as product and process innovation. Informational asymmetries reflect the absence of informational (indeed any kind of) advertising, the absence of well-defined brands, trademarks and copyrights to induce private entrepreneurs to cultivate brand loyalty, and the dissatisfied consumer's inability to seek redress through official channels.

These developments in the private sector were accompanied by what might be called the etatization of Poland's cooperative sector. During 1949–1956 small, independent cooperatives were amalgamated into larger units whose management was selected from the PUWP *nomenklatura*, and whose autonomy was administratively subordinated to national co-operative congresses complete with their own central and intermediate-layer organs. In 1985, for example, the 12,000 cooperatives then func-tioning in Poland were grouped into one of 16 intermediate-layer "central cooperative associations," which in turn answered to the "Supreme Council of Cooperatives."[10] Prior to 1989, intermediate-layer cooperative organs were present at the regional level as well.

These "state cooperatives" functioned in essentially the same regu-latory environment as state enterprises. In contrast to the USSR and Hun-gary, where cooperatives in the 1980s had come to function as proxies for private enterprise in numerous industrial and agricultural branches, the Polish cooperative sector had more in common with the state sector than with the private sector. Prior to 1989, the state and cooperative sectors both had three-tiered organizational structures (central administration, intermediate layer, producers), high levels of industrial concentration, extensive wage regulations, political control through the PUWP *nomen-klatura*, administrative redistribution of profits, and few incentives for entrepreneurial behavior. It is instructive that, prior to 1990, official Polish statistics traditionally combined data from the state and coopera-tive sectors under the heading of the "socialized" (*uspoleczniony*) sector, often without distinguishing between the two.

Economic Reforms in the 1980s

The economic reforms introduced during the 1980s evolved out of the political and economic crisis of the 1979–1982 period. Facing catastrophic declines in income and output, the loss of the country's external credit-worthiness, the political challenge posed by Solidarity and intense popu-lar demands for change, the PUWP agreed in 1981 to introduce economic reforms.[11] Prior to 1987, these reforms were directed primarily at the state and cooperative sectors. The "Law on Cooperatives" approved by the Sejm (parliament) in September 1982 made cooperatives (like state enter-prises) legally "self-reliant," "self-managed" and "self-financing."[12] Increased legal autonomy for cooperatives came at the expense of the central and intermediate-layer organs; the authorities' prerogatives in issuing obligatory plan quotas were circumscribed; and financial instru-ments like taxes, subsidies and bank credits became more important. As in the state sector, however, inflationary pressures, shortage conditions, and formal and informal rationing programs administered by the central and local authorities reduced the influence of financial instruments. Also, the authorities' unwillingness to break up cooperatives that effectively monopolized wholesale trade on a regional basis helped preserve the highly-concentrated, administrative nature of many cooperative activities.

As mentioned above, the economic crisis of the late 1970s and early 1980s was largely responsible for these reforms. The specter of empty shelves during the economic collapse of 1979–1982 cemented the liberalizing trend towards the private sector begun after the 1976 strikes in Radom and Ursus. In particular, the Polish private sector experienced a period of rapid expansion (relative to the state and cooperative sectors) during the early 1980s (see Table 2.1) and the diversity of private activities broadened to include the following:[13]

1. Direct Foreign Investment: The 1979–1982 economic collapse convinced the PUWP leadership to encourage direct investment in Poland via small-scale "Polonia" firms, theoretically owned by Poles living abroad. After a period of rapid expansion during 1982–1984, the end of a three-year tax hiatus and a more restrictive administrative environment slowed the growth of the "Polonia" firms and reduced employment levels after 1984. However, 1986 legislation authorizing large-scale joint ventures between Polish and Western firms, followed by December 1988 liberalization of this law, resulted in the appearance of 250 large-scale joint ventures by June 1989.[14]

2. Leasing: Private individuals became authorized to lease facilities from the state and manage them privately for the duration of the lease. Originally restricted to shops, restaurants and kiosks in the 1970s, leasing after 1987 came to be practiced on a larger scale. In early 1989, for example, the state-owned electronics firm *Omig* in Warsaw was leased in its entirety to its manager.[15]

3. Economic Working Groups: Workers employed in state enterprises were permitted to contract with management to work overtime as a separate organization (*zespol gospodarczy*) and perform tasks that were not profitable or otherwise possible during the normal work day. Workers received higher payments that were subjected to lower wage taxes than day labor, thus reducing enterprise tax liabilities. These groups were similar in principle to the enterprise contract labor associations (VGMKs) introduced in Hungary during the early 1980s (see Chapter 4), although they did not acquire the significance of the Hungarian groups. In any case, many of these groups had been active in the underground economy prior to their legalization.

4. Corporations (*spolki*): The Economic Activity Act, passed in December 1988, permitted all economic organizations, regardless of their form of ownership, to engage in any legal business activity, as well as enter into partnerships with firms from other sectors. Poland's 1986 joint venture law was simultaneously liberalized as well. Together with the 1935 Commercial Code (which had never been formally annulled) and other laws passed during 1981–1989, this legislation led to the rapid formation of thousands of corporations and created the legal framework for the dramatic expansion in the private sector that began in 1989.

Sectoral Development in the 1980s

Despite the above-described enrichment of the private sector's organizational profile, the private sector according to official Polish statistics did not register significant increases in its legal share of aggregate economic activity (as measured by national income produced) during the 1980s. The private sector's expansion during this time is quite visible in industry, retail trade, and services to the population (Table 2.2), as well as in the growth rate of non-agricultural employment (Table 2.1). On the whole, however, the private sector's share of national income produced (Table 2.3) in 1989 was actually below its 1983 share. No clear pattern is present in agricultural production (Table 2.2): growth in the private sector's share relative to other sectors during 1980–1982 was followed by the socialized sector's resurgence during 1983–1984. After an increase in 1985, the private sector's share of agricultural output declined again during 1986–1989.

These data imply that claims about rapid private sector growth during the 1980s should be viewed with some reservation. Kaminski, for example, argues that the private sector experienced a transformation of sorts, as part of the state's loss of control over the Polish economy during the 1980s. While this argument may be true, it is difficult to sustain on the basis of the official Polish data on changes in the private share of national income produced, the most general measure of aggregate economic activity available for the 1980s (see Table 2.3).[16] Kaminski supports his case for the private sector's expansion by using official data describing the expansion of the non-agricultural private sector (see Table 2.1).[17] As we have seen, this provides a less than complete, and therefore somewhat misleading, view of the overall picture. Instead, as Table 2.3 shows, the official data indicate that the private sector's share of national income produced in 1989 was lower than it had been in 1983, and was only marginally higher in 1989 than it had been in 1980.

Official data also indicate relatively poor private-sector performance

Table 2.2
Sectoral Shares of Private Output

Year	Industry[a]	Agriculture[b]	Domestic Trade[c]	Consumer Services[d]
1980	1.5%	76.9%	1.6%	25.0%
1981	1.9	79.2	1.8	26.0
1982	2.1	80.0	1.9	29.8
1983	2.3	79.4	2.1	29.0
1984	2.6	78.4	2.3	29.7
1985	3.2	80.0	2.5	30.1
1986	3.4	79.8	2.3	31.7
1987	3.6	79.3	2.5	32.5
1988	3.9	79.5	2.9	34.3
1989	4.8[e]	79.0[e]	4.8[e]	42.4[e]
	16.2[f]	77.6[f]	59.5[f]	--
1990	11.6[e]	68.1[e]	26.3[e]	--
	17.4[f]	76.0[f]	63.9[f]	--

[a]Data for 1985-1989 are for gross sales (produkcja sprzedana przemyslu) measured in 1984 prices. Data for 1980-1984 are for gross output (produkcja globalna przemyuslu) measured in 1982 prices.
[b]Globalna produkcja rolnicza for 1985-1989 in 1984 (old) prices, and for 1989 - 1990 in constant (new) prices.
[c]Sprzedaz w handlu rynkowym detalicznym, (or sprzedaz detaliczna w handlu wewnetrznym), current prices.
[d]Sprzedaz uslug dla ludnosci, current prices.
[e]old
[f]new
Source: Rocznik Statystyczny (1985), 211, 282-283, 374; (1990), 260, 331, 415, 423; (1991) xvi, xviii.

in terms of labor productivity and efficiency of material usage. A comparison of Tables 2.1 and 2.3 shows that the relative constancy of the private sector's share of national income produced during the 1980s was accompanied by rapid increases in the share of labor inputs. Since real output essentially stagnated during the 1980s, this implies that labor productivity in the private sector declined during this period, in real terms. By contrast, real labor productivity in the socialized sector increased during 1985–1989.[18] This differential can not be explained by more rapid growth in the socialized sector's capital stock, either.[19] A similar story can be told for the material-intensity of production in the private and socialized sectors. While the material intensity (the "material cost" associated with 1000 zloty of national income produced) declined during 1985–1989 in both sectors, the 46 percent drop in the socialized sector dwarfed the 4 percent drop the private sector experienced during that time.[20] Moreover, by 1989 the material cost of producing 1000 zloty of national income in the private sector (818 zloty) actually exceeded the cost of producing 1000 zloty of national income in the socialized sector (651 zloty).[21]

There are non-efficiency explanations for the apparently greater mate-

Table 2.3
National Income Produced: Sectoral Distribution[a]

Year	State	Cooperative	Private
1980	72.4%	9.6%	17.5%
1981	61.2	8.0	30.4
1982	70.6	9.2	20.0
1983	71.1	8.9	19.6
1984	71.8	9.1	18.8
1985	71.5	9.9	18.2
1986	71.7	9.7	18.2
1987	72.5	9.8	17.2
1988	71.5	8.9	18.8
1989	69.9[b]	9.1[b]	19.2[b]
	--	--	23.1[c]
1990	67.7[c]	--	32.2[c]

[a]*Dochod narodowy wytworzony,* in current prices.
[b]1984 (old) prices.
[c]1989-90 constant (new) prices.
Source: *Rocznik Statystyczny* (1985), 79; (1988), 80; (1990), 118; and (1991), xiv.

rial intensity of the private sector, of course. One lies in distortions in the price system, in that state enterprises were more likely to purchase inputs at lower (subsidized) prices than private firms.[22] Another is monopsony: large state enterprises with market and bargaining power were better able to force lower prices out of suppliers than smaller, less well-connected private firms, although the sellers-market conditions prevailing until 1990 worked against the exercise of this monopsony power. Still, while the proposition that the private sector in the 1980s was inherently more efficient and productive than other sectors may be intuitively appealing, it can not be readily supported by the official data. Given the burdens under which the private sector labored, this should not be particularly surprising.

It should be noted, however, that the quality of the official statistics cited here is hardly above reproach. Suspicion is raised, for example, by the fact that the row data in Table 2.3 (as well as the official data on output shares produced by the state and cooperative sectors that underlie the data in Table 2.2) rarely sum to 100 percent, and the deviations from 100 percent are too great (in excess of 0.5 percent) to be attributed to rounding off. While the extent and direction of the biases implicit in these errors are not known, they imply that conclusions based upon these data can not be made with great certainty.

The official data also omit much economic activity. For example, the data on the private sector refer only to the legal private sector. The inclusion of activities that were illegal prior to the 1989 liberalization (including unregistered activities carried out by legal private firms) would certainly increase the private sector's share of output in different branches, although its effect upon the dynamics of sectoral growth would be unclear. In addition, the data on national income produced do not include services, where the private sector has been relatively well-represented. This omission is particularly important in light of the private sector's growth in services to the population and domestic trade (see Table 2.2).

Official Polish data on the growth of the private sector during the 1980s are thus ambiguous enough to be read in different ways. Problems with data quality and interpretation muddle the picture further. The only reasonable conclusion here seems to be that a strong case for the private sector's quantitative expansion (or lack thereof) during the 1980s cannot be made solely on the basis of these data.

The Private Sector Since 1989

The quantitative expansion of the indigenous private sector since 1989 has been impressive. According to one source, the total number of private firms (including corporations, peasant farms, proprietorships, foreign firms and other registered privately-owned commercial organizations) had reached 1.5 million by mid-1991.[23] The number of privately-owned corporations had risen to 54,267 by June 30, 1992, with the largest concentrations in domestic and foreign trade (34.5 percent), industry and construction (19.1 percent each).[24] As Table 2.4 shows, according to official statistics, the private sector's share of the output produced by industry, construction and transport at the end of the first quarter of 1992 had reached 26.6 percent, 73.2 percent and 31.0 percent, respectively. The private sector also accounted for 46.1 percent of Poland's imports and

Table 2.4
Shares of Private Activities in Selected Sectors[a]
(beginning of year)

Sector	1991	1992
Industry	18.9%	26.6%
Construction	58.0	73.2
Transportation	23.0	31.1
Foreign Trade: Imports	14.4	46.1
Foreign Trade: Exports	4.9	19.8

[a]The shares for industry, construction and transportation are from the first quarter of 1991 and 1992, respectively. The shares for imports and exports are from the ends of 1990 and 1991, respectively. All are for the "new" private sector.
Source: "J. Eysymontt: Sa przeslanki lekkiego ozywienia w gospodarce," *Polska Agencja Prasowa* (April 29, 1992); and Ada Kostrz-Kostecka, "GUS o handlu zagranicznym w 1991 roku: Wzrost importu, spadek eksportu," *Rzeczpospolita* (February 10, 1992).

19.8 percent of exports in 1991. The share of the private sector in whole-sale and retail trade had reached around 75 percent by the third quarter of 1991 as well,[25] although this was primarily the result of the small pri-vatization program discussed in Chapter 9.

While there is little doubt that the private sector has grown rapidly since 1989, care must be taken in interpreting official data measuring this growth. First, a share of the post-1989 growth reflects the legalization or surfacing of previously-existing illegal activities, which tends to exag-gerate the extent of the private sector's expansion. Second, the Central Statistical Office in 1990 changed its methodology for classifying private and non-private activities.[26] The traditional division between the "social-ized sector" (sektor uspoleczniony), which included the state and coopera-tive sectors, and the "non-socialized sector" (sektor nieuspoleczniony) was abolished. In its place a new taxonomy, consisting of the "public sector" (sektor publiczny) and "private sector" (sektor prywatny) was introduced, thus doing away with the cooperative sector (spoldzielczosc) as a separate statistical category. Most activities that had formerly been classified as "cooperative" were reclassified as "private," as were commercial activi-ties owned by labor unions, and "social and political organizations."[27]

In addition to automatically increasing the private share of economic activity in many sectors, this reclassification included in the private sec-tor a wide variety of firms, some of which (e.g., large cooperatives) had previously been closely identified with the institutions of state socialism. For this reason, official data on the private sector since 1990 appear in two different guises: as the "old" (pre-1990) private sector, consisting es-sentially of proprietorships and spolki in which the majority of shares are owned by private actors; and as the "new" (post-1989) private sector, consisting of the "old" private sector plus cooperatives, social and politi-cal organizations. Correspondingly, the "socialized" sector has been replaced by the "public" sector, which includes firms owned by the cen-tral government (wlasnosc panstwowa) and the local authorities (wlasnosc komunalna).[28] Private capital can be included in these firms, provided that at least 50 percent of the stock is owned by the state.

On the other hand, the official data reflect only those firms and activ-ities registered with the local or tax authorities. They thus ignore the hundreds of thousands of unregistered private traders—many of whom collect unemployment benefits—who have appeared on city squares throughout Poland since 1990, as well as other forms of informal or ille-gal private activity. Moreover, there is much evidence (discussed below) indicating that legal private firms continue to under-report sales, em-ployment and profit, in order to avoid taxes. The Central Statistical Office estimated that, in 1991, the shadow economy consisting of illegal or unreported activities comprised 10 percent of national income; other specialists put the figure as high as 30 percent.[29] It is generally accepted therefore that, on balance, the official statistics underestimate the true size of the private sector.

How large is the private sector in Poland? Because of these and other statistical issues, it is impossible to give anything other than an approximate answer to this question. However, simple, reasonably conservative calculations suggest that the private sector at the end of 1991 accounted for 38 to 53 percent of aggregate economic activity, figures roughly consistent with the "conventional wisdom" placing the private share of the Polish economy somewhere in the range of 40 to 45 percent.[30] Combined with official data showing that half the workers employed at the end of 1990 were working in the private sector,[31] these numbers portray a private sector poised to play, in quantitative terms, a dominant role in the Polish economy in 1992. In comparative terms, a 40 to 45 percent share for the private sector in 1991 dwarfs the private sector of all the other post-communist economies, with the possible exception of Hungary.

Increases in the private share of economic activity since 1989 also reflect the fact that the private sector's expansion has occurred during a recession that decimated the state sector. Although a part of the decline in output and income generated by state firms can be seen as the result of statistical quirks,[32] the recession is linked to Poland's stabilization program (developed in cooperation with the International Monetary Fund) which was designed to squeeze hyperinflationary pressures out of the economy. Although the high interest rates and reductions in consumer demand produced by the stabilization program did not leave the private sector unscathed, the damage done to the private sector by the recession was much less than that done to the state sector. Similar developments occurred during 1980–1981 as well (see Table 2.1). As in 1980–1981, the private sector's tax and regulatory environment was significantly liberalized after 1989. In addition to the 1988 Economic Activity Act and other legislation discussed above, support for the private sector took the form of a Finance Ministry declaration on May 18, 1990 granting one- to three-year sales and turnover tax holidays for private proprietorships.[33]

The private sector's post-1989 expansion has not been without controversy. While these tax holidays contributed to the private sector's post-1989 expansion, they have also been used as tax dodges, allowing private corporations to channel their most profitable activities through dummy proprietorships. Entrepreneurs have also been known to create dummy enterprises for the purpose of conducting a single transaction. Once the transaction is completed, the dummy vanishes without a trace, and the entrepreneur avoids paying taxes and customs duties. These factors helped keep tax revenues from the private sector during 1990–1991 well below what many regard as the private sector's "fair share."

According to Finance Ministry officials, private firms were providing only 8.4 percent of the state's budgetary revenue through taxes and tariff duties in October 1991, despite the fact that the private sector accounted for 46.1 percent of all imports at year's end.[34] Losses to the state treasury resulting from tax evasion and underground economic activity are estimated to be in the 40–60 trillion zloty (approximately $3–4.5 billion) range—a sum larger than the budget deficit in 1991.[35]

The private sector's unwillingness to part with its liquidity may in part reflect the fact that most private firms function largely in isolation from Poland's official financial system. The vast majority of private firms have virtually no access to the banking system, which remains dominated by state-owned institutions. As of mid-1991, nine state-owned commercial banks allocated some 90% of Poland's commercial credits,[36] and were devoting some 90% of this pool to state firms in early 1992.[37] This lack of access to credit hampers the indigenous private sector's ability to expand and invest in more modern, efficient production methods. It also prevents private firms from becoming better integrated into the international economy.

The private sector's problems are not limited to financial questions. According to investigators in the State Work Inspection Agency, working conditions in most private firms are worse than in state firms. Work on private farms is more than twice as dangerous, in terms of the number of accidents, than in any other area of the economy.[38] Private owners, too, often seem unwilling to permit labor unions or workers' councils to function in their firms. On the other hand, private employers complain about being unable to find qualified, hard-working and honest workers. According to press reports, owners of private trading firms are unwilling to hire workers with long experience in state stores, since these workers:

"are often demoralized, expect compensation 'on the side' in addition to their base pay, are rude to customers, are not concerned about protecting the firm's property, and look for any occasion to cheat the boss."[39]

While younger workers entering the labor force may not have these bad habits, they may also be inexperienced and unaccustomed to doing careful work.

Corruption and the Post-Communist Private Sector

The rapid expansion of corporations since 1988 has had three positive implications for the development of the private sector in Poland. First, this expansion signified a major liberalization in the regulation of enterprise creation and mergers, regardless of ownership. Second, the spread of corporations made possible rapid increases in the numbers of market actors in most branches of the economy, thus improving competitive market conditions. Third, corporations also promote capital-market development, in that transactions pertaining to ownership or expansion involve buying and selling stock.

On the other hand, the rise of the corporation exacerbated the Polish private sector's traditional problems of corruption. Various corporations by mid-1991 found themselves in the center of a sensational series of scandals which, according to Poland's Supreme Control Office NIK, could cost the state treasury as much as 50–75 trillion zloty ($4.5–6.8 billion at current exchange rates).[40] Moreover, prior to the July 1990 passage of landmark privatization legislation, the corporation was the mechanism through which the spontaneous privatization of 1989–1990 occurred (see Chapter 9). Because this process enfranchised members of the PUWP *nomenklatura* as owners of newly-privatized firms (the so-called *uwlaszczenie nomenklatury,* or "propertization of the *nomenklatura"*), it linked privatization and the expansion of the private sector in general with popular outrage over what was widely regarded as a socio-economic injustice.

The scandals associated with the post-1989 expansion of the private sector go well beyond spontaneous privatization, however. The financial and legal environment for Poland's indigenous private sector was liberalized during 1988–1990 even though regulatory mechanisms appropriate to the new setting were not put into place. Corporations owned by enterprising, often privileged, individuals straddling the public and private sectors were able to take advantage of loopholes and lax enforcement of fiscal and financial regulations to bilk the state treasury out of trillions of zloty. While the scandals have been many and varied, the Art-B and FOZZ scandals are perhaps the best known and most instructive.

Art-B was established as an import-export company in the town of Cieszyn in February 1989 with all of $20 (reported) as founding capital.[41] The firm experienced meteoric growth during 1990, earning some 360 billion zloty (approximately $38 million) in profits on sales of 3 trillion zloty ($300 million). By mid-1991, only two years after its inception, Art-B had established one of Poland's largest business empires. Art-B had obtained a controlling interest in some 200 private firms, and through holding companies had acquired indirect control over another 2000 firms employing almost 100,000 people. While astute use of conventional business tactics and political connections played important roles in Art-B's rise to the top, criminal investigations into Art-B's activities subsequently alleged that manipulation of Poland's banking system was a crucial element in the firm's success.

Art-B allegedly exploited the primitive technical state of Polish banks to earn millions of dollars in interest on "float"—the time required for Bank X to inform Bank Y that a check written on an account in Bank Y has been deposited or cashed in Bank X. Art-B's kiting scam was possible because the Polish banking system did not possess electronic facilities for clearing checks. Inter-bank check clearing had to be done by mail, thus creating long periods of float. Art-B developed a computer program called the "oscillator" to simulate the inter-bank check clearing mechanism, so that by moving funds back and forth between banks, Art-B could earn interest on the same money in various accounts. The Polish press reported that as much as 500 billion zloty (approximately $53 million) may have been bilked out of the banking system by running this scam in over 100 bank accounts.

This scandal led to the August 1991 arrest of Wojciech Prokop, First Deputy Director of the National Bank of Poland (NBP), Poland's central bank, allegedly for providing Art-B with unwarranted credit guarantees prior to his tenure at NBP. Prokop's arrest was followed by the dismissal and subsequent arrest of Grzegorz Wojtowicz, the President of NBP, on grounds of failure to exercise effective supervision over the banking system.

The FOZZ scandal revolved around the state-owned Fund for Servicing the Foreign Debt (*Fundusz Obslugi Zadluzenia Zagranicznego*). FOZZ was established in 1985 and received independent legal status in February 1989. According to press reports, the repurchasing (and annulment) of Poland's foreign debt was the real reason for FOZZ's existence.[42] Although not in itself illegal, such repurchases by debtor nations are not looked upon favorably by international creditor agencies, and Poland in 1988 explicitly agreed to refrain from such activities. FOZZ's dealings could therefore have further weakened Poland's already suspect international creditworthiness.

FOZZ's success as a debt-repurchasing institution is somewhat difficult to gauge, since the costs the Fund allegedly incurred in covertly repurchasing Polish debt through Western intermediaries exceeded the market price of Poland's debt by a factor of two to three. However, these losses were probably small potatoes compared to the chicanery engineered by the Fund's own officials. Between February 1989 and FOZZ's abolition in December 1990, FOZZ management allegedly lost, embezzled or misappropriated up to 9.5 trillion zloty (approximately $864 million). This malfeasance led to the August 1991 arrest of the Fund's General Director and Vice Director who, although they were removed from their positions in 1990, had apparently continued to spend money in FOZZ's name in an unsupervised manner through the private firm TRAST. This corporation, which had worked closely with FOZZ, was owned by none other than FOZZ's General Director, Vice Director and other members of FOZZ's supervisory board. So while the FOZZ affair is primarily a story of government incompetence, the role played by TRAST and its owners acting in the name of the Polish government is another case of rapacious corporations vandalizing the state treasury to line the pockets of a few privileged individuals.

Combined with the outcry against spontaneous privatization, these scandals deepened public cynicism about private enterprise and did not promote the private sector's post-communist regeneration. On the other hand, the media's ability to scrutinize the sordid details contrasts sharply with the public ignorance about the details of official corruption that existed in communist Poland. How many FOZZ-like cases of hard-currency malfeasance by the PUWP *nomenklatura* went unreported prior to 1989? Seen in this light, the strong public reaction against post-communist corruption in the private sector is somewhat ironic, to say the least.

Conclusion

The commitment of the governments of Prime Ministers Tadeusz Mazowiecki (August 1989–December 1990) and Jan Krzysztof Bielecki (January 1990–December 1991) to the growth of the private sector was undeniable, and the quantitative expansion of the indigenous private sector since 1989 has been impressive. However, it is also clear that problems remain. The private sector's greatest breakthrough came in the trade sphere. Official and unofficial private firms broke the state's hold on wholesale and retail trade in 1990 and, thanks to import liberalization and the introduction of internal zloty convertibility,[43] filled the shelves of Polish stores with goods from all over the world. Equally impressive is the fact that, some three years after the abolition of the state monopoly on foreign trade, private firms in 1991 accounted for close to half of Poland's imports.

On the other hand, the state's hold on industry as of 1992 had not been broken. In quantitative terms, this is apparent in the relatively small private share of industrial production (see Table 2.4). In an important sense, however, the data underestimate the size of the problems that large, state-owned industrial firms continue to pose for Poland's economic prospects. Some three years into the economic transition, virtually all the large factories, farms and mines that dominated Poland's industrial policies in the communist period, and were responsible for much of the environmental devastation the country has suffered, were still intact. As explained in Chapter 9, post-communist governments were unable during 1990–1992 to devise viable privatization programs for these firms, nor were they able to increase efficiency through restructuring them. By 1991 most of these giants had been pushed into insolvency by the recession, and the government seemed to have no viable strategy for dealing with them. Along with the gathering crisis in the (still state-owned) banking system, the problems of these firms seemed in late 1992 to pose the greatest structural threats to Poland's economic transformation.

Politically, the pieces for an anti-private backlash had fallen into place by late 1991. Public outrage over the Art-B, FOZZ, and other scandals, the legacy of spontaneous privatization in 1989–1990, and the incongruities of tax loopholes for private firms during a period of budgetary austerity, convinced Polish policy makers to adopt more restrictive tax and regulatory standards for the private sector in late 1991 and early 1992. Anti-privateer sentiments were echoed by Prime Minister Jan Olszewski, who told the Sejm in February 1992 that "the invisible hand of the market has often turned out to be the hand of the swindler, garnering public funds from the state treasury."[44] Regulations issued December 7, 1991 restricted private firms' abilities to produce, import and sell alcoholic beverages, non-ferrous metals, and intellectual property.[45] Additional restrictions on the private import of spirits, tobacco and fuels came into effect on March 31, 1992.[46]

Some of these restrictions, such as those meant to crack down on the piracy of intellectual property, may have been inevitable, and even desirable.[47] However, they can also be seen as a return to the unstable environment that characterized the regulation of the private sector under socialism. While the fourth post-communist government of Prime Minister Hanna Suchocka (which took power in July 1992) loosened some of these restrictions, it remained to be seen whether the corrections introduced by the Olszewski government will significantly constrain the development of the private sector. If so, this would tend to reinforce the uncertainty facing private enterprise inherited from the communist era.

Fundamental change does not occur quickly, and the private sector will not be transformed overnight. Instead, behavioral change is likely to be slow and evolutionary. As one observer put it:[48]

> The schizophrenic world of fraud and trickery has changed somewhat thanks to the buyer's market, zloty convertibility and new accounting systems. This does not mean that corruption and tax evasion have disappeared. New varieties of corruption and tax evasion have arisen, especially where the nascent private sector is difficult to control. On the other hand . . . small-scale fraud, label-switching and other forms of chicanery are becoming less profitable. A buyer's market requires large sales volumes, where better quality, brand loyalty, advertising and service can compensate for lower profit margins.

Optimism about Poland's private sector must therefore be guarded. As of mid-1992, the private sector had become less dysfunctional and much larger, but it still had a way to go before it could assume a truly dominant—and completely healthy—role in the Polish economy.

Notes

1. According to the official statistics, the private sector on December 31, 1990 accounted for 50.0 percent of total employment, and the private share continued to grow in 1990–1991. (Source: *Rocznik Statystyczny 1991*, xiv.)

2. Methods used to encourage "voluntary" collectivization included: 1) requiring peasants with no heirs to sell their land to the state land fund in order to receive a retirement pension; and 2) linking the size of the pension to the volume of grain sales made to the state. See Andrzej Korbonski, *Politics of Socialist Agriculture in Poland: 1945–1960* (New York: Columbia University Press, 1965).

3. Anders Aaslund, *Private Enterprise in Eastern Europe* (London: MacMillan, 1985), 227–228.

4. National income produced is the measure of aggregate economic activity typically applied in Soviet-type economies. Because of its roots in Marxian political economy, national income produced purports to measure "productive" activities while excluding "non-productive" activities. The resulting exclusion of services, and some transportation and communications activities, account for the largest differences between national income produced and gross national (domestic) product.

5. The arbitrary use of the tax system to promote the PUWP's goals vis-a-vis the private sector was most visible during the immediate post-war era. A sudden "once-for-all" (lump sum) tax was imposed during 1945 on wealth acquired during the war. Its rates varied from 15 to 75 percent. A second lump sum tax was levied in 1946, yielding revenues equal to those produced by the turnover tax that year. In Aaslund's words, "The lasting consequences of the complex tax system, once-for-all taxes and high tax pressure have been massive tax evasion and distrust between authorities and entrepreneurs." See Aaslund, 24.

6. *Trybuna Ludu*, the PUWP daily paper, joined the attack on the freedoms obtained by the urban private sector during 1956 with a newspaper article entitled "Shall Speculators Go Unpunished?" in its March 2, 1957 edition. See Aaslund, 60.

7. Bogdan Mroz, "Poland's Economy in Transition to Private Ownership," *Soviet Studies* 43, no. 4 (1991): 677–688. Quotation is from pp. 678, 680. See also Chapter 7 for a microeconomic analysis of the causes of similar behavior among Russian entrepreneurs.

8. Bartlomiej Kaminski, *The Collapse of State Socialism: The Case of Poland* (Princeton: Princeton University Press, 1991): 180.

9. Marek Misiak, "Kondycja 'drobnych'," *Firma* (September 1987): 28.

10. Despite its "etatization," the cooperative sector in Poland functioned on a significant scale until the late 1980s. In 1985, for example, approximately 40 percent of the population belonged to at least one cooperative; cooperatives comprised at least 75 percent of the productive capacity in such sectors as retail trade, restaurants and housing construction. See Andrzej Chajecki, "Zmiany w strukturach organizacyjnych spoldzielczosci: ewolucja form koncentracji"

(Warsaw: Institute of Organization, Management and Personnel Training, 1985), 2–4.

11. For an account of these reforms' impact upon the state sector, see Paul Marer and Wlodzimierz Siwinski, *Creditworthiness and Reform in Poland* (Bloomington: Indiana University Press, 1988).

12. Chajecki, 4.

13. For an excellent analysis of the private sector's expansion in Poland, see Jacek Rostowski, "The Decay of Socialism and the Growth of Private Enterprise in Poland," *Soviet Studies* XLI, no. 2 (April 1989): 194–214.

14. Bogda Zukowska, "Wejscie eksperymentalne: Rozmowa z Zdzislawem Skakujem—Prezesem Agencji ds. Inwestycji Zagranicznych," *Zycie gospodarcze* (August 27, 1989): 24; Aaslund, 103–113.

15. Michal Federowicz, "Social Barriers of Ownership Transformations: Case Study," (Warsaw: Economic Research Program for Central and Eastern Europe, 1990).

16. Although gross domestic product (*produkt krajowy brutto*) data is available for the 1980s, statistics about changes in sectoral shares during this time are not.

17. Kaminski, 179.

18. Labor productivity in real terms increased by 13.6 percent during 1985–1989. *Rocznik Statystyczny 1990,* 123.)

19. The capital stock in both the private and socialist sectors declined in real terms during 1980–1989. Decapitalization actually occurred more rapidly in the socialized sector, where the gross value of the capital stock (*wartosc brutto srodkow trwalych*) declined by 19.9 percent. The corresponding figure for the private sector was 16.7 percent. (Source: *Rocznik Statystyczny 1990,* 244).

20. Ibid., 249.

21. Ibid.

22. A similar argument can be made about the private sector's less favorable labor productivity data.

23. "Prywatnych przybywa," *Gazeta wyborcza* (September 7–8, 1991).

24. "Statystyka Polski" supplement to *Rzeczpospolita* (August 4, 1992): iv.

25. *Polska Agencja Prasowa* (September 30, 1991).

26. For more on the methodology of this reclassification, see *Rocznik Statystyczny 1991,* xii–xiii.

27. Ibid.

28. References in Tables 2.1 through 2.4 to the share of the "old" state sector refer to activities conducted by firms falling under the traditional (pre-1990) taxonomy, while the "new" state sector refers to the "public sector."

29. The 10 percent figure is given by Bohdan Wyznikiewicz, former president of the Central Statistical Office, and refers to gross national product. The 30 percent figure comes from Krystyna Doliniak, "Szara strefa," *Kurier Polski* (December 3, 1991).

30. See, for example, "Survey: Business in Eastern Europe," *The Economist* (September 21, 1991): 9.

31. *Rocznik Statystyczny 1991,* xiv.

32. See Jan Winiecki, "The Inevitability of a Fall in Output in the Early Stages

of Transition to the Market: Theoretical Underpinnings," *Communist Economies and Economic Transition* 3, no. 4 (1991): 397–416.

33. Grazyna Nasierowska, "Sprawa jakich wiele," *Firma* (December 1991): 35. These holidays contrast sharply with onerous wage and asset taxes for state firms.

34. "GUS o handlu zagranicznym w 1991 roku," *Rzeczpospolita* (February 10, 1992); and "Podatki bez mitow," *Polska Agencja Prasowa* (October 24, 1991).

35. Krystyna Doliniak, "Strefa cienia," *Kurier Polski* (March 26, 1992).

36. Alina Bialkowska, "Banki w prywatne rece," *Gazeta Wyborcza* (July 12, 1991); and "Prywatyzacja bankow," *Prywatyzacja* (November 1991): 3.

37. Slawomir Lipinski, "Jak pozbyc sie balastu," *Gazeta Bankowa* (February 2, 1992). See Chapter 8 regarding similar capital allocation issues in Hungarian banking.

38. "Praca, kalectwo, smierc," *Gazeta Wyborcza* (October 11, 1991).

39. Krystyna Milewska, "Uczciwego zatrudnie . . . ," *Zycie Warszawy* (August 20, 1991).

40. "Lawina afer," *Tygodnik Solidarnosc* (August 23, 1991). By way of comparison, Poland's gross foreign debt, prior to the debt-reduction agreement negotiated between Poland and Western governments in April 1991, stood at approximately $45 billion. See "Bad Supervision Given as Reason for Debt Negotiator's Dismissal," *Reuter* (August 25, 1991).

41. For more on the Art-B story, see David McQuaid, "Art-B and the Pathology of Transition," *Report on Eastern Europe* 2, no. 38 (September 20, 1991): 15–21; and Jerzy Andrzejczak, Przemyslaw Cwiklinski and Jacek Ziarno, *Art-B Bluff* (Warsaw: Polska Oficyna Wydawnicza BGW, 1991).

42. The debt of many heavily-indebted countries circulates on secondary markets, where it is bought and sold at some fraction (in the Polish case, 15–30 per cent) of its face value. This made it possible for the Polish government to repurchase one dollar worth of its foreign debt at a cost of 15–30 cents.

43. The zloty was made internally convertible (meaning that Polish citizens and firms were allowed to purchase Western currencies on demand) on January 1, 1990. Internal convertibility was preceded by the March 1989 legalization of black-market currency trading. The January 1990 announcement also unified the official and (black) market exchange rates, bringing the former to the level of the latter.

44. "Wystapienie Premiera Olszewskiego," *Polska Agencja Prasowa* (February 26, 1992).

45. Malgorzata Niezgodka-Medvoda, "Zmiany ustawy o dzialalnosci gospodarczej," *Firma* (December 1991): 20–21.

46. "Obowiazuja koncesje na import alkoholu, tytoniu i paliw," *Polska Agencja Prasowa* (April 1, 1992).

47. For more on intellectual property rights and piracy, see Anna Sabbat-Swidlicka, "Intellectual Piracy in Poland," *RFE/RL Research Report* 1, no. 16 (April 17, 1992): 57–60.

48. Milewska, "Uczciwego zatrudnie . . ."

3

Privatization in Post-Soviet Russia: The Politics and Psychology of Reform

John E. Tedstrom

Perestroika, Glasnost', and Property Rights

The numerous impressive achievements of the Soviet system came at a tremendous, in some cases tragic, social price: severe restrictions on personal liberties, low living standards, and isolation from the rest of the world. In essence, Gorbachev's *perestroika* was an effort to modernize that traditional system in hopes of simultaneously improving economic performance and reducing the social price of the Soviet experiment. In contrast, the post-*perestroika* period has, for most purposes, abandoned efforts merely to *reform* the system. Finally, leaders in a number of the Soviet successor states have embarked on programs to *replace* the traditional Soviet system with one that is predicated, first of all, on a fundamental shift of authority from the state to the individual.

A key element in this transition is the reform of property rights and the development of a significant private economy. Besides all of the purely economic advantages to a private economy over a state-owned one, the shift of property rights from the state to the individual is, arguably, a necessary element in the development of a middle class that will have strong vested interests in seeing the process of democratization continued and maintained. For these reasons, the development of the private sector in the former Soviet region represents an exceptionally important goal.

Achieving this goal will be as problematic as it is important. For some 70 years the Soviet system all but totally prohibited legal private businesses. Citizens of the former Soviet Union have little experience with the institutions and traditions of capitalist economies. Moreover, the private enterprise that did take place existed mostly in the vast black market. The fact that private business activities took place within this illegal enclave reinforced the socialist message that private business was bad economics by saying that it was also immoral. Those who would replace the traditional socialist system thus have not only to introduce the concepts and principles of capitalist economics (that is, effect an intellectual transformation), but must also erase its negative stigma (that is, effect a psychological transformation). The reason for addressing this point is that many view the privatization process in Russia and the other Soviet successor states as a purely technical matter. In reality it involves a much more complicated and problematic reorientation of people's understanding of their place and role in society, economic relations generally, economic and social justice, and the individual's relationship to the state. As such, privatizing the former Soviet socialist economy is bound to be an exceedingly long and difficult exercise. As this chapter discusses various aspects of privatizing the Russian economy, it emphasizes the many difficult cultural as well as economic problems that must be overcome in the process.

Glasnost' (the spread of information), more than *perestroika* (the restructuring of the economic system), has fostered the birth of the still nascent private sector in the former Soviet Union. To be sure, *perestroika*'s economic decentralization, along both branch-ministerial and regional lines, served an important purpose. In fact, a convincing argument can be made that the adoption of the State Enterprise Law in June 1987 initiated a significant shift of property rights from the central planners to their agents in state-owned firms. But what most Western economists are comfortable calling "privatization" began only after a major conceptual, some might say spiritual, hurdle had been jumped in Soviet society. It is in this vein that *glasnost'* played the pivotal role. The notion of private property— the antithesis of the socialist concept of collective property—could arise as part of the economic reform debate only when economists and other social scientists were allowed to speak and write more freely.[1]

A comprehensive discussion of privatization in the Soviet successor states is beyond the scope of a reasonably sized book, let alone a chapter such as this.[2] To narrow the focus somewhat, this chapter examines privatization in the Russian Federation, discussing some of the more important specifics within a context that comprehends both the economics and politics of the problem and gives due attention to the important Soviet legacy.[3] Russia is chosen because it is by far the largest economic region in the former USSR and represents the largest economic policy concern among Western governments and international financial organizations. Also, Russia takes on special importance because it has in many respects taken the lead in developing privatization legislation, and could well serve as a model for other Commonwealth of Independent States (CIS) members. Finally, because the Soviet successor states are likely to be closely intertwined economically for the foreseeable future, what happens in Russia in terms of economic policy and development will have significant effects on at least some of the other former Soviet republics.

The Politics and Psychology of Privatization

As the April 1992 shakeup of the Russian government underscored, both the direction and pace of economic reform in Russia are highly contentious issues. At the end of 1991, in response to the public opinion survey question "If we lived in a society where everyone builds his life by his own choice, where would you prefer to work?" only 31 percent said that they would prefer to work in a private firm while 43 percent preferred to work for a state firm.[4] In fact, it appears that in the early 1990s, public opinion toward the private sector was becoming less positive.[5] By late 1992, the political situation, too, had become quite unstable. A major clash between the president and the parliament, largely over the latter's dissatisfaction with the former's management of economic reforms, threatened to force changes in top government personnel and to slow or in some cases even reverse parts of the reform program.[6]

Nevertheless, the prospects for privatization throughout the Russian Federation seem brighter than ever before. The major turning point in this respect was the failed coup of August 19–22, 1991, in which a group of conservatives temporarily overtook the Gorbachev government only to be overthrown themselves three days later by a popular movement led by Russian president Boris Yeltsin. One of the most significant and immediate results of the failed coup was that central policy and central policymakers lost virtually all authority. Policy was increasingly formulated on a republican or even subrepublican level. In many republics—certainly in the Russian republic (RSFSR)—this resulted in a radicalization of policy generally as conservative elements increasingly lost influence and the ability to block reform. In the RSFSR, the republican leadership replaced a large share of local and regional authorities beginning in November 1991. The new leaders were generally young and supported a stronger commitment to market-oriented reforms. At the same time, the international community supported reform by making progress on privatization a condition for economic and financial aid.

The coup also provoked a situation of pseudo-lawlessness throughout the former Soviet region. Many individuals, organizations, and administrative regions were asserting themselves in ways that were inconsistent with existing law. In terms of economics and business, a good deal of this activity, including laying claim to property, went unchallenged. Within Russia herself, there ensued a constitutional crisis which in many ways replicated that of the USSR prior to its disintegration. The economic dimensions of this crisis included general confusion and struggle over property rights claims within the federation's various administrative regions.[7]

This shifting and uncertain environment created a fertile breeding ground for energetic and imaginative entrepreneurs. Fledgling business people began to take advantage of poorly-written, vague regulations on business and privatization, and exploited the opportunities created by the general political, constitutional, and legal disarray. As a result, the non-state sector grew relatively rapidly after the coup, though often in ways that were neither approved nor expected.

Many political figures as well as social commentators and economists noted the "spontaneous," "unorganized," and "inefficient" way in which privatization was taking place. On the one hand, observers could point to considerable bureaucratic foot-dragging, lack of public support, and the absence of important institutions such as commercial banks—all of which stood in the way of efficient business creation. On the other hand, the same observers noted with despair that a large share of privatization was of the *nomenklatura* variety (i.e., property ended up in the hands of former Communist bosses), and that the mafia was often playing a decisive role in what was privatized and by whom.[8] Thus, the private sector in Russia has developed in part because of, and in part in spite of, the confusion in the legal and economic spheres.

Because of legal confusion and a general decentralization of political power, Russian privatization is increasingly being managed on the local level. The federal government has officially delegated a sizable part of its authority on these questions to local officials. In addition, where gaps in property rights legislation exist, local authorities tend to be the ones who step in. Current regulations stipulate that municipal governments receive only 50 percent of receipts of privatized municipal enterprises and 10 percent of the receipts from the privatization of regional and federal enterprises. Local authorities will have strong incentives to organize these transactions in such a way as to retain as much of the proceeds as possible—all the more so as the federal budget has largely been relieved from meeting local needs. Local decisionmaking will also lead to large disparities in the share of privatized industry among regions. Tatarstan, Moscow, and St. Petersburg are examples of regions that are taking an aggressive approach to privatization, sometimes in conflict with existing Russian Federation legislation.[9]

An additional result of legal and political turmoil is that much of Russia's privatization so far has been of an immature, unsophisticated variety that focuses on short term gains and gives much less attention to investment and growth in the longer term. One example of this trend that is now visible is the practice of "rolling" or "stripping" state enterprises.

This entails the purchase of state and municipal firms largely for the purpose of stripping them of their capital stock and selling it piecemeal at higher prices to others. In the Russian cultural context, this obviously smacks of "speculation" (unfair gains from buying low and selling high), and is something many people would like to see stopped. The reason "stripping" takes place, however, is because the buyers of this property calculate that its future value is less in real terms than its present value. As long as the Russian economy suffers from severe macro-disequilibrium— including a severe inflation which discourages long-run investment strategies—stripping is likely to continue.

Industrial Privatization: Goals and Achievements

Before the failed coup of August 19–22, 1991, some progress on privatization had been made in the Soviet Union. The progress was uneven, though, both in terms of sectoral coverage and in terms of geographical distribution of privatized businesses. This unevenness reflected the Soviet public's lack of understanding of, and ambivalence toward, private enterprise. Despite the increasing numbers of "private" businesses (of whatever variety), an organized private business culture failed to develop in the USSR. Business licenses continued to be awarded or denied based on arbitrary rulings by officials with little appreciation for, or understanding of, business or market economics. In too many cases, these officials made their decisions based on how they felt their own interests might be affected. Not surprisingly, private business managers as often as not operated primarily in ways designed to circumvent the state economic bureaucracy, not to best serve customers or to maximize long-run profits. Marketing was an important aspect of business management that had not developed, and managers often had little idea of what products were in demand. Production decisions were often a matter of "supply-push," and depended on what materials were in inventory or were readily attainable. When looking at the growth of the private sector in Russia and the USSR, then, it is important to keep in mind that behind the statistics lay a disorganized system based on only a partial transformation of economic and social relationships.

As of September 1, 1991, some 45 large enterprises had been privatized in the USSR. These firms produced some 1.8 billion rubles in annual output (sales, not value added), and employed some 37 thousand people. As a rule, however, the privatization of large, low-profit enterprises has taken place mainly in the manufacturing sector, though it is going more slowly even in that sector than most reformers would like.

In the first half of 1991, the number of cooperatives in the USSR decreased from 245,000 to about 197,000. Some of this loss, however, was due to the rechartering of cooperatives into other types of businesses, such as fully-private partnerships and joint-stock companies. In 1990, cooperatives produced some 67 billion rubles worth of goods and services, with about 4/5 of that going directly to state enterprises. Approximately 90 percent of cooperatives work directly for state enterprises, often in industrial branches, largely because they are able to negotiate favorable terms on space and equipment and because they enjoy the benefits of serving a primary customer that can have a significant share of its sales coming from state orders (*goszakazy*), which usually means that they have privileged access to material inputs.[10]

Within Russia, firms worth approximately two billion rubles were privatized in 1991.[11] This included 127 enterprises in trade and social catering, 47 repair and craft shops, and about 500 industrial enterprises (most of which were small, employing less than 200 people). In all, roughly 80,000 new businesses were registered over the course of 1991.[12] While not all of these were "privatized" in the strict sense of the term, they did contribute to a growing non-state sector. These new businesses included nearly nine thousand joint stock companies, about three thousand associations, 227 concerns, and 123 consortia. Also registered were approximately 1,300 commercial banks, and more than 110 exchanges.[13] The non-state sector acquired approximately four percent of the total Russian capital stock in 1991, and approximately 14 percent of total Russian output. Table 3.1 shows how the Russian industrial sector was divided by ownership form at the beginning of 1992.

Meaningful values for privatized assets (and private-sector output for that matter) are difficult to calculate, due to administratively-fixed prices and an underdeveloped capital market. Thus, it is important to look at other indicators for a more complete picture of the growth of the non-state sector. Employment figures are particularly useful in this regard. By the end of 1991, the non-state sector was employing approximately 23 percent of the total employed population in Russia. The private and individual labor sector claimed some 1.7 million people, (the private and individual labor sector's share in total employment increased from 1.6 percent to 2.3 percent over the course of 1991). For comparison purposes, figures for the USSR in September 1990 and September 1991 are presented in Table 3.2.

Taken together, employment in leased firms, joint stock companies and associations grew roughly three times in January–September 1991 over the same period in 1990. It is noteworthy that the private/individual labor activities sector employs a significantly lower share of the total employed population in Russia than it did in the USSR as a whole.

The initial goals for industrial privatization in Russia in 1992 were ambitious and, frankly, unrealistic given the cultural obstacles to be

Table 3.1
The Ownership Structure of Russian Industry
(As of January 1, 1992)

Type of Ownership	Number of Enterprises		Volume of Production in Current 1991 Prices	
	Number	Percent of All Enterprises	Billions of Rubles	Percent of Total
State Property	21945	95.7%	1045	95.7%
Republican	13674	59.6	340	31.1
Communal	287	1.3	5.1	0.5
Leased Enterprises	3042	13.1	134	12.3
Non-State Property	992	4.3	46.7	4.3
Citizen's Property	70	0.3	0.1	--
Collective Property	922	4.0	46.6	4.3
Collective Enterprises	272	1.2	4.0	0.4
Joint-stock Companies	162	0.7	16.1	1.5

Source: *Ekonomika i zhizn'*, no. 14 (1992): 1.

Table 3.2
Growth of Employment in the State
and Non-State Sectors in the USSR

	September 1990		September 1991	
	Million Persons	Percent of Total	Million Persons	Percent of Total
Total Employed	138.2	100%	135.7	100%
by:				
State Enterprises	108.8	78.7	98.9	72.9
Leased Enterprises			9.0	6.6
Joint Stock Companies, etc.	3.8	2.7	1.0	0.7
Concerns, Associations	--	--	0.7	0.5
Social Funds	1.8	1.3	1.8	1.3
Joint Ventures	0.1	0.1	0.2	0.2
Kolkhoz-Cooperative Sector	18.8	13.6	17.6	13.0
including:				
Producer Cooperatives	4.0	2.9	3.2	2.4
Private & Individual Activities	4.9	3.6	6.5	4.8
including:				
Fermery (Farmers)	0.1	0.1	0.2	0.2
Private Plots	4.6	3.3	4.6	3.3
Individual Labor Activities	0.2	0.2	1.7	1.2

Source: "Predprinimatel' na rasput'e," *Ekonomika i zhizn',* no. 2
(1992): 1,8.

overcome, including political opposition to wide-scale industrial privatization. Seventy percent of the enterprises in light industry were targeted
for privatization, as were sixty percent of all Russian enterprises in the
food processing industry. In the construction and construction materials
branches, seventy percent and fifty percent, respectively, of the enterprises were to be privatized, though the figures varied by region.[14] Revenues from privatization in 1992 were originally planned to total some 92
billion rubles, or about 1.5 percent of Russian GNP for the year.[15] This
represented a tremendous increase over the 2 billion rubles recorded in
1991. For 1993 and 1994, the amount of revenue was scheduled to increase to about 350 billion rubles and 470–500 billion rubles, respectively.
Already by Spring 1992, though, these ambitious goals had been re-

vised in the face of experience with privatization in the first months of the year. Virtually all of the privatization targets were revised downward, and it remained to be seen whether even these new figures were realistic. The total value of enterprises scheduled for privatization in 1992 was reduced by nearly 25 percent (apparently in real terms) to 72 billion rubles. Of that total, only about 21 percent was expected to be invested by private individuals. Just 7.2 percent was expected to come from foreign investors. In contrast, 32 billion rubles, or over 44 percent of total investment in privatization projects was to come from the "stimulation fund" of state and municipal enterprises.[16] As discussed below, state enterprises, as representatives of their labor collectives, were encouraged to use their own funds for "self-privatization," distributing ownership shares among the workers and employees. Problems of "unjust" *nomenklatura* privatization, the maintenance of old management structures and practices, and the dangers associated with employee-owned firms (such as an emphasis on current wages over capital investment) were bound to arise under these circumstances.

Nevertheless, this type of "self-privatization" went some way toward getting around another problem in Russia's privatization experiment. The price liberalization and credit policies pursued by the Russian government since January 1992 contributed to a hyperinflationary situation that erased a large share of the savings balances held by the population. The Russian private sector was seriously undercapitalized (i.e., it possessed low real net wealth) as a result, and entrepreneurs found it difficult to arrange venture financing.

Even though the overall target value was lowered to a more achievable level, there were signs that the Russian privatization program was still not well designed and reconciled with other planned and unplanned trends in the Russian economy. In particular, a full 40 billion rubles, or nearly 56 percent of total privatization was to take place in the following branches: light industry (9 billion rubles or 12.5 percent); food processing (19 billion rubles or 26.4 percent); and construction (12 billion rubles, or 16.6 percent). Yet, for several reasons, these branches were among the least attractive for private investors. For example, profitability in these branches suffered in the wake of liberalized energy prices in Russia. Further, some studies indicated that demand in these industries' markets remained weak.[17] Business closures in these branches were bound to become more frequent as bankruptcy legislation took effect. Also, very little output from these branches was competitive on world markets. On a more general level, the political and economic uncertainty in Russia was a strong negative factor in any foreign investor's decisionmaking process.[18]

The Role of Foreign Capital

An important factor affecting the pace of privatization is foreign investment. As of the end of 1991, there were some 13 operating free economic zones in Russia, intended to attract foreign capitalists via low taxation and other incentives. These zones covered approximately 1.2 million square kilometers, with a population of 18 million people (12 percent of Russia's total).[19] Although there are indications that these regions do outperform other areas, foreign partners often complain about cumbersome bureaucracies, overreliance on planning, and skepticism about market-oriented business practices among the local populations. There is also the all too common xenophobia that inhibits efforts to attract foreign partners. These problems, coupled with the general political and economic instability in the region, go a long way toward explaining why there are so many more joint ventures registered on paper than operating in the Russian economy.

As of the end of 1991, there were some 2600 joint ventures registered in Russia.[20] Foreign partners represented over sixty countries. Total capital investment was about six billion rubles, only a third of which was from the foreign partners.[21] Active joint ventures employed some 135,000 people (125,000 Russians) at the end of 1991, and generated about 11 billion rubles in sales.[22] As regards joint ventures in industry, special problems have arisen concerning the development of firms in the primary manufacturing branches such as machine building and metal working (MBMW), fuel and energy, etc. The main difficulty is that these businesses require relatively large capital outlays which the foreign partners are not terribly eager to make. Recent changes in the regulations governing hard-currency earnings and taxes hit capital-intensive operations especially hard, and there are strong indications that growth in this sector will continue to be slow. On the other hand, the performance of joint ventures in labor-intensive computer technologies (including software) has been more impressive. Joint ventures in this field are earning 40–50 percent of all joint venture earnings in Russia, although their shares in total number of firms and in capital investment are only 13 percent and 8 percent, respectively.[23]

The Role of the Underground Economy[24]

The gradual legalization of economic activities traditionally proscribed under Soviet law has been a major element of the overall reform effort in the USSR and its successor states, and is important for two basic reasons. First, the Soviet underground economy was large, and operated in both the domestic and the foreign sectors of the economy. Indeed, some authors in the former USSR implicate virtually all of their compatriots in illegal economic activity.[25] Other experts likewise estimate that many millions of citizens systematically (i.e. full- or nearly full-time) participated in the underground economy of the former Soviet Union.[26] To one degree or another, then, virtually all Soviet citizens had some experience with, and knowledge of, the illegal side of the Soviet economy. The value of "black market" economic activity in the late 1980s is estimated at between 50 billion and 150 billion rubles, with most estimates falling in the 90–100 billion ruble range—at least 10 percent of "official" GNP.[27] Since then, all observers agree that the figure has grown significantly, though reliable estimates do not exist.[28] Whatever its exact magnitude, the underground economy clearly operated in all sectors of the Soviet economy and ran from the garden plot up into Kremlin offices. By bringing these illegal activities above ground, recorded national income would be larger, and the state would be able to collect revenues on a larger tax base.

A second, and even more important, reason for attention to the formerly underground economy is that it operated on principles which were fundamentally different from those which prevailed in the official economy. In fact, the market system which existed in the underground economy (minus the drug dealing, prostitution, and other forms of vice) in large measure represented the goal which many Soviet reformers were striving toward. The key question, then, was not whether the legalization of the underground economy would make Soviet national income "bigger," but whether the legalization of this sector, and the adoption of its operating principles throughout the official economy would help create a system that worked "better" than the traditional Soviet model.[29]

Adopting market principles and institutions in the official economy is not easy, but it may prove easier than rooting out illegal private businesses. A point that many Soviet analysts make is that the Soviet system itself represents a specific case that generates a particular type of underground economy, one that may be difficult to bring above ground. The reason the underground economy may be so entrenched in Russia is that the mafia and the *nomenklatura* have become partners. One observer has even gone so far as to assert that the underground economy is "genetically linked to the economic system of developed socialism," and "the bosses of the shadow economy are the illegitimate children of our ideological 'chastity,' of the planned, socialist economy . . . . It is precisely the state that is the chief organizer of the shadow economy."[30] In fact, official involvement in the underground economy has been rife, even at the highest levels of the Party and state bureaucracy, and in some instances implication in these affairs has contributed to the de-deification of former Soviet leaders and the execution of high-ranking state officials who were caught operating in the underground economy.[31] Activities at such high levels do not take place spontaneously, but require organization. As one Soviet economist put it, "... in specifically Soviet conditions, a situation formed whereby the 'informal management structure' began to develop and work independently, and gradually turned into an exclusively corrupt, mafia structure. This merger of the informal and mafia elements constitutes a glaring feature of the Soviet economic system."[32]

As Gregory Grossman points out, the underground economy had a mixed impact on the Soviet system.[33] On the one hand, Grossman notes that it served as a training ground for would-be entrepreneurs. It also tended to grease the wheels of the inefficient and cumbersome state economic machine. On the other hand, by stealing materials and other goods (including time) from the state, the underground economy was a drain on the official economy.

A rapid shift of activities out of the underground economy into the legal sector is not to be expected. Economic and legal instability, the chance for tax-free incomes, and cooperation between government officials and organized crime will all slow the legalization of now-underground businesses. In fact, the growing presence and influence of the Russian mafia and the authorities' apparent inability to control organized crime suggest that this part of the economy may well expand. Finally, it is worth noting that the long experience with the illegal economy has no doubt tainted private business generally in the minds of many former Soviet citizens. This is another serious cultural obstacle to the growth of the private sector that could take years to effectively erase.

The Legal Framework for Privatization

Since mid-1991, there have been numerous legal measures devoted to the process of privatizing state-owned industry in Russia. The most important of these are the RSFSR Law on Privatization and the RSFSR Basic Provisions.[34] In mid-1992, the Russian government issued its program for deepening the country's reforms, and although this program does not carry the force of law, it does represent the thinking of the reformers in the government and gives a good indication of how they would like to see the reforms progress.[35] Finally, it should be noted that some influential groups outside the Russian government have also issued their own proposals for economic reform, including privatization. The most prominent of these groups is the Union of Industrialists and Entrepreneurs who argue that the government's privatization program is too ambitious and would result in the collapse of Russian industry, an erosion of enterprise managers' authority, and a dramatic increase in unemployment.[36]

The fact that so many programs for privatizing the Russian economy have emerged in the last year and a half both reflects and contributes to an almost debilitating lack of consensus on this key issue. In essence, Russian society has fractured into numerous interest groups, the strongest of which, the former *nomenklatura*, state enterprise managers, and the mafia, all see real privatization as a threat to their economic interests. The main fracture, however, seems to be that between policymakers on the one hand and the general public on the other.

Simply put, privatization has been imposed on the Russian population *a la Russe*, from the top down, and many Russians have little or no idea about how they as individuals fit into the new socio-economic order. Until Russian society can more fully grasp the essence of capitalism and come together in support of privatization, it is highly likely that the current pattern of disorganized, extra-legal privatization activity will continue. Nevertheless, the laws on the books in Russia now do set a broad, if vague, framework for privatization upon which any improvement will be based. It is therefore appropriate to outline the key points of current legislation.

The Basic Provisions were issued following the demise of the USSR, and they recapitulate many of the points contained in the RSFSR Law on Privatization, and expand the Russian Federation's privatization program. The Basic Provisions set the foundation for privatization at the local and regional levels, and stipulate binding instructions on local and regional governments, which are responsible for designing their own detailed privatization programs within the framework established by the Law on Privatization and the Basic Provisions. To the extent that these laws directly address local leaders, they help to prevent conservative officials at that level from blocking privatization efforts.

The program for industrial privatization in Russia is predicated on the following goals. First, privatization is seen as an important step toward macroeconomic stability. Privatization is intended to help tackle both the stock and the flow aspects of the current financial disequilibrium by (1) generating significant revenues for the state through the selloff of state-owned enterprises, and (2) relieving the state of the financial burden created by loss-making enterprises. Further, the government believes that budgetary revenues will increase (in real terms) due to privatization. Experience elsewhere has shown, though, that corporate income tax revenues tend to fall in the short run at least, as the effective tax rate falls, and tax evasion increases in the face of a complexification of tax legislation and the absence of a trained tax inspectorate. Second, privatization is seen as a way of generating higher efficiencies in production and in resource allocation.[37] Third, privatization is seen as a component part of the more general effort to combat monopolies. Fourth, privatization is seen as a way to help develop a middle class that has a clear vested interest in seeing the reform program pursued.

The Basic Provisions establish a two-phase program for privatization, with 1992 serving as a period in which "the conditions for a significant widening of the privatization process in 1993–94" will be set. The program divides state-owned enterprises into four categories.[38] The first group is comprised of those enterprises and organizations that must be privatized, preferably in 1992. These are the enterprises and organizations that make up the bulk of the market infrastructure. In the first three quarters of 1992, wholesale and retail trade, public catering, services; food processing, and unfinished and late construction are scheduled to be turned over to private owners. In the second half of the year, that group will expand to include auto transport and some auto repair; construction and the construction materials industries; and small enterprises (200 employees or less) in the light and food industries.

A second group of enterprises and organizations can only be privatized by a decision of the Russian Federation government. These include all enterprises which dominate in their market sector, i.e., monopolies or near monopolies. Also included in this group are the largest enterprises (those with either a net worth of 200 million rubles or more on January 1, 1992, or with more than 10,000 employees), any of the defense industry enterprises (including nuclear machine building), enterprises in the fuel and energy complex (including enterprises concerned with the supply of natural gas) and enterprises involved in the extraction of precious ores and metals. This group also includes drug and pharmaceutical enterprises, certain construction organizations of all-Russian significance, graduate schools and other higher education institutions, and stud farms and cross-breeding centers.

Enterprises which require the approval of state government, administrative bodies and local authorities include city passenger transport organizations and their repair shops, pawn shops, bath houses, laundry services, hotels, funeral homes, pharmacies, movie houses, and waste processing factories.

Finally, the list of assets that may not be privatized includes land, water, forest and continental shelf resources, airspace, and the territorial waters of the Russian Federation and the Russian Federation economic sea zones. Also included are the State Treasury of the Russian Federation, the public fisc, the Central Bank, the country's gold reserves and diamond fund, banks and other entities which service money circulation, and enterprises and institutions which ensure the release of bank notes, state treasury notes, shares, bonds, and other securities. This group also includes property of the armed forces, enterprises and entities dealing with electrical energy and pipeline transportation, enterprises of communication (with the exception of *Soiuzpechat'*) and television and radio broadcasting centers, port facilities, enterprises which sell and produce jewelry and State decorations, and enterprises in the space field or in space research and development. In sum, it seems clear that the Russian government remains committed to a significant state-owned sector.

Methods of Privatizing Russian Industry

Russian Federation legislation provides for several methods of privatization depending on the type of enterprise (that is, its activities) and its size.[39] Essentially, these fall into three categories (1) privatization by auction; (2) privatization by commercial competition; and (3) transformation into a joint stock company. The method selected depends on the activity of the firm (services, catering, manufacturing, oil and gas exploration, etc.) and its size. Generally, larger enterprises (those valued at more than one million rubles) are to be transformed first into joint stock companies. Only after that are they truly privatized through the issuance of shares. Commercial competitions exist for cases in which the government wants the new owners to have special qualifications. Auctions can be used in many cases, though they are most commonly reserved for smaller firms in the service sector. It is important to keep in mind, however, that the methods of privatization are also extremely contentious in Russian society, and it is highly likely that these regulations may change.

A major theme running throughout the rules and regulations on privatization is preferential treatment for labor collectives. For example, a labor collective may successfully bid for a firm, even though its bid may not be the highest.[40] Also, worker collectives can be given a one-time distribution of the firm's preferred stock, in an amount up to 25 percent of the capital value of the firm.[41] Workers may also be sold as much as 10 percent of the total value of the stock offering at a 30 percent discount on the nominal value of the shares. The purchasers of this stock may pay for it in 12 monthly installments. During the sale of joint stock company stocks on the open market the employees of the privatized firm receive 10 percent of the proceeds from the sale of these shares, though all of these revenues must be kept in their personal privatization accounts.

In cases where a firm is being privatized by auction or competitive sale, there are also benefits for the workers. For example, state and municipal enterprises may create privatization funds from their profits and the personal funds of the workers of the enterprise, though there are restrictions on how much money the firm can funnel into the privatization fund. Also, a joint stock company that includes at least one-third of the employees of the privatized enterprise is granted a 30 percent discount off the selling price and the opportunity to repay the amount by installment over a year's time, though the first payment must equal 30 percent of the total price.

A good deal of attention has been devoted to the Russian voucher program. This program, which gives every Russian citizen a privatization voucher worth 10,000 rubles, is another attempt to spread ownership rights throughout society as equally as possible. The vouchers may be invested directly in firms, may be invested in mutual funds, or may be sold to other investors for cash. Today, 10,000 rubles seems a small sum compared to the total asset value of the enterprises scheduled for privatization in Russia (even if asset values are calculated in pre-inflation rubles). Moreover, because of the serious deficit of information regarding businesses in Russia it is questionable whether most Russians will have knowledge of investment opportunities outside their city or region. Although this need not be a serious problem in the short term, capital markets and good flows of information on business activity must develop so that the global Russian investment portfolio is as efficient as possible.

The favorable treatment of labor collectives and the widescale distribution of privatization vouchers attack two problems discussed above. First, these methods help mitigate any feelings that privatization violates the traditional norms of social justice because they help to spread ownership shares more widely through society than would a policy that distributed equity shares based on the ability to pay. Further, such policies attack the problem of ambivalence toward and lack of understanding of private enterprise because they give more people a vested interest in the success of the private sector.[42]

Privatizing Soviet Housing: 1985–91[43]

The above discussion has shown that industrial privatization is extremely complex and is bound to move slowly; privatizing agriculture has proved so problematic that progress in this area should not be expected soon, even though advancements in this area would go a long way toward broadening and strengthening the ownership class in Russia.[44] The privatization of housing has, however, proven to be a more efficacious process, and could well distribute property throughout society more quickly. This is due in part to the low capital requirements involved, the fact that special business experience is not necessary, the absence of ideological opposition to private housing, and the failure of the state to provide adequate housing for its citizens.

Solving the housing shortage problem emerged as one of the most prominent socio-economic policy matters for the Soviet government during the Twelfth Five-Year Plan period (1986–90). As the plan was being drafted, increasing attention was given to investment in the housing sector. At the 27th CPSU Congress in February 1986, the Party platform declared that "practically every family would have its own house or apartment by the year 2000." Indeed, there was progress in the total number of square meters of housing built in the first years of *perestroika* (see Table 3.3). Housing space completed grew from 113.0 million square meters in 1985 to 132.3 million square meters in 1988. But by 1988, constraints in the construction industries generally began to take their toll on the housing industry in particular, and by 1990, only some 115.0 million square meters of housing space were built. For 1991, figures from the CIS indicate that housing space completed fell a further 17 percent, while in the RSFSR alone, housing was off 22 percent.[45] In 1989, there were some 38 million households[46] without their own apartment in the Soviet Union, and the situation has not improved since then.

This downturn in housing construction came at a time when the queues for housing were growing. An important new factor in the last two years of the Gorbachev period was the return of Soviet service personnel from abroad. Many of these—the estimates reach as high as many tens of thousands—remain without homes.[47] The dislocation of ethnic minorities in many areas (particularly within the Caucusus and from non-Russian regions to Moscow) exacerbates the housing shortage in some areas, while somewhat alleviating it in others.

By the beginning of 1991 the shortage of housing had grown to about 40 million apartments.[48] At the same time, wages and incomes generally were growing much faster than prices, and Soviet savings accounts were holding hundreds of billions of "excess" rubles that represented unsatisfied consumer demand. In the face of the growing disequilibrium in the housing market, the leadership gradually came to terms with the fact that, as with so many other social and economic programs, the centrally administered system was hopelessly inadequate and stood no chance of meeting housing policy goals. Selling off state-owned apartments came to be seen as a way not only of relieving the state of its self-imposed re-

Table 3.3
Housing Construction in the USSR

Year	Total Space (mln. meters^2)	Total Apts. (1000s)	Built by: State (1000s)	Coops (1000s)	Private (1000s)	Kolkhozy (1000s)
1985	113.0	1991	1327	137	226	122
1986	119.8	2099	1413	142	239	115
1987	131.4	2264	1545	155	258	110
1988	132.3	2230	1522	150	296	99
1989	128.9	2120	1463	134	311	85
1990	115.0	1800	1207	113	302	70

Source: Goskomstat SSSR, *Press vypusk*, no. 159 (May 27, 1991): 1-3.

sponsibility for housing, but as a way of satisfying at least part of the demand, of soaking up some of the excess cash held by Soviet citizens, and of relieving pressure on the state budget for housing construction and maintenance.[49] Further, and no less important, private ownership of the housing stock would contribute to the development of a middle class that would have strong vested interests in the continuation of democratic and market-oriented reforms. Finally, it is worth noting that some influential, if unofficial, policy advisors began to argue that there was a significant positive correlation between income and the benefits derived from subsidies on many consumer goods. In particular, the traditional system of providing state-owned housing at subsidized rents that grossly understated true market value came under attack for violating the very concept of social justice the policy was meant to defend.[50] This became an increasingly common theme among reformist economists, but the government was slow to understand their point.[51]

The leadership took several measures in 1988–91 to shift the burden of housing from the state to the individual. In 1988, the USSR government issued three decrees aimed at (1) spurring private housing construction; (2) encouraging cooperative takeovers of state and municipal housing; and (3) selling off—privatizing—state and municipal housing. Interestingly, these policy steps were not the radical departures from established party orthodoxy that one might have thought. The 1977 Soviet constitution, for example, guaranteed Soviet citizens access to state and socially-owned housing and assistance for cooperative and individual housing construction.

Non-state construction of housing grew after the introduction of the three decrees in 1988, as did the sale of state-owned housing. Growth was slow, however, in part because construction materials were difficult to obtain and in part because there was a good deal of skepticism among the population about the notion of private housing. Nonetheless, the number of privately built apartments in the Soviet Union increased by over 33 percent from 1985 to 1990, when they accounted for about one-fifth of total housing space brought on line.[52]

The RSFSR Law on Privatizing the Housing Stock

The RSFSR Supreme Soviet passed a law on the privatization of the housing stock in the RSFSR in July 1991.[53] In part, this law was an attempt to exercise control over state-owned assets on RSFSR territory in the ongoing struggle for power with the USSR government. The very existence of the law presupposed RSFSR ownership over the housing stock on its territory, reconfirmed in a very concrete way RSFSR stewardship over assets that were formerly the uncontested property of the USSR, and stripped the USSR of an important asset (and potential tax) base.[54]

The law calls for the voluntary sale and distribution (free of charge) of housing units in the state and municipal housing stock into the private property of people who occupy those units. The law further provides for the future sale of housing in a secondary market. Additionally, owners may rent out their apartments (houses) and bequeath them to their heirs as they see fit. According to the law citizens are entitled to at least eighteen square meters plus nine square meters for a family free of charge, though local and regional authorities may establish higher levels.[55] Families wishing to buy apartments must pay for any additional space at a per-square meter rate specified by independent commissions that are attached to (*pri*) local *soviets* (councils). That rate is to be based on the "average value" of housing space in the region, and does not necessarily vary to account for any type of quality differentials between housing units. However, the Russian government *did* issue some methodological recommendations to local officials for calculating the value of privatized housing. These recommendations include some administratively set quality differential coefficients which attempt to factor consumer preferences into the initial selling price of the property.[56]

In today's Russian economy, plagued by financial disequilibrium, it is impossible to determine the amount of capital available to privatize the housing stock or the distribution of capital through the population. Monetary emissions in the RSFSR in 1991 were nearly five times the 1990 level, and bank credits were two times larger in 1991 than in 1990.[57] Nonetheless, in the wake of the January 1992 price liberalization, as many as 90 percent of all Russian Federation citizens are living below the poverty line, and there are many more for whom buying an apartment at market prices is out of the question.[58] Further, the absence of a sizable, active, housing market, and the hyperinflationary conditions prevailing in 1992 further complicate pricing. In such a circumstance, only a second-best solution, based on administered prices for the initial purchase of housing space, and wide access to credit for those who do not have enough of their own capital, may be practical. In this way, *nomenklatura* privatization, and the purchase of housing units by enterprises, might well be avoided.

The selloff of the housing stock, even below market-clearing prices, will generate sizable revenues for the Russian budget. In January–April 1991, some 27,000 apartments were sold in the RSFSR, generating about 144.5 million rubles.[59] If even a half-million apartments are sold at roughly 5400 rubles each, this would generate revenue of nearly 3 billion rubles, roughly one percent of total budgetary revenue for the RSFSR in 1991. Sales of this magnitude are not unrealistic. For example, in February 1992 alone, roughly 51,000 apartments were privatized in Russia.[60] However, it is likely that the main financial benefit will be the relief of carrying the aging housing stock on the books in years to come, and the relief from generating new housing.

The outlook for privatized housing in Russia is good compared to privatization in other sectors and to housing development in the state sector. Private housing is a relatively safe investment, though threats of immanent monetary reform and serious price instability might inhibit people from going heavily into debt. The further development of markets, both for housing and credit, will improve housing's attractiveness as an investment alternative. Also, private housing is not a "productive" asset and thus represents much less of an ideological problem for conservatives than does private industry. Finally, the existing legislation makes the privatization of housing easy, at least in principle, and could avoid the problem of *nomenklatura* privatization.

Outlook for the Future

This essay has taken a brief and broad look at some of the key issues involved in Russia's movement away from state socialism and toward a private, market-based economy. Several important themes emerge to paint a complex, unstable, and, often, contradictory picture. Many of the complexities and contradictions are unavoidable. For one thing, political decentralization within the vast Russian Federation has often resulted in slow progress toward privatization in the provinces, where legislation concerning property rights has often lagged behind federal regulations. Another problem that has arisen independently of government reform programs is the growth of a sizable organized crime system that casts a dark shadow on the Russian private economy, damaging its reputation among the population and discouraging would-be entrepreneurs from becoming involved. Other problems—such as the rapid decapitalization of the economy in the wake of the January 1992 price liberalization— point to the intricate way in which various aspects of economic reform are interdependent. It remains to be seen if savings balances in Russia will be adequate to support wide-scale privatization. But the most important obstacle, as we have seen, has been the cultural predisposition against private enterprise in Russia. Overcoming that obstacle will take several years at best, and must be carefully managed.

It is worth pointing out that Russia has only pursued its current line of reform since December 1991. Prior to that date, Russian economic policy was constrained (though to an ever-decreasing degree) by Soviet federal policies. Thus, the process of transformation is still in its early phases. Experience thus far has shown that the path is complex and littered with difficult problems and choices. But despite its flaws, the Russian economic legislation is impressive and is increasingly competent and sophisticated.[61] Although the constant revisions in economic law are confusing and off-putting to many investors, most of the changes have been in the right direction. Finally, it has become clear from experience in Eastern Europe that privatization, especially when it comes from below and is not over-orchestrated from the top, is a self-supporting process that has its own dynamic. Although the privatization of large enterprises is proving to be especially difficult in Russia, small scale privatization, usually with less government involvement, is likely to be more promising and will develop more rapidly.[62]

Still, much is left to be done. Russia must pursue her fiscal and monetary policies with strict discipline. The institutional components of a market economy—such as a modern banking system, capital markets, antitrust legislation, and business regulations that are supportive while not repressive—must be established. Many of these issues are now under discussion in Russia, and others have already been dealt with. All of these elements are necessary for the successful development of the Russian private sector, and seem to be falling into place. However, even all these institutional changes in sum are not sufficient to produce a prosperous and stable Russian economy. A major psychological transformation must take place among Russians that will change the individual's perception of his role in society and the economy. That is a longer-term exercise, but one which—fortunately—has also begun to be reflected in Russian policy on privatization.

Notes

1. Although *samizdat* literature on the topic kept a few economists thinking in terms of capitalist-oriented economics, its scope and immediate impact were relatively limited. See Elizabeth Teague, "Redefining Socialism," in *Socialism, Perestroika, and the Dilemmas of Soviet Economic Reform*, edited by John E. Tedstrom, 22–39 (Boulder, CO: Westview Press, 1990); and Philip Hanson, "Ownership Issues in *Perestroika*," in same, 65–96.

2. A major complicating factor is that data on economics and privatization in the USSR and its successor states is extremely sparse. The Russian Federation has the most extensive and competent statistical services of all the Soviet successor states because it inherited the bulk of the USSR Goskomstat. Still, the Russian Goskomstat, as well as the Russian State Property Committee which also collects and publishes information on privatization, do not yet have adequate facilities and methodologies for tracking the privatization process, though reforms are underway.

3. The special case of agricultural privatization is not addressed in this chapter because even less progress has been made in this area than in others.

4. *Novoe vremia*, no. 50 (1991): 8. The remainder chose cooperatives. Only in Estonia and Georgia were the percentages of respondents wanting to work

in private firms higher than those who wanted to work in state enterprises. In Turkmenistan, the vote was 84 percent for state enterprises and 8 percent for private firms.

5. See *Pravitel'stvennyi vestnik,* no. 27 (1991): 4–5.

6. To the extent that the political situation in Russia is so unstable, future trends in economic policy are difficult to predict.

7. The Russian government issued a statute on the division of property between the federal and subfederal administrative regions, though the debate continues. See *Ekonomika i zhizn',* no. 3 (1992): 17. In general terms, the federal government retained for its own property natural resources such as the continental shelf, air space, etc., some key industries (including all of the defense industries and most of the fuel and energy complex) and parts of the Russian economic infrastructure such as federal highways. Republics within Russia were allocated most of the major enterprises not claimed by the federal government. Local jurisdictions received small enterprises and most of the social infrastructure.

8. See the complaints of Russian president Boris Yeltsin, in *Sovetskaia Rossiia* (October 29, 1991): 3. See also Chapter 2 for a detailed description of similar scandal and corruption in the Polish reforms.

9. See Carla Thorson, "The Politics of Privatization in Moscow," *RFE/RL Research Report,* no. 17 (1992): 51–57.

10. See "Predprinimatel' na rasput'e," *Ekonomika i zhizn',* no. 2 (1992): 1, 8.

11. This number includes all types of non-state-owned firms.

12. "Sotsial'no-ekonomicheskoe polozhenie Rossiiskoi Federatsii, v 1991 godu," *Ekonomika i zhizn',* no. 4 (1992: 4–5.

13. The large number of exchanges is somewhat worrisome in that it points to and underscores the fractious nature of the Russian economy. By mid-1992, Russia possessed some 700 such exchanges. These are described in Perry L. Patterson, "Financial Markets in the Soviet Union, 1987–1991," manuscript, Wake Forest University, May 1992; and Paul Klebnikov, "A Market Grows in Russia," *Forbes* (June 8, 1992): 78–82.

14. *Ekonomika i zhizn',* no. 2 (1992): 20.

15. The Russian GNP estimate of roughly 6.3 trillion rubles is from report of a government cabinet meeting in early March, 1992. ITAR-TASS, March 6, 1992.

16. The remaining 15 billion rubles (21 percent) is expected to come from other state enterprise funds.

17. See the RSFSR Goskomstat report for the first quarter of 1992 in *Ekonomika i zhizn',* no. 17 (1992): 14–15.

18. *Ekonomika i zhizn',* no. 14 (1992): 1. As this source notes, applications to privatize firms increased significantly in early 1992, from 1430 in January, to over 3500 in February, and to some 11,000 in March. However, it is unclear how many of these were approved, what sort of profit opportunities may have motivated these applications, and whether such firms were likely to continue operating.

19. "Zony dlia predprinimatelei," *Ekonomika i zhizn',* no. 48 (1991): 7.

20. Vladimir Ranenko, "Sovmestnoe predprinimatel'stvo v Rossii," *Ekonomika i zhizn',* no. 5 (1992): 13. As of April 1991, Russia had by far the largest number of active joint ventures (733), with Ukraine and Belarus' the next in line (125 and 52 respectively). See "Zony dlia predprinimatelei."

21. The share of foreign partner investment in Russia is below the average in the former USSR of about 60 percent toward the end of 1991. About 80 percent of the total foreign investment came from Western partners in the US, FRG, Finland, and Italy.

22. Assuming that by the end of the year there were about 850 active joint ventures in Russia, these figures imply that the active joint ventures are relatively small, averaging only about 160 employees and 13 million rubles in annual sales per firm.

23. See "Regulirovanie vneshneekonomicheskoi deiatel'nosti v Rossii," *Ekonomika i zhizn'*, no. 5 (1992); and "Sovmestnoe predprinimatel'stvo v Rossii," for more on this issue.

24. The term "underground economy" is meant here to encompass all of those economic activities that take place but that are not sanctioned by the state. Understood as such, the underground economy includes such activities as padding production reports, taking or giving bribes, dealing in foreign currencies, and stealing goods from state stores to sell on black markets, in addition to what most Westerners would call private businesses that happen to be illegal under Soviet law.

25. See B. Golubev, "Boi s ten'iu," *Trud* (September 25, 1991), for example.

26. See Valeryi Rutgaizer, "Sizing Up the Shadow Economy: Review and Analysis of Soviet Estimates," *Berkeley-Duke Occasional Papers on the Second Economy in the USSR*, no. 34 (1992); and Gregory Grossman, "Sub-rosa Privatization and Marketization in the USSR," *Berkeley-Duke Occasional Papers on the Second Economy in the USSR*, no. 17 (1989).

27. The largest single component of the total is moonshine sales, worth approximately 23 billion rubles in 1990, compared with official production of alcoholic beverages of 55.2 billion. See Vladimir Kostakov's article in *Kultura*, no. 16 (n.d.): 4.

28. Valeryi Rutgaizer, "Sizing Up the Shadow Economy."

29. Of course, most policy makers in Russia now believe that a shift to market relations is the only answer to the country's economic survival. See Grossman, "Sub-rosa Privatization."

30. V. Golubev, "Boi." Another Soviet observer, Gavril Popov, has characterized the operators in the underground economy as the "legitimate" children of the system. See Gavril Popov, "Perspektivy i realii," *Ogonek*, no. 51 (1991).

31. Examples of such scandals include Yurii Churbanov, Leonid Brezhnev's son-in-law being implicated in the cotton affair, the minister of the Ministry of the Fishing Industry being executed for involvement in the "fish affair," and members of the military-industrial complex organizing to sell tanks abroad. Further, former Soviet president Gorbachev has been under investigation for possibly "mismanaging" USSR and CPSU funds.

32. A. Bunich, "'Tenevaia' chast' byurokraticheskogo aisberga," *Ekonomika i zhizn'*, no. 3 (1992): 15. This is the first in a two-part series on the black market. Part two, by the same author, is published as "Kak tenevaia ekonomika stala legal'noi," *Ekonomika i zhizn'*, no. 4 (1992): 13. Together, they provide a very useful overview of this topic.

33. Grossman, "Sub-rosa Privatization."

34. "Zakon RSFSR: O privatizatsii gosudarstvennykh i munitsipal'nykh pred-preiatii v RSFSR," *Ekonomika i zhizn'*, no. 31 (1991): 15–17; and "Osnovnye polozheniya programmy privatizatsii gosudarstvennykh i munitsipal'nykh predpriatii v RSFSR na 1992 god," *Ekonomika i zhizn'*, no. 2 (1992): 18–20. Prior to that, the USSR law "On the basic principles of enterprise denationalization and privatization" governed the privatization process. See *Izvestiia* (August 9, 1991) for the text. For a summary of relevant legislation in 1989 and 1990, see Philip Hanson, "Property Rights in the New Phase of Reform," *Soviet Economy* (April–June 1990): 95–124. For a discussion of the economic implications of laws affecting the Russian (Soviet) cooperative sector, see Murphy, Chapter 8, this volume.

35. *Programma uglubleniia ekonomicheskikh reform*, Moscow, June 1992.

36. This is the group headed up by Arkadii Volskii. The chief economist of this group is Evgenii Iasin, a very able academic and policy analyst. It is interesting to note that Iasin's team of economists has close contacts with the government "Working Group" on economic reform headed by Sergei Vasilev. In some instances, members of these two groups have overlapped, and they occasionally share other resources as well.

37. See Hanson, "Ownership Issues in *Perestroika.*"

38. The following discussion of the four categories is only partial, and is intended to give a representational sample of the complete list of enterprises and organizations in each group.

39. This discussion is based on material available in March 1992. If past trends are any indicator of future developments, we can expect further revisions in the details, if not the fundamentals, of the Russian reform program over the course of the next several years. The instability of the privatization program and its legal framework is a problem not only for academics who study the Russian economy, but is also a major inhibiting factor for would be entrepreneurs and investors.

40. The law stipulates that the bid has to come "reasonably" close to the highest auction price, though.

41. Preferred stocks are non-voting stocks which must be paid back to investors when a firm is going bankrupt.

42. This is not to say that these policies are perfect. For example, many Russians may sell their vouchers to others who have ready cash, leading to a concentration of equity in a smaller share of the total population.

43. This section draws on the following sources: Aaron Trehub, "Housing Policy in the USSR/CIS: *Perestroika* and Beyond," *RFE/RL Research Report*, no. 6 (1992): 30–42; and Aaron Trehub, "*Perestroika* and Social Entitlements," in *Socialism, Perestroika, and the Dilemmas of Soviet Economic Reform*, edited by John E. Tedstrom, 207–232 (Boulder, CO: Westview Press, 1990). See also Gregory Andrusz, "Housing Policy in the Soviet Union," in *Housing Policies in Eastern Europe and the Soviet Union* (London: Routledge, 1990).

44. There are indications that the movement to privatize agriculture is beginning to take root. President Yeltsin is publicly committed to serious agrarian reform, and some of the opposition in the Russian parliament seems to be eroding or at least losing influence. It is clear, however, that there is substantial skepticism about the government and its reforms in rural areas, many of which are still run

by former CPSU hacks and many of which lag seriously behind more urban areas in terms of social, political, and economic modernization.

45. See the USSR Goskomstat report in *Ekonomika i zhizn'*, no. 6 (1992): 13, and the Russian Federation Goskomstat report in *Ekonomika i zhizn'*, no. 4 (1992): 4.

46. Families plus single member households. See Trehub (1992).

47. Some authoritative Soviet observers have warned of the destabilizing political force the homeless service personnel could embody. See Stephen Foye, "Soviet Armed Forces Face Housing Crisis," *Report on the USSR*, no. 13 (March 30, 1990): 5–7.

48. Based on data for 1989 in *Zhilishchnye usloviia naseleniia SSSR: Statisticheskii sbornik* (Moscow: Goskomstat, 1990); *Vestnik statistiki*, no. 8 (1991): 52; and the Goskomstat report for economic performance in 1991, in *Ekonomika i zhizn'*, no. 6 (1992): 13.

49. It is worth stressing that the initial selloff of state-owned assets only attacks the problem of excess money stocks. It does not, in the absence of other measures such as price liberalization, deal with the "flow" problem, i.e., of incomes rising faster than output. See Wolfram Schrettl, "Structural Conditions for a Stable Monetary Regime and Efficient Allocation of Investment: Soviet Country Study," in *Transformation of Planned Economies: Property Rights Reform and Macroeconomic Stability*, edited by Hans Blommestein and Michael Marrese, 109–126 (Paris: OECD, 1991).

50. See Tat'iana Zaslavskaia, "Chelovecheskii faktor razvitiia ekonomiki i sotsial'naia spravedlivost'," *Kommunist*, no. 13 (1986): 71–73.

51. Western economists have explored the theme as well. See Michael Alexeev, "The Effect of Housing Allocation on Social Inequality: A Soviet Perspective," *Journal of Comparative Economics*, no. 2 (1988): 228–34; and Michael Alexeev, "Market versus Rationing: The Case of Soviet Housing," *Review of Economics and Statistics*, no. 3 (1988): 414–420.

52. In 1985, private apartments represented 14 percent of total housing space brought on line.

53. "Zakon Rossiiskoi Sovetskoi Federativnoi Sotsialisticheskoi Respubliki, O privatizatsii zhilishchnogo fonda v RSFSR," *Ekonomika i zhizn'*, no. 33 (1991): insert, 3. This was followed by regulations that detailed the mechanics of privatizing the housing stock. "Primernoe polozhenie, O privatizatsii zhilishchnogo fonda v RSFSR," *Ekonomika i zhizn'*, no. 1 (1992).

54. The RSFSR asserted its right to ownership of assets on its territory in June 1990, when it issued its declaration of sovereignty. See "Deklaratsiia o gosudarstvennom suverenitete Rossiiskoi Sovetskoi Federativnoi Sotsialisticheskoi Respubliki," *Sovetskaia Rossiia* (June 14, 1990): 1.

55. Trehub, "Housing Policy," notes that some local and regional authorities have set higher minimums on the amounts of both the basic free living space and the family supplement, and have granted the family supplement to each family member, not the entire family unit as the RSFSR law stipulates.

56. *Ekonomika i zhizn'*, no. 2 (1992): 16.

57. *Ekonomika i zhizn'*, no. 6 (1992): 13.

58. ITAR-TASS, March 18, 1992. The share of Russian citizens living below the

poverty line is based on the estimate that only 7 percent of the population received income of at least the minimum subsistence level of 1500 rubles per month. The estimate is admittedly rough, but indicative of the situation, nonetheless.

59. *Ekonomika i zhizn'*, no. 28 (1991): 6.

60. *Ekonomika i zhizn'*, no. 15 (1992): 11. Most of the privatization of housing has taken place in large urban areas such as Moscow.

61. It also reflects the influence of Western economists, including those from international financial institutions such as the International Monetary Fund and the World Bank.

62. A similar conclusion for Poland is reached in Chapters 2 and 9.

4

Struggles over a Growing Private Sector: The Case of Hungary

*Catherine Sokil-Milnikiewicz**

As the country with the longest history of comprehensive economic reform during the Communist period, Hungary provides an interesting case study of the evolution of the private sector in Eastern Europe from the Communist period to the present. As such, the lessons learned by Hungary are valuable for the other fledgling democracies of the new Eastern and Central Europe. Since the comprehensive economic reform program of 1968, Hungary's leadership tried to boost personal initiative in the economy through reforms limiting the state's involvement in the economy and tolerating—even supporting—some forms of private economic activity. Legal and institutional support of the private sector has evolved gradually in Hungary since then, as the following account testifies.

Because attempts to stimulate the private sector and to energize state industry began earlier there, the Hungarian example stands as a unique case in Eastern and Central Europe where a significant, growing private sector coexisted with a dominant state sector over an extended period. Authorities allowed the private sector to exist in some forms, and even promoted development of new forms of private effort, for the simple reason that it performed so well. The private sector not only contributed to economic growth on its own; it also served the state sector, making an important contribution to the growth of the economy overall. The

*The author gratefully acknowledges research and other support provided by Middlebury College. Erik Whitlock and Perry Patterson provided extremely useful comments on an earlier draft. Many thanks also to Mrs. Csilla Hunyadi, who generously provided up-to-date statistics on the course of Hungarian privatization.

Hungarian experience shows that private initiative can be a potent force contributing toward economic growth, even under socialism.

Furthermore, in Hungary, in which the private sector flourished in response to economic reforms,[1] authorities gradually attempted to reform the state sector to make it as productive as the private sector. Nonetheless, authorities' attempts to make state sector firms behave more like private firms did not work. Inadequacies of the reform effort led to a "dual economy" consisting of a more highly regulated state sector competing unequally with a less regulated private sector. Inconsistencies in the regulation of these two sectors precluded true competition and the benefits thereof.

Political authorities in Hungary have finally concluded that "political pressures and ill-devised managerial incentives condemn state-owned enterprises to perform substantially worse than privately-owned firms."[2] Specifically, the evidence shows that in Hungary state-owned industry has used and invested capital much less efficiently than have private firms in market economies; that the Hungarian government has allocated investment poorly; and that Hungarian managers have used existing capital less efficiently than have their market economy counterparts.[3] Hungarian policymakers have finally concluded that, in order to improve economic performance, not only should new, private firms be allowed to compete in the Hungarian marketplace, but state-owned firms must also be privatized.

Although the general policy decision to privatize on a grand scale may have been reached, differences—largely political—remain as to the precise scope and pace of privatization. Although the Hungarian leadership has made great strides in the development of legal and other institutions to promote large-scale privatization, the slow pace of privatization is perhaps best explained by social conditions. For example, given the shortage of domestic savings and high interest rates in Hungary, entrepreneurs and ordinary citizens lament that they are handicapped relative to foreigners also wishing to buy privatized Hungarian assets.[4] How are political authorities to prevent alienation of their constituencies, when Hungarians see their state assets being sold off, largely to foreigners? Hungarian entrepreneurs have begun to seek political empowerment through, for example, the lobbying efforts of the National Association of Entrepreneurs.[5] The politico-economic questions regarding equity versus efficiency seem likely to plague all transition governments. Any political regime must now ask whether the benefits of allowing people to enrich themselves through privatization are worth the costs of alienating those who perhaps are unable or unwilling to participate in the process.

The Hungarian example, then, is one of introducing political reform—

i.e., allowing many voices in the society, who may now openly criticize policymakers for economic and other decisions—at the same time that leaders must grapple with tough economic issues. Economic constraints to speedy privatization include a lack of sufficient domestic savings to allow many Hungarians to participate in the privatization process, at the same time that external debt and other macroeconomic considerations have ruled out the kind of mass distribution of shares to the public which has been widely debated in Hungary and Poland, and which may still be a possibility in, say, Czechoslovakia and Russia. The political and social dilemmas of privatization on a grand scale in a society controlled by Communism for decades will undoubtedly take many years to be re-solved, and Hungary will continue to set an example in its decades-long struggle to become a society based on democracy and private ownership.

Post-War Nationalization of Industry and Agriculture

The challenges of reconstruction led Hungary as well as other Euro-pean countries to extend state control over the economy after World War II. As the Hungarian economic historian Gyorgy Ranki explains,[6] the Hungarian Communist Party's program initially called for partial state control and only later for a fully centralized, planned economy. Although the coal mines and major industrial Hungarian companies were quickly nationalized, the private sector dominated the Hungarian economy under the three-year reconstruction plan introduced in August 1947. In agriculture, peasant plots were the prevailing form of land tenure since the 1945 land reform which abolished the age-old feudal landholding system. The three-year plan represented a combination of a large albeit declining private sector working with a small yet growing state sector.

By 1948–49, however, having achieved a monopoly on political power, the Hungarian Communist Party changed course.[7] The Party gave up the idea of achieving socialism gradually and opted for the establishment of a socialist economic and social system in the shortest time possible. Full-scale introduction of state property was seen as a prerequisite to a socialist economic system; private property was viewed as an obstacle to this aim.

In March 1948, all private firms employing 100 or more persons were nationalized; by December 1949, all firms employing more than ten workers were expropriated.[8] Even smaller-scale industry was eventually brought into state hands, not by direct expropriation but by administra-tive pressure. Small-scale industry had played a very important historical role in Hungary; even in 1948, there were 180,000 artisans employing 188,000 workers.[9] Although these tiny shops were not directly national-

ized, taxation, price controls, materials allocation, and occasional bureaucratic harassment led to a precipitous drop in the number of private artisans by 1950.

In Hungary as in the other countries of Eastern and Central Europe
which fell under the Soviet sphere of influence after World War II, the
Soviet model of the centrally planned economy (CPE) was introduced.
Market mechanisms were replaced with an administrative-command
system based on central planners' preferences. Through a process of
nationalization of industry, capitalist property was virtually eliminated in
Hungary. By the end of 1949, virtually the entire economy, with the exception of agriculture and retail trade, fell under state ownership. The
managers of these new state enterprises were chosen and dismissed by
officials of the dominant Communist Party. The Stalinist model was
further implemented during the 1950s, as heavy industry predominated,
beginning with the First Five Year Plan enacted on January 1, 1950. Production targets as well as the allocation of resources were handed down
in the form of central directives originating at the National Planning
Office, the top of the economic hierarchy. In agriculture, centralization
was achieved by attempting to force peasants to join large state and cooperative farms.

These changes took their toll on the Hungarian people, who responded to their economic and political lot in the bloody uprising of 1956.
The 1956 Hungarian uprising, a popular response to the shortcomings of
the Stalinist political economy model, was quelled by Soviet tanks and
the installment of Janos Kadar as the country's leader. Yet the Kadar leadership, which finally ended in 1988, was characterized by compromise:
Domination of politics and economics by a Communist Party leadership
loyal to the Soviet Union was tolerated in exchange for experimentation
with economic reform and steady improvement in the population's standard of living.[10]

Under Kadar, a set of economic reforms was quickly elaborated, but it
was tabled until 1968, with the exception of some reforms in agriculture.
In the meantime, however, the private sector already began to show its
strength early on in the Kadar regime. Under a fifteen-year housing program announced in 1960, one million new flats—an ambitious target—
were to be built. Whereas the program envisioned two-thirds of these
being built in the framework of the government program, and one-third
through private efforts, in fact experience was just the opposite. State
efforts during the workweek produced only 350,000 flats, while private
efforts on the weekend, to a large extent substituting sweat for machinery, produced 650,000 new homes. A similar wonder occurred in agriculture, where 1.7 million small-scale farms operated by the mid-1970s. This
figure implies that 80–90% of agricultural workers and 40% of industrial

workers possessed their own private plot. It is estimated that these small farms were the source of 80–90% of the grapes, 60–70% of the pork, and at least 50% of the fruits, milk, and beef produced in the country.[11]

During 1959–61, agriculture was collectivized, but the forced collectivization of the 1950s was replaced by voluntary collectivization using material incentives. This voluntary method of collectivization stands in sharp contrast to the forced collectivizations in the Soviet Union imposed by Stalin. Given the success of these reforms in agriculture, industrial reform was renewed by the mid-1960s. The major reform program was begun in 1968 under the title of the New Economic Mechanism. While this reform program focused on reforms within the state sector, it also involved the limited reintroduction of some forms of private economic activity.

The New Economic Mechanism

The New Economic Mechanism, or NEM, introduced in 1968, sought to introduce certain market-economy benefits, most notably efficiency, into the Hungarian centrally planned economy. Directive central planning was eliminated; in its place, the government was to maintain indirect control over enterprises via financially-based instruments, known as "regulators." These included prices, wage and tax rules, credit, and subsidies. In other words, under the old system, authorities would elaborate, and would then send, detailed quantitative targets to state enterprise managers regarding how much to produce, with what inputs, and at what prices. Under the new system, it was hoped that the same plans might be achieved by authorities who instead indirectly guided enterprise managers' behavior via financial instruments, that is by instructing top management of firms to be profitable, and then by setting rules for such things as how much they could pay to their workers, and how much they would have to pay in various kinds of taxes, etc. The price system was also reformed, with the goal of making prices more important economic signals. The NEM also encouraged the formation of agricultural cooperatives with limited government regulation, as well as limited forms of private enterprise in the retail sector.[12]

Thus the economy under the NEM could be divided into sectors of varying size based on ownership form. Large state-owned enterprises, subject to central control, dominated industry. However, state-owned industry coexisted with cooperative and private forms of ownership, which performed successfully under the NEM. In agriculture, cooperatives were dominant; cooperatives also contributed a share of production in industry, construction, and industrial services.

Legally, cooperatives were established under the following terms.

They had equal rights to state enterprises; they were formed voluntarily; they exhibited socialist ownership along with democratic self-government in internal affairs; and they were subject to state regulation. A basic condition of a cooperative was that members must contribute their wealth and personal services to it. Although under the cooperative form the land was to be farmed jointly, in a substantial share of these cooperatives the land technically belonged to the individuals rather than to the cooperative. This technicality is significant for subsequent privatization efforts, as we shall see.

Another 11.5 percent of agricultural land in Hungary remained in the form of household plots and a few remaining private farms.[13] These private farms as well as officially licensed small-scale industry facing limits on the number of employees they could hire made up the so-called formal private sector. The informal private sector included all remaining, unregistered, private undertakings. Thus what is typically termed the "black market" would fall into this category, and would not be captured in official statistics. Hence we see the difficulty in measuring the true size of the private sector, which in the wake of the NEM was officially measured as contributing only a few percentage points to the national income. For example, by 1970, according to official Hungarian statistics, the private sector accounted for 0.8 percent of retail trade; this share amounted to only 1.9 percent by 1985.[14] The corresponding shares were 65.5 and 33.7 percent for the state and cooperative sectors, respectively, in 1970; and 61.9 and 36.2 percent by 1985.[15]

Retrenchment and Renewal of Reform

By the early 1970s, domestic and international considerations led to retrenchment in economic reform, although the principles of the NEM were not formally abandoned.[16] The retrenchment was initiated by the state and party bureaucracy and supported by managers of large state enterprises whose economic positions had deteriorated as a result of economic decentralization. In addition, Hungary's difficulty in dealing with the world-market explosion in energy prices and subsequent Western recession played into the hands of those who favored greater economic centralization.[17]

Faced with an impending economic crisis as a result of rapidly rising convertible currency trade deficits, reforms returning to the principles of the NEM were reintroduced by 1979. At the same time, it was recognized that this time around, economic reform had to establish policies and institutions which were the preconditions for freer competition between the state and private sectors. These involved three basic types of reforms: first, reforms within the socialist sector, to reduce the central controls on it; next, reforms to promote and expand the second economy; and finally, reforms to equalize competition between the socialist and nonsocialist sectors. The latter would include capital market reforms and the development of institutions and instruments which would service both the state and private sectors, as well as labor market reforms which would reduce wage controls in the state sector.

Legal Changes of the Early 1980s

Having finally resolved to continue the reforms initiated under the NEM, Hungary embarked on a series of legal changes in the early 1980s. These legal reforms included introduction and reintroduction of various forms of private activity, which "took off" during this period, as well as reforms within the state sector, which met with limited success.

Reforms Within the Private Sector

In 1982, various new forms of second-economy activities were either introduced or revived in Hungary, creating, in effect, a continuum of ownership forms. These forms could be distinguished on the basis of the degree of regulation by authorities. State enterprises and large, traditional cooperatives formed the first economy, which was heavily regulated. New entrepreneurial forms, including small cooperatives, the private sector (legal and illegal), and the so-called "combined" forms of enterprise ("combined" in that they involve an arrangement between a state or cooperative enterprise with a private activity and/or firm, such as in leasing arrangements) formed the second economy, which was relatively free from government regulation.

Among these new forms, several deserve mention, as they would subsequently undergo considerable growth, and as their growth has had important implications for subsequent privatization efforts. The most prolific of the new combined forms have been the so-called enterprise contract work associations (*vallalati gazdasagi munkakozosseg* or *VGMK*). These are groups of two to thirty workers from a state enterprise who voluntarily organize to perform duties for that enterprise in their spare time. They are not independent legal entities. They do not have independent financial means, nor do they take risks; they make use of the facilities and capital of the enterprise. Conversely, in the so-called economic contract work association (*gazdsagi munkakozosseg* or *GMK*), members are not affiliated with any single enterprise, cooperative, or farm; thus they are essentially private undertakings.[18] Members invest their own capital and find work without assistance; hence they undertake risk. Industrial and service cooperative groups correspond to the VGMK in the cooperative sector. Small cooperatives consist of ventures established by groups of 15–100 private persons, perhaps by seceding from some large organization. These small coops often accommodate parttime workers, including students and retirees. Their regulation is simpler than that of the traditional cooperatives. The civil law association (*polgari jogi tarsasag* or *PJT*), already in existence prior to 1982 but revived under the new rules, are usually associations of private professional people. Under a leasing arrangement, a private individual or groups (for example, artisans) may pay a fee to use the assets of a larger state enterprise. Under a similar arrangement, an enterprise might hire a private person under a contractual agreement. In the contract, the entrepreneur would commit himself to achieve a certain income within a predetermined period, paying some proportion of this income to the enterprise for the use of its assets.[19]

These new forms of enterprise grew at a fast pace in the first half of the 1980s. Table 4.1 provides figures on the considerable growth of these second-economy activities from 1982 to 1985 as measured by the number of various types of new firms in existence. As for their contribution to the Hungarian economy, Kornai estimates that by the mid-1980s the Hungarian labor force spent one-third of its total working time on second economy activities.[20] And, although the formal private sector contributed only a small portion to officially-recorded GNP, the informal (i.e., not those forms listed here) private sector contributed up to 20 percent of gross national output.

This dual economy, in which many Hungarian citizens participated by holding a state-sector job while engaged in the second economy, created the "half-way house" of Hungarian reform.[21] While the second economy registered remarkable growth, the net result included perverse economic behaviors and limited competition. For example, the most widespread of the new enterprise forms, the enterprise contract work association (ECWA), allowed groups of employees of state enterprises to work after hours at high wages which were not subject to state limits. Often, only by hiring workers under the ECWA system could a state enterprise retain its most productive employees, who would otherwise be bid away by another state enterprise. Ironically, this system accentuated the perverse incentives of the planned economy: workers were even more likely to shirk their regular-time, state-sector work, and to put more effort into their overtime, second-economy job.

Unequal regulation and access to factor markets created unequal competition between the first and second economies. The first-economy firms continued to resemble firms in the traditional, unreformed centrally planned economy. Managers of enterprises were appointed by ministries, and therefore were accountable to them. Their budgets were "soft": should they experience financial difficulties, the ministries would bail

Table 4.1
Growth of New Enterprise Forms in Hungary,
1982-88 (no. of firms)

	1982	1983	1984	1985	1986	1987	1988
Form of Association:							
Enterprise contract work associations (VGMK)	3,531	9,836	17,770	20,267	21,490	19,120	16,978
Economic contract work associations (GMK)	2,289	4,592	7,316	9,314	10,941	11,186	11,815
Industrial and service cooperative groups	536	1,346	2,335	2,634	2,768	2,336	1,838
Small cooperatives	140	238	356	713	1,185	2,230	2,890
Civil law associations (PJT)	227	216	190	154	68	527	476

Source: Szirmai, "First Steps," 16, 19.

them out.[22] On the other hand, the second-economy firms enjoyed managerial independence but were subject to a "hard budget constraint." The second economy had more restricted access to capital and material inputs—they did not share the perks of managers in the first economy—but they enjoyed advantageous access to labor. Many workers kept their first-economy jobs for the perquisites that state enterprises had to provide to their employees, but they worked much harder at their private-sector jobs. In short, second-economy firms were more responsive to market signals, including prices—they had to be, for their own survival. To the extent that second-economy firms competed with each other, a limited "market" was created. However, the lack of competition between the first and second economies precluded true functioning of a "market mechanism."

Regulations changed frequently, and often unexpectedly, in both sectors. In this uncertain environment, paradoxically, first-economy firms became even less profit-oriented, and second-economy firms more, at least in the short run. Because second-economy firms were restricted in size, and because they had no access to a capital market which would allow reinvestment of their profits, second-economy firms tended to use their profits to increase wages and bonuses. Workers who either voluntarily or involuntarily worked only in the state sector became envious of the "conspicuous consumption" of private incomes. The mentality of "Grab the profits while you can"[23] contributed to popular resentment of the private sector which colored the population's views about markets in general.

Reforms Within the State Sector

Although a deconcentration program was instituted to break up some monopolies, Hungarian industry remained one of the most concentrated in the world. A new pricing system artificially linking domestic and world market prices was introduced in 1980. Intended to force international competition onto Hungarian firms, this "competitive pricing system" failed, as prices continued in practice to be essentially formed by bargaining between the enterprise and the central body responsible for price formation. Restrictions on enterprises' production profiles (product assortments) were relaxed and eventually eliminated, allowing enterprises to compete with new products. Still, few did. In 1983, enterprises began filling important managerial positions through advertised public tenders. In the same year, enterprises were given the right to issue bonds to raise capital.

In 1985, the managerial system of state enterprises was further reformed in an effort to improve the performance of state enterprises. For approximately 80 percent of state enterprises (many of the largest enterprises were not included), an elected enterprise council composed of representatives of workers (50 percent) and management (50 percent) became the new managerial authority. The managerial change, involving greater devolution of managerial authority to workers, would subsequently contribute to the uncertainty over property rights which has accompanied the onset of privatization in Hungary.

In 1986 a bankruptcy law was also enacted. Institutions were established by which a state enterprise might actually be liquidated; unfortunately, they were cumbersome and rarely used. Despite all of the foregoing attempts by the Hungarian government to make state enterprises behave more like their market economy private sector counterparts, authorities finally acknowledged that in order for state enterprises to behave like private firms, they had to directly compete with them. In part to help eliminate the state sector's edge in the capital markets, a two-tier banking system was established in which specialized new financial institutions would service industrial, agricultural, and consumer cooperatives. However, these new "banks" were limited in the capital they could raise relative to the traditional banks which served the state sector.[24] In part to help eliminate the private sector's advantage in the labor market, a personal income tax was introduced in 1988 which would tax the excessive incomes in the private sector.

Reforms within the state sector had only limited success in making state firms behave more efficiently. And, despite these and other changes, unequal competition for resources remained. Faced with the remarkable growth of the second economy and popular resentment of the incomes gained there, the authorities responded by increasing substantially the tax burden on the second economy. These taxes took the form of personal income taxes levied on the entrepreneurs themselves as well as taxes on the state enterprises ordering services from the second-economy enterprises. The net result of these taxes and other restrictive public policies was a significant drop in the number of several of the new forms of second economy enterprises in the latter half of the 1980s, as shown in Table 4.1.

The Post-1989 Legal Framework

By the end of the 1980s, faced with growing social tensions created by unequal tax and other treatment of the first and second economies, the political leadership in Hungary had to act. To help combat unequal taxation and legal status of second- versus first-economy firms, in 1989 three important laws were introduced. The Laws on Economic Association, Foreign Investment, and Transformation were designed to promote entry and to put all enterprises on equal legal footing.[25] An examination of these laws shows that they also paved the way for privatization to begin in Hungary.

Act VI of 1988, the Law on Economic Associations, or the Company Act (in Effect as of January 1, 1989)

This law allows freedom of enterprise; anyone, including private persons, may form a business association simply by registering it. Contrary to past practice, no approval of the Ministry of Finance or local councils is required. The Law on Economic Associations represents the first legal code that uniformly governs and regulates all forms of "business companies" or economic associations, and thus strives to create equal competition among all enterprise forms. Patterned after the (West) German model, the Act recognizes six company forms that may be formed on an equal legal and tax footing by both domestic and foreign legal entities and/or individuals. These are, from simplest to most complex:

1. Unlimited Partnership
2. Deposit (Limited) Partnership
3. Union
4. Joint Enterprise
5. Limited Liability Company (LLC)
6. Company Limited by Shares (Co., Ltd.)

The differences among these forms are primarily legal and financial. In unlimited partnerships, the partners have unlimited liability. (The economic work group, or *gazdasagi munkakozosseg (GMK)*, of Table 4.1 falls into this category.) In the deposit partnership, one partner may have limited liability but then cannot be involved in management. The union is a non-profit organization. Although all members have to be legal entities and the union has a separate legal personality, each of its members has unlimited liability. The joint enterprise can be a for-profit enterprise but, as in the union, its members must be legal entities and must have unlimited liability. (Therefore, it seems unlikely that the foregoing are likely to be popular vehicles for foreign investment.) The limited liability company (*korlatolt felelossegu tarsasag* or *KFT*) is a flexible form of association which already exists in Hungary. All shareholders participate in management. While there is no limit on the number of shareholders, these may not be obtained by invitation to the public. Minimum share capital of a LLC is one million forints, with a minimum subscription of 100,000 forints for each shareholder. The company limited by shares (joint-stock company) has a more formal structure, but provisions are in place to allow it to issue various forms of securities to the public. Minimum share capital for a company limited by shares is ten million forints.[26] At present, the most popular legal forms of private business in Hungary are the partnerships, both limited and unlimited, joint stock companies, and private entrepreneurs.[27]

The Act is a watershed in that it formally allows private and mixed capital ownership. At the same time, it does not apply to state enterprises, state farms, and cooperatives (small and large, including agricultural)—leaving these to operate parallel to the six forms, pending the subsequent Transformation Act.

Act XXIV of 1988, On Foreign Investment in Hungary (in Effect as of January 1, 1989)

This Act allows companies to be 100 percent foreign-owned and protects foreign investors from nationalization or expropriation of their investments. The act also allows special tax exemptions to be granted to the private sector.

Act XIII of 1989, On the Transformation of Economic Organizations and Economic Associations, or the Transformation Act (in Effect as of May 30, 1990)

The Transformation Act supplements the Act on Economic Associations, as it provides for the transformation of existing state enterprises and cooperatives into economic associations (companies).

Taken together, these three Laws established the necessary legal framework for privatization to take place. State enterprises could be transformed into corporate forms with private, including foreign, ownership, at least on paper.

It is important to note that this legal framework preceded non-Communist rule in Hungary. Yet, although the Communist government embarked on the program, given the fall of Communism in Eastern and Central Europe, the task of undertaking massive privatization of the Hungarian economy would be left to the new, non-Communist Hungarian government. At least, the new government was well-poised, relative to most of the other new governments of East and Central Europe, to begin the chore. Moreover, the new government had the benefit of the so-called Blue Ribbon Commission (BRC), a multilateral effort to develop a comprehensive program for Hungary's transformation. The directors of the Commission sought to articulate a program in advance of the March and April 1990 democratic elections, with the participation of Hungary's major political parties, namely the center-right Hungarian Democratic Forum and the "Western-style liberal" Alliance of Free Democrats. That way, regardless of the outcome of the elections, the new leaders would have the benefit of an internationally sanctioned, integrated program for the unprecedented task of the transformation to a market economy. The BRC's report recommended a comprehensive, pre-announced transition program as well as speedy privatization, to include considerable foreign participation.[28] Nonetheless, the speed of privatization became a major issue in the election campaign. The Free Democrats supported rapid privatization, while the Hungarian Democratic Forum emphasized a slower pace to ensure that asset sales generate the best possible price.[29]

Moreover, despite the best intentions of the organizers of the BRC to be perceived as independent and non-partisan, the BRC was only partially successful in achieving its goals. Although "the incoming government of Prime Minister Antall never formally rejected [the BRC's policy recommendations], it never considered them as policy guidance either."[30] Perhaps ironically, however, "in his first speech to Parliament outlining the program of the newly-formed government, Prime Minister Antall cited the BRC report as an input in formulating what the government wished to do in the economic realm."[31] Moreover, Antall subsequently endorsed the reconstitution of the BRC in order to serve as an independent international advisory body to Hungary on economic affairs.[32] In all, the entire experience with the BRC may constitute yet another lesson for the countries of East/Central Europe regarding the delicate political climate in which seemingly sound economic advice may find itself during the transition phase.

The End of Communist Rule in Hungary and
the Future of Privatization

The March 1990 Parliamentary elections resulted in a coalition government led by Prime Minister Jozsef Antall of the Hungarian Democratic Forum (holding 164 of 386 seats), with the Alliance of Free Democrats constituting the major opposition party (92 of 386 seats). The new, non-Communist Hungarian leadership committed itself to full-scale restructuring of the ownership system, although the details and pace of this restructuring were at first uncertain.

Early progress was slowed down by abuses in some of the first privatization cases. Specifically, existing managers and Socialist Party members were accused of profiteering from the sales of state-owned companies at depressed prices in so-called "spontaneous privatizations." Enterprise councils had the power—given the legal possibilities created by the Acts on Economic Associations and Transformation in the absence of a true capital market—to sell off enterprises to themselves and to their friends at bargain-basement prices. An example of such a case involved the proposed sale of *HungarHotels*, a chain of 50 hotels in Hungary and

Western Europe, to a Swedish-Dutch consortium, *Quintus*. In that case, a joint venture headed by *Quintus* and *HungarHotel's* management team emerged as the successful bidders when the hotel chain was offered for sale by its managers. The Hungarian government took the joint venture to court, however, as the price bid appeared to be much lower than the market value of the chain. The Hungarian Supreme Court found that the supposedly independent auditor in the deal, hired to assess the fair market value of the firm, was actually employed by the joint venture. The sale was declared null and void.[33] The government attempted to put the privatization process back under control by subsequently limiting privatizations pending renationalization, as ownership rights were explicitly given back from enterprise councils to the state.

The State Property Agency (SPA) was founded on March 1, 1990, under the January Law on Protection of Property Entrusted to State Enterprises. The agency, which was initially placed under the direct jurisdiction of Parliament and later placed under government control, was entrusted with monitoring the privatization process by protecting state assets. It was thought that the privatization process could be brought under greater control, and the abuses of spontaneous privatizations could be corrected, through centralization in the SPA. The State Property Agency's First Privatization Program, begun shortly thereafter, sought to sell to the private sector in Hungary and abroad the majority of shares of a selected group of manufacturing, tourist, commercial, trade, and transport sector enterprises. These enterprises represented $507 million in total equity, $1.1 billion in total assets, $1.4 billion in annual sales, and $92 million in before-tax profits, and were expected to generate $385–615 million in revenues for the state.[34]

The SPA has yet to achieve these goals, and has seen its own share of scandals. The Agency has been accused of being bureaucratic and slow in finding sellers, and of attempting to sell off firms at unrealistic prices. Recently, it has been criticized for selling several large Hungarian firms without revealing the sales price to the public, claiming that these are confidential.[35]

Moreover, under the Retail Privatization Act passed in the fall of 1990, the SPA has been charged with selling some 10,000 small retail outlets to Hungarian citizens on a large scale, to reduce state ownership quickly (within about 2 years). The program got off to a slow start, as only 272 outlets were sold in the first 9 months of the program. (Most of these "sales" technically involve some sort of leasing of assets, rather than their direct sale.) Two years into the program, progress has quickened. However, the SPA is still under heavy criticism. To correct these shortcomings, decentralized privatization methods have been instituted to bypass the SPA, or at least to speed up its operations.[36]

Under self-privatization, state enterprises are given more freedom to initiate their own privatizations; the technique involves using consulting firms to manage the privatization, instead of the SPA. According to Tamas Szabo, minister without portfolio responsible for privatization, forty firms have been converted into corporate entities under the self-privatization program since September 1991. Under investor-initiated privatization, outsiders are invited to bid for companies "over the head of existing managers." The SPA evaluates these bids and may approve them with or without the endorsement of the enterprise's management. Finally, sales via the Budapest Stock Exchange (opened in June 1990) have been very limited, as only twenty companies are actively traded on the exchange.

The progress of privatization has been stalled by confusion over property rights, especially in agriculture. Contributing to the confusion was a lengthy political debate over how to compensate former owners of properties confiscated under the Communist regime. This issue has begun to be resolved by the Compensation Law of August 11, 1991. Under this law, previous owners of properties nationalized after June 8, 1949 (i.e., land and assets of small business owners and former peasants, primarily) could submit claims for partial compensation in the form of compensation bonds.[37] These bonds are transferable certificates which entitle the holder to purchases of state properties being privatized by the SPA. Special rules apply to the compensation of farmers. Cooperatives and state farms must auction off farmland they obtained through confiscation under the Communist era if the original owner submitted a claim for it. Coops can use the compensation vouchers thus obtained to buy shares in privatized food processing plants.

In all, one-fifth of the book value of Hungarian state assets (370 billion forints', or $4.8 billion, worth) was converted into corporate entities during 1991. According to Lajos Csepi, Managing Director of the SPA, half of that amount had been privatized. Attesting to lack of domestic capital, 85 percent of the privatization revenues came from foreign investors, the largest portion being Americans, followed by Germans, Austrians, French, Swedes, Italians, and Japanese.

Given these statistics, the Hungarian government is not likely to reach its plans to privatize half of its state-owned assets (including 2300 firms) by 1994. The government's privatization strategy, published in October 1991, calls for speedy privatization, in large part bypassing the State Property Agency. The control of state ownership rights is to be taken away from the SPA and given instead to competing state holding companies. In 159 state enterprises, the state is to retain control via majority or at least significant ownership through a new "State Ownership Corporation" (*Allami Vagyonkezelo Rt.*).[38] State enterprises are instructed to

Table 4.2
Number of Businesses in Hungary, by Legal Status

	end-1989	end-1991
Limited Liability Companies (KFT)	5,978	41,206
Joint Stock Companies (RT)	362	1,072
Ordinary Partnerships (GMK)	5,769	71,000[a]
Limited Partnerships (BT)	--	1,125[b]
Entrepreneurs	21,794	400,000

[a]This figure includes both ordinary and limited partnerships.
[b]Private only.
Source: Hunyadi, "Transformation," 29; and Hunyadi, *Hungary Today,* 4, no. 3-4 (March-April 1992).

transform themselves into corporate entities speedily, to assist in the privatization process. Still, the government is deeply divided over how to proceed with privatization.

In the meantime, the number of private entrepreneurs in Hungary grows steadily, as do LLCs and partnerships. Given that newly founded and reorganized firms often are owned by two or three different sectors (private citizens, municipalities, social organizations, etc.), the Central Statistical Office (CSO) in Hungary as of 1990 no longer classifies firms by ownership form, but rather by legal status.[39] Table 4.2 provides evidence of the remarkable growth in the number of enterprises, particularly limited liability companies, partnerships, and private entrepreneurs (proprietors) since the institution of the Laws on Economic Association, on Foreign Investment, and on Transformation.

Conclusions

The foregoing has shown how the Hungarian leadership, before the collapse of one-party Communist control, attempted with limited success to introduce market mechanisms into the Hungarian economy. Instead, a "dual" economy was created. The success of reforms allowing and expanding private enterprise, combined with less successful reforms within the state sector, created unequal competition which is now gradually being eliminated. Legal institutions have also been established to ensure a smoother road toward private ownership (as well as various mixed sectoral forms).

The Hungarian example illustrates well the failure of economic reforms constrained by state ownership and the monopoly power of the Communist Party. Whereas central authorities were willing to give up some managerial functions of the firm, or those concerned with current operations (i.e., decisions over what to produce and how, over how to acquire inputs, which workers to hire and fire, etc.), they were not willing through economic reform to give up ownership functions, or strategic decisions concerned with long-term assets (authority to raise capital, make new investment, establish new enterprises, etc.)[40] Thus, the first lesson of the Hungarian experience is that although the authorities allowed the state and private economies to coexist, they were unable and/or unwilling, for social and political reasons, to equalize competition between the two economies, and thus to allow the private sector to drive the state sector to greater efficiency.

While the centrally planned socialist system in Hungary could accommodate private initiative to a limited extent, it could not easily stomach some of the resultant social problems, particularly exacerbated income inequality. The authorities responded with discriminatory taxation and other policies which dealt serious blows to the private sector. The second lesson of the Hungarian experience, then, is that government policies which attempt to mask some of the results of private initiative, including greater income inequality, can seriously hurt the private sector (and, in so doing, the economy as a whole). The eventual decision to embark on a full-scale privatization effort for the Hungarian economy amounts to an admission that discriminatory policies toward the private sector were counterproductive for the economy as a whole.

Eventually succumbing to the merits of private ownership, the Communist leadership itself embarked on a privatization program for the Hungarian economy. By large-scale privatization, the admission has been made that the only way to make state enterprises behave like private firms is to turn them into private firms. Now that a new, non-Communist leadership has emerged, one which is unconstrained by socialist principles such as strict income equality, privatization can presumably proceed at an even faster pace. Indeed, the new government has embarked on a program of comprehensive privatization. Nonetheless, the pace of privatization has been slow. The third lesson of the Hungarian experience, then, is that the pace of large-scale privatization is likely to be constrained by various socio-political as well as economic factors. These include legacies of the past, including how to compensate previous owners.

Debate over the pace and method of privatization is likely to be long and drawn out, and to include such issues as whether "privatization" might mean not only individual, but also various forms of "mixed"—i.e., worker, institutional, individual, municipal—ownership. Macroeconomic considerations such as lack of adequate domestic savings and budgetary constraints may rule out or at least hinder some of the debated methods of privatization, and might necessitate politically unpopular reliance on foreigners to purchase domestic firms undergoing privatization. As a result, a clear privatization strategy may emerge very slowly, as confusion sets in over who really exercises property rights.[41] And, finally, social consequences of privatization, such as rising income inequality, which these countries have historically sought to avoid, are likely to become politically charged issues. The difficult issues raised by massive privatization, including large-scale unemployment as well as growing income inequality, are not palatable for any political regime. Indeed, considering all these complicated issues, this small country of ten million people has pioneered the difficult and uncharted journey toward a private market economy reasonably well to date, setting an example for the other emerging market economies of Eastern and Central Europe as well as the former Soviet Union.

Notes

1. In all, according to Bertlan Diczhazy, advisor to the Prime Minister, the private sector is expected to account for 31–35 percent of Hungary's GDP in 1992, compared to 25 percent in 1991, 19 percent in 1990, and 16 percent in 1989. See *Hungary Today* (July–August 1992): 2.

2. Keith Crane, "Property Rights Reform: Hungarian Country Study," in *Transformation of Planned Economies: Property Rights Reform and Macroeconomic Stability,* edited by Hans Blommestein and Michael Marrese, 69–94 (Paris: Organisation for Economic Co-operation and Development, 1991).

3. Ibid.

4. Interview with Mrs. Ilona Zsiday, June 1989, Budapest.

5. Interview with Peter Szirmai, June 1989, Budapest.

6. Gyorgy Ranki, "The Introduction and Evolution of Planning in Hungary," in *Market Reforms in Socialist Societies,* edited by Peter Van Ness (Boulder, CO: Lynne Rienner Publishers, 1989).

7. Ibid.

8. Ibid.

9. Gabor Revesz, *Perestroika in Eastern Europe: Hungary's Economic Transformation, 1945–1988* (Boulder, CO: Westview Press, 1990).

10. Paul Marer, "Hungary's Political and Economic Transformation (1988–89) and Prospects after Kadar," in *Pressures for Reform in the East European Economies,* 42–51 (Washington, DC: Joint Economic Committee, 1989).

11. These examples, and the accompanying statistics, are from Peter Szirmai, "First Steps Toward a Bourgeois Democracy in Hungary," manuscript, 1991.

12. Joseph Wolfe and Joszef Poor, "A Socioeconomic Note on Hungary in 1990," manuscript, March 6, 1990.

13. Crane, "Property Rights Reform."

14. *Statisztikai Evkonyv* (Hungarian Statistical Yearbook) (Budapest: Kozponti Statisztikai Hivatal, 1976).

15. By 1989, however, the private sector's share officially amounted to 13 percent. See Csilla Hunyadi, "Transformation from Socialism to Capitalism: Privatization in Hungary," manuscript, presented at the Allied Social Science Associations Annual Meeting, New Orleans, January 1992.

16. Paul Marer, "Economic Reform in Hungary: From Central Planning to Regulated Market," *East European Economies: Slow Growth in the 1980s* (Washington, DC: Joint Economic Committee, 1986).

17. Ibid.

18. A good source for definitions of the forms is Eva Szita,, "New Types of Entrepreneurial and Organizational Forms in the Hungarian Economy," in *The Unofficial Economy: Consequences and Perspectives in Different Economic Systems,* edited by Sergio Alessandrini and Bruno Dallago (Hants, U.K.: Gower, 1987).

19. Ibid.

20. Janos Kornai, "The Hungarian Reform Process: Visions, Hopes, and Reality," *Journal of Economic Literature* 24, no. 4 (December 1986): 1687–1737.

21. Tamas Bauer, "Economic Reforms Within and Beyond the State Sector," *American Economic Review* 78, no. 2 (May 1988): 452–456.

22. Reference is made here to the so-called "soft budget constraint," a term attributed to the Hungarian economist Janos Kornai. Under a centrally planned system, many of the financial constraints imposed on the firm by central authorities (such as tax and wage rules) are not binding. Should the firm fail to comply with the rule, or even if it should be insolvent, authorities have no choice but to accept noncompliance and, in the extreme case, to "bail out" the firm.

23. Paul Marer, "Hungary's Reform and Performance in the Kadar Era (1956–88)," in *Pressures for Reform in the East European Economies,* 1–15 (Washington, DC: Joint Economic Committee, 1989).

24. For a full discussion of the role of the banking sector in the Hungarian reform process, see David Bartlett, Chapter 8, in this volume.

25. The following description of the three laws borrows heavily from Catherine Sokil, "Hungary's Economic Transformation," in *Comrades Go Private,* edited by Michael P. Claudon and Tamar L. Gutner (New York: NYU Press, 1992).

26. Simon MacLeod, "Recent Hungarian Legislation," *International Financial Law Review* (October 1989): 25.

27. Hunyadi, Csilla, "Transformation from Socialism to Capitalism: Privatization in Hungary," manuscript, presented at the Allied Social Science Associations Annual Meeting, New Orleans, January 1992.

28. Blue Ribbon Commission (BRC), *Hungary: In Transformation to Freedom and Prosperity,* Economic Program Proposals of the Joint Hungarian-International Blue Ribbon Commission. (Indianapolis, IN and Budapest, Hungary: Hudson Institute, 1990).

29. Crane, 84.

30. "An Interview on the Experiences of the Hungarian Blue Ribbon Commission," (interview with Ivan Major, General Secretary of the Hungarian Blue Ribbon Foundation) *Transition: The Newsletter About Reforming Economies* 3, no. 5 (May 1992).

31. Paul Marer, "Comment on the Article on the BRC in *Transition*," manuscript, 1992.

32. *The Joint Hungarian-International Blue Ribbon Commission* (Indianapolis: The Hudson Institute, 1992).

33. Hunyadi, 10.

34. *First Privatization Program (FPP)* (Budapest: Allami Vagyonugynokseg [State Property Agency], September 1990).

35. Hunyadi, 11.

36. This and following paragraphs are based on Csilla Hunyadi, ed., *Hungary Today: Business, Economic, and Political Newsletter* 4, no. 3–4 (March–April 1992).

37. Michael Marrese, "Progress in Transforming Hungarian Agriculture," *Comparative Economic Studies* XXXIII, no. 2 (Summer 1991): 159–177.

38. Hunyadi, *Hungary Today.*

39. Janos Arvay, "Classification of Ownership Forms in the Transition Period," manuscript, delivered at the October 1991 World Bank-Trento University Workshop on Measurement of the Private Sector's Contribution in Transition Economies, Budapest, September 1991.

40. See Chapter 7 in Catherine Sokil, *Markets and "Market-Type" Instruments in a Modified Planned Economy: Hungary, 1982–85,* Ph.D. dissertation, Indiana University, December 1989.

41. Marrese, "Progress."

5

Private Enterprise Development and the Transition to a Market Economy in the Czech and Slovak Republics

Dennis A. Rondinelli

The ability of Central European countries like the Czech and Slovak Republics to transform themselves successfully over the next decade from command- to market-oriented economies will depend in large part on their ability to spawn a strong small business sector and to transform their state-owned enterprises into private companies. The emergence of a vigorous private sector will be crucial in absorbing labor and generating income lost from the inevitable restructuring and eventual demise of state monopolies.[1]

Although both political leaders and a vast majority of the public realize that private enterprise development is a precondition for economic progress in the Czech and Slovak Republics, re-creating the private sector as the foundation for a market-oriented economy has not been easy. For 40 years Czechoslovakia was ruled by a Communist regime that wiped out nearly all forms of private enterprise. In the pre-Communist era, Czechoslovakia had developed an industrial economy resembling those in Western Europe. During the 1930s more than 330,000 small firms employed between one and five people. About 40 percent of labor employed in industrial enterprises worked in private companies with less than 100 employees.[2] But by the end of Communist rule in 1989, Czechoslovakia had only about 1500 large state-owned industrial and agro-industrial enterprises employing nearly 4 million people and an additional 750 state commercial enterprises employing about 750,000 workers. The average firm size exceeded 2500 employees.[3] Nearly 90 percent of all manufacturing firms had more than 500 workers in 1988.[4] About 95 percent of national production came from state enterprises, most of which were operating inefficiently with obsolete equipment and bloated labor forces.

Many survived only by supplying mass-produced goods to the former Soviet Union and other Communist states.

During the period of Communist domination virtually no incentive or opportunity remained for people to engage in self-employment or entrepreneurial activities in Czechoslovakia and thus, unlike in Poland and Hungary, the private sector virtually disappeared. In 1988, nearly 89 percent of employment was in the state industrial and service sector, with an additional 10 percent in state-dominated agricultural cooperatives. Less than one percent of the population was self-employed.[5] Even more than two years after the "Velvet Revolution" of 1989, services and retail activities were still provided largely by state-owned enterprises (SOEs). Individual enterprises and small businesses began to re-emerge in 1990 as a result of economic reforms, but most entrepreneurs faced serious problems in coping with uncertain economic conditions.

Statistics on the number of private businesses operating in the Czech and Slovak Republics are still unreliable. The government estimated that at the end of September 1990 about 285,000 small businesses were officially registered. The number grew rapidly to about 500,000 by the end of 1990, and by mid-1991 increased to nearly 921,000. But many of these small businesses were registered only for tax purposes and remained inactive. Their owners registered quickly, fearing that fees would increase, but many were really employees (who called themselves "consultants") of other small enterprises whose owners were looking for ways around paying the substantial social benefit taxes for workers, or they were waiting to accumulate enough capital and access to property to start their own businesses. Moreover, the overwhelming majority of newly registered businesses were in services rather than production. Only about 27 percent of the registrations identified the businesses as manufacturing or production industries; nearly 25 percent were in construction; and an additional 45 percent were in other services and trade.[6] Most small businesses consisted of consultants, street vendors, and self-employed people who worked as beauticians, photographers, carpenters, masons and in similar trades.[7]

Foreign investment helped privatize some companies and, by 1991, resulted in many joint ventures with Czechoslovakian businesses. The Central Bank estimated that more than $600 million in foreign investment, mainly from Germany, Austria and other European countries, flowed into the country during 1991.[8] The government reported that from 1990 to the end of 1991 the number of joint ventures between Czech and Slovak companies and foreign investors grew from virtually none to nearly 3,000.[9] Despite the apparent large number of new business starts, however, the private sector still accounted for less than 10 percent of total employment in Czechoslovakia and produced less than 9 percent of national output by the end of 1991.[10]

This chapter describes the re-emergence of the private sector in the Czech and Slovak Federal Republic (CSFR) during the transition period from late 1989 to mid-1992, a period when a democratic national government under the leadership of President Vaclav Havel and Finance Minister Vaclav Klaus attempted to initiate widespread economic reforms to re-create an environment conducive to private enterprise development. At the same time, ethnic and nationalistic—as well as economic—differences resulted in the decision in mid-1992 to split the federation into two sovereign and independent states. Although these multiple transitions were far from over by mid-1992, the experience of Czechoslovakia in developing private enterprise during this period may hold lessons for other socialist economies undergoing transformation. In addition, this chapter assesses the problems of implementing transitional economic reforms; explores the challenges facing small- and medium-scale business owners and managers of privatizing SOEs during the transition; and discusses actions that must be taken in the Czech Lands and Slovakia in the future to assist entrepreneurs and managers to expand in an emerging market economy.

Private Sector Development and Economic Reform

Business expansion in Czechoslovakia from 1989 to mid-1992 depended in large measure on the overall performance of the national economy and on the emergence of an economic and political structure that would support entrepreneurial activity. Despite the devastation of the private sector during the Communist regime, the CSFR emerged from the Velvet Revolution with some strong potential advantages on which to build a market economy and a larger private sector during the 1990s. These included relatively low levels of hard-currency foreign debt (less than $10 billion in 1992) compared to other former socialist economies; a skilled industrial labor force that was relatively well educated and almost completely literate; a basic system of health services that could maintain the productivity of the labor force; and a relatively low wage level that made the country competitive with Western European and some East Asian countries in labor-intensive industries.[11] The ability of the CSFR to build on these advantages, however, depended on the successful implementation of economic reforms that would allow entrepreneurship to emerge and flourish.

Economic Reforms

The economic reforms undertaken in Czechoslovakia in early 1990 were based in part on conventional economic principles for structural adjustment tested by the World Bank, the International Monetary Fund and other international financial agencies in developing countries during the 1980s; partly on political exigencies and pressures in the Czech and Slovak Republics; and partly on economic and political experiments, the results of which even the initiators could not predict.[12] The acknowledged architect of Czechoslovakia's economic reforms, Finance Minister Vaclav Klaus, readily admitted in 1991 that, despite the application of well-known principles of development economics, the reformers were operating under a high degree of uncertainty, especially about how to sequence reforms; how to create appropriate incentives for entrepreneurship and international trade and investment; and how to maintain some degree of social equity during a transition period when a few people might reap enormous windfall profits from the dismantling of the socialist system while many others would suffer the adversities of inflation, unemployment and loss of real income.

Despite these uncertainties, Klaus argued for rapid, comprehensive and transparent reforms that could be adjusted as they were implemented. In response to political critics who feared that Czechoslovakia would suffer the seemingly intolerable consequences of more radical reforms such as those adopted in Poland and who argued for more detailed planning and gradual implementation, Klaus insisted that Czechoslovakia could not wait; it had to implement reforms quickly, based on what economists already knew about transformation:

> When we stress a comprehensive reform, it doesn't mean that we must wait for an all-embracing reform blueprint. In my opinion, waiting for an ambitious, intellectually perfect, all-details-elaborated reform project is a suggestion to start the reform in the year 2057. It means postponing the reform process to eternity; there will never be a reform. What is even worse, when the reform process has already started, is to wait for the blueprint; it leads very quickly to a chaotic disintegration of the economy . . .[13]

Thus, at Klaus's insistence and with strong pressures from the International Monetary Fund and other international financial institutions, the Federal Assembly passed a variety of economic reform laws in early 1990.[14] It gave citizens the right to create businesses without restrictions on number of employees or amount of property owned. The government began removing price controls from many goods and made the *koruna* (crown) internally convertible, allowing business owners in Czechoslovakia to exchange limited amounts of crowns for hard currencies. Under a restitution policy, the government reinstated ownership rights for 70,000 properties expropriated by the Communists between 1955 and 1961. It began returning to previous owners farmland that was not being used by agricultural cooperatives and state farms. The agricultural land law allowed about 3.5 million former owners and their heirs to reclaim up to 150 hectares (370 acres) of land and the property on it that was confiscated between 1948 and 1990.

The Federal Assembly also authorized under the "small privatization law" the auctioning of 100,000 small state-owned service businesses to individuals. By early 1992 nearly 22,000 small businesses in the Czech Republic and a little more than 6700 small businesses in the Slovak Republic were privatized. Under the "large privatization law" the government began restructuring large state-owned companies such as *Skoda*, a diversified heavy manufacturing conglomerate, into smaller companies and transforming them into joint-stock companies owned entirely by the state. Shares in these restructured companies were offered to private individuals and foreign investors through a variety of privatization procedures, including a voucher scheme. *Skoda*'s automobile division, for example, was purchased by *Volkswagen*.

Early in 1990, the federal government had also begun to address many of the institutional issues that were critical to creating a market-oriented economy. Extensive changes were made in the structure of government in Czechoslovakia, aimed at decentralizing administrative and political power. They included shifting some authority from the federal government to the republics; replacing centrally directed National Committees with local self-governments; and abolishing a number of federal ministries and shifting their responsibilities to the republics. The Federal Assembly allowed the republics to control their own budgets and levy their own taxes. Municipal assemblies of elected local representatives were to form the foundation for a new system of local self-government. Municipalities could choose their own mayors directly in elections in Slovakia and by elected assemblies in the Czech Republic.[15] And because serious political tensions between the Czech and Slovak Republics surfaced quickly, negotiations were initiated on constitutional changes, the form of the central and republic governments, and the relationships between the republics and the federal government.

In June 1991, the Czech Republic announced its goal of privatizing fifty leading Czech enterprises through total or partial sale by the end of the year. Targeted companies included engineering, chemicals, building materials, paper, printing, textiles, electronics and metal processing firms.[16] At the same time, the Parliament strengthened the social safety net to protect Czech and Slovak citizens from the most serious adverse effects of the change from a command- to a market-oriented economy—especially unemployment and loss of real income.

The government also began developing new laws to expand business and trade in 1991 by proposing bills to revise and strengthen the patents and copyright protection laws, to legalize joint ventures and permit joint ownership by foreign companies and private Czechoslovakian companies and individuals, to allow foreign nationals to set up businesses, and to obtain both credit and property needed to conduct their business activities. Tax reductions were made to attract foreign businesses and joint ventures. The Parliament began overhauling the tax system by scheduling a value added tax (VAT) and personal income tax to take effect in January 1993; and began creating a legal framework for business, including laws pertaining to bankruptcy, contract and dispute resolution, anti-trust, international and domestic trade, and company status.

In early 1992, Parliament approved a voucher scheme allowing all citizens over eighteen years old to obtain coupons at a nominal cost (about $33) that could be used to bid on shares in joint stock companies that would be privatized by the voucher method. The coupon booklets with vouchers containing 11,000 points would be tradeable on a stock market that was expected to begin operating in early 1993. Although the voucher sales had been slow during the early offerings, a strong government advertising campaign and aggressive marketing by private investment funds spurred sales. By March 1992, more than 8.5 million citizens (about 80 percent of the adult population) had purchased vouchers, far more than had been expected to participate.[17] The strongest stimulus to sales came from the vigorous campaign by private investment funds to attract subscribers, who delegated their coupons to the companies in exchange for promises of payments of up to 10 times their value within a year.[18] Using the pooled vouchers, the investment companies would bid on shares and manage the portfolio much like mutual funds in the United States.

Foreign banks were allowed to operate in the CSFR in 1992 without creating subsidiaries. Branch banks that were not previously restricted by their licenses could accept deposits, extend credits, invest in securities, issue credit cards and travelers' checks, and grant guarantees and letters of credit. The banking reform law also allowed branch banks to engage in brokerage and financial services activities and trade in and purchase foreign currencies.[19] The law made the central bank, *Statni Banka*, independent of both the federal and republic governments.

In order to promote foreign investment and international trade, the government also adopted a new set of accounting laws which made procedures compatible with those of the European Community, and regulations which standardized the annual financial statements of companies doing business in the CSFR.[20] Import surcharges were reduced from 20 to 10 percent.

Difficulties in Implementing the Economic Reforms

Although the CSFR made steady progress toward reforming economic policy and restructuring the economy, not all of the reforms were widely supported and effectively implemented. Economic uncertainties spawned serious differences in both the Czech and Slovak Republics among political cal parties and various factions within them over the scope and pace of economic reform.[21] The economic uncertainties remained a strong force affecting private sector development in CSFR throughout the early transitional period.

The willingness of entrepreneurs to start new businesses and of investors to bid on privatizing state enterprises was tempered by a dim economic outlook in Czechoslovakia. The crown was devalued in early 1991 by 14.5 percent after having been devalued by 50 percent the year before. The devaluations and announcements of limits on wage increases intensified the opposition of those concerned about social and economic adversities of reform.[22] During 1991 nearly all macroeconomic data reflected the seriousness of the recession that had begun in 1990. Gross national product declined by 16 percent, personal consumption dropped by 28 percent, gross industrial output decreased by 22 percent, and gross investment fell by 30 percent.[23] Real average monthly wages fell by 28 percent at the same time that the consumer price index increased by nearly 58 percent. Exports fell by 7.5 percent and unemployment increased to 6.6 percent.[24] (See Table 5.1.)

The harsh consequences of the rapid and radical economic reforms in Poland made many people and some of the political leaders in Czechoslovakia wary of adopting Polish-style adjustments.[25] At the beginning of 1991, as the opinion poll results shown in Table 5.2 indicate, about 40 percent of Czechoslovakians thought that economic changes were coming too fast, and only 48 percent were convinced that a free-market economy would produce a better standard of living for everyone in the long run.

Progress on economic reform was slowed by the tensions between those disenchanted with the sluggishness of change and those fearing the adverse consequences of rapid change. These tensions were exacerbated by the fear of Slovaks that their poorer economy would suffer harsher effects than would the Czech Republic's. Opinion polls released in early 1991 indicated that people in the Slovak Republic were far more pessimistic about the success of political and economic changes than those in the Czech Republic. Less than a majority of those interviewed in the Czech Republic thought that, overall, the country was moving in the right direction. Only 58 percent of the Slovaks, compared to 75 percent of the Czechs, believed that conditions would get better over the next five years. And 41 percent of the Slovaks, compared to 22 percent of the Czechs, believed that political change was occurring too fast. Table 5.2 shows that far more Slovaks than Czechs preferred a mixed socialist-market system than a free market system, and a majority of Slovaks believed that a free market economy would not produce a better standard of living. Far fewer than a majority of people in the Slovak Republic

Table 5.1

Macroeconomic Trends in the Czech and Slovak Federal Republic
1984-1991

Annual Growth in Percent

Indicator	1984	1985	1986	1987	1988	1989	1990	1991
Gross National Product	2.4	0.7	2.1	1.1	1.8	0.0	-1.0	-16.0
Gross Industrial Output	4.0	3.5	3.2	2.5	2.1	0.8	-3.1	-22.0
Gross Agricultural Output	4.4	-1.6	0.6	0.9	2.9	1.9	-3.5	-10.6
Gross Investment	-4.2	5.4	1.4	4.4	4.1	1.6	4.0	-30.0
Retail Trade Turnover	2.1	1.5	2.2	2.8	4.8	2.3	1.7	-35.5
Real Average Monthly Wages	-0.5	-2.0	-0.4	0.4	0.4	-0.9	-6.3	-28.1
Retail Price Index	0.9	2.3	0.5	0.1	0.2	1.4	10.0	57.0
Total Exports	8.9	3.8	0.5	1.7	6.1	1.7	-1.0	n.a.
Exports to Former Socialist Countries (excl. E. Germany)	12.8	5.4	1.8	5.0	6.5	-5.0	-18.4	n.a

Source: Compiled from *PlanEcon Report* VII, nos. 41-42 (November 9, 1991) based on figures supplied by Czech and Slovak Federal Republic, Statistical Office, Bulletin No. 8.

Table 5.2
Summary of Results of Public Opinion Poll on Political
and Economic Situation in Czechoslovakia
January 1991

Percent Responses

Question	Response	CSFR	Czech	Slovak
Is overall development of the country moving in the right direction?	Yes	58	66	42
	No	23	17	37
	Don't Know	19	17	21
Do you think that conditions will get better, worse or stay about the same in the next five years?	Better	70	75	58
	Worse	6	3	13
	Same	8	7	9
	Don't Know	16	15	20
Do you believe that political change is occurring too fast or not fast enough?	Too Fast	28	22	41
	Just Right	24	26	20
	Too Slow	37	41	28
	Don't Know	11	11	11
Do you believe that democratic systems will be stabilized in Czechoslovakia relatively quickly and without serious problems?	Yes	4		
	No	88		
	Don't Know	8		
Do you believe that economic changes are occurring too fast or not fast enough?	Too Fast	40		
	Just Right	17		
	Too Slow	35		
	Don't Know	9		
What type of economic system do you prefer for Czechoslovakia?	Free market	48	52	39
	Socialist	4	3	6
	Mixed	36	33	43
	Don't Know	12	12	12

(Table continued on next page)

Table 5.2 (continued)

Percent Responses

Question	Response	CSFR	Czech	Slovak
Will a free market economy produce a better standard of living for all Czechoslovakians in the long run?	Yes	48	53	36
	No	42	36	56
	Don't Know	10	11	8
Are you afraid that the economic reforms will fail?	Afraid	50		
	Not Afraid	45		
	Don't Care	5		
Do think there should be ownership of large businesses by individuals?	Yes	43	44	40
	No	41		
	Don't Know	16		
Do you think there should be investment in and ownership of companies by foreigners?	Yes	40	44	32
	No	46		
	Don't Know	14		
Do you believe that people should be able to do well in business and become rich?	Yes	57	63	44
	No	37		
	Don't Know	7		

Source: Adapted from Association for Independent Social Analysis,
"Democracy, Economic Reform and Western Assistance in
Czechoslovakia," in *Democracy, Economic Reform and Western
Assistance in Czechoslovakia, Hungary and Poland* (Washington:
Penn and Schoen Associates for Freedom House and The American
Jewish Committee, 1991).

believed that people should be able to do well in business and become rich.

Given these beliefs, it is not surprising that strong factions within political parties in the Slovak Republic were skeptical of federal policies promoting privatization, private enterprise and economic reform. Slovak Prime Minister Vladimir Meciar's resignation from the Public Against Violence political party, and his dismissal from the government in April 1991, resulted largely from Meciar's belief that the federal government's economic reform policies would produce higher inflation and more unemployment in the Slovak Republic than in the Czech Republic. These sentiments were widely shared. As a result, opposition to the application of national economic reforms in the Slovak Republic became widespread and continued to be a major point of contention between the National Council of the Slovak Republic and the federal government until the elections of June 1992 led to the split between the two Republics.[26]

Political opposition to rapid economic transformation and privatization in Slovakia seemed to be justified by economic trends. In March 1991, unemployment in the Slovak Republic was twice as high as in the Czech Republic. By June, unemployment in Slovakia rose to 6.3 percent compared to only 2.6 percent in the Czech Republic and by early 1992 reached nearly 13 percent in the Slovak Republic while rising to 4.3 percent in the Czech Lands.[27] Prices of industrial goods were 13 percent higher and of food 4 percent higher in Slovakia than in the Czech Republic. And industrial output in Slovakia during the first three months of 1991 was 14.3 percent lower than the same period during the previous year, compared to 11.9 percent lower in all of Czechoslovakia.[28] For 1991, inflation in the Slovak Republic was at least 5 percent higher than in the Czech Republic. Moreover, little of the foreign investment needed to revitalize companies in the CSFR went to the Slovak side. Of the more than 5500 companies that had foreign participation in 1991, only about 20 percent were located in Slovakia, which attracted only about 5 percent of the total amount of foreign investment in the CSFR.[29] All of this evidence reinforced the belief among Slovak leaders that their people would bear the brunt of economic adversities arising from rapid and extensive reforms.

As the impacts of economic reform were felt, the public's confidence in the government dropped. Although President Havel remained popular in 1991, his ability to transform that popularity into influence over public policy declined.[30] Also, polls taken by the Czechoslovakian Institute for Public Opinion Research in February 1992 indicated that the share of the population who said they trusted the Federal Assembly plummeted to 26 percent. Only about 25 percent of Czechs and 29 percent of Slovaks trusted the Parliament to deal effectively with economic and political problems.[31]

Moreover, the implementation of privatization was slowed by the opposition of some managers and workers in state-owned enterprises. Many of the managers who were used to operating under socialist principles and with assured markets in the former Soviet Union and CMEA (Council for Mutual Economic Assistance) countries feared the removal of state subsidies and the uncertainty of working within a market system. In 1989, nearly 61 percent of exports went to, and more than 62 percent of imports came from, socialist states. The USSR accounted for about 30 percent of the total in each category. Principal exports were machinery and equipment, fuels, minerals and metals, and non-food consumer goods.[32] Many of the state enterprise managers whose traditional markets were now cut off knew that they could survive only by cutting production costs, eliminating the large number of excess employees that state enterprises had been required to hire, and limiting wage increases. Most of those managers were ill-prepared technically or administratively, however, to deal with market-based competition during a period when state subsidies were being phased out and exports to the former socialist countries were dropping steadily.[33]

Despite the government's desire to eliminate subsidies to state-owned enterprises, it had to bail out some inefficient companies to limit unemployment and prevent the demise of some large producers. Many companies were reluctant to release excess labor and cut wages for fear of antagonizing trade unions.[34] Moreover, in an agreement reached in March 1991 among the Federal and Republic governments, employers, and the trade unions, the government backed off its 3 percent ceiling on wage increases for 1991.[35]

In order to overcome opposition to privatization by managers of state-owned enterprises, the Federal Finance Ministry ordered them to develop their own sell-off plans or be fired. They could choose among auctions, voucher schemes, or joint ventures with foreign firms.[36] At the same time, the government placed some state enterprises off-limits for sale or for joint ventures with foreign companies, and denied permission to some companies to move beyond the stage of transforming themselves from joint stock companies owned entirely by the state. These restrictions limited the capacity of foreign companies to buy up strategic enterprises and reduced the level of employee layoffs in sensitive industries and regions of the country.

Finally, the operation of the voucher scheme for privatization raised doubts about its success in the minds of many who purchased coupon booklets. The unregulated investment funds made questionable but eagerly accepted promises in early 1992 about their ability to return 10 times or more the cost of the voucher booklets within a year. The investment funds based their promises on generous estimates of the book value of the companies that would be privatized—a value that was questionable to begin with and that was eroded by recession and bankruptcies—and on what turned out to be very low estimates of the number of people who would ultimately register for the vouchers.[37] This created the potential for a volatile situation during 1993 and 1994 if the investment funds failed to deliver on their promises, or if the process of privatization was slowed seriously by adverse economic conditions, or if the stock market failed to function effectively. Public confidence in the entire economic reform package could easily be undermined.

The Challenges of Private Sector Development

During the transitional period from 1989 to 1992, small businesses were being created and state enterprises were being restructured in an environment of serious economic uncertainty. With devaluation of the crown in January 1991, prices increased by about 50 percent. Consumer prices in the Czech Republic were 60 percent higher in February 1991 than in January 1989. The average salary in Czechoslovakia was only about 3300 crowns, or about $113 a month. Not only did consumer goods prices increase rapidly, but considerable uncertainty over the supply and price of energy made assessments of the cost of production for both privatizing SOEs and small businesses difficult. Coal production decreased substantially and oil supplies were cut as a result of the former Soviet Union's demand for purchases in hard currency during 1990 and the reallocation of supplies after the disintegration of the Soviet Union in 1991.

Most of the heavy manufacturing companies lost their protected markets in former socialist countries and at the same time saw declining markets at home because of secondary insolvency: their customers were also facing export losses and thus manufacturers were not paid for deliveries; they, in turn, could not pay their suppliers. In highly integrated manufacturing companies, the loss of markets for primary goods sent a ripple of production cutbacks through the whole system of intermediate goods producers and suppliers.

Constraints on Business Owners and Managers

In mid-1991, 48 small-business owners and SOE managers whose companies were being broken up into smaller businesses were asked to identify the most serious problems and challenges facing them in establishing and operating their enterprises.[38] About half of the respondents (54 percent) were owners of private businesses—sole proprietorships, private partnerships, cooperatives and family-owned businesses—and 46 percent were managers of SOEs undergoing privatization, joint stock companies, and mixed ownership companies. More than half of these businesses (almost all of the small enterprises) began operations after 1990. The general characteristics of the respondents' companies varied— they represented products and services from nearly all sectors of the economy, from small personal service activities to large-scale manufacturing and production. About 46 percent reported an increasing volume of sales since they started their businesses, and 54 percent reported decreased or stabilized sales. An overwhelming majority of the business owners believed that the most important factor in the sale of their products was low price and high quality.

   Most of the business owners and managers identified a long list of
potential constraints on their ability to survive and compete during the
transitional period. The most frequently mentioned ones are summarized
in Table 5.3. Business owners and managers were also asked to identify
the factors that they believed would most seriously affect their operations *over the next five years*. Those results are summarized in Table 5.4.
Existing constraints and perceived future problems can be classified in
three categories: market, informational, and credit problems; difficulties

Table 5.3
Principal Constraints on the Growth of Companies
Identified by Small Business Owners and Managers

Constraint	Percent of Respondents Identifying Problem (n = 48)
-- Assessing the feasibility of business opportunities	50.0%
-- Finding sources of capital	47.9
-- Developing business plans	39.5
-- Managing financial and accounting activities	39.5
-- Obtaining efficient equipment	39.5
-- Expanding into international markets	37.5
-- Developing a marketing strategy	37.5
-- Obtaining market information	35.4
-- Employee motivation and training	35.4
-- Participating in government procurement programs	33.3
-- Obtaining production inputs and supplies	27.0
-- Improving production efficiency	27.0
-- Obtaining adequate physical space	27.0
-- Skilled labor recruitment	27.0

Source: D. Rondinelli, S. Dougherty and J. VanSant, *Management
and Technical Assistance Needs of Small Businessess in
Czechoslovakia* (Washington, DC: Central European Small Business
Enterprise Development Commission, 1991).

Table 5.4
Business Owners' and Managers' Perceptions of Current
and Anticipated Problems Affecting Business Operations
over Next Five Years

Problem	Percent of Respondents (n=48)
-- Old equipment needing replacement	72.9%
-- Changing government economic and business policies	58.3
-- High Price of raw materials	50.0
-- Low quality of raw materials and inputs	43.7
-- Too few salesmen and distributors of company products	33.3
-- Compliance with government rules and regulations too costly	29.2
-- Inadequate telecommunications services	29.2
-- High cost of transportation and shipping	20.8
-- Difficulties obtaining government licenses and permits	18.7
-- Lack of skilled workers	10.4

Source: D. Rondinelli, S. Dougherty and J. VanSant, *Management and Technical Assistance Needs of Small Businesses in Czechoslovakia* (Washington, DC: Central European Small Business Enterprise Development Commission, 1991).

in planning and operating a business; and uncertainties affecting the business environment. Let us review each of these in detail.

Markets, Information, and Credit

Almost all of the respondents worried about how to increase their competitiveness, expand their markets domestically and overseas, and gain access to financial resources, information, and management know-how. Nearly half of the respondents reported that finding and assessing business opportunities and obtaining access to credit and financing were the principal constraints on the growth of their companies. Several types of marketing problems were also frequently reported. Gaining access to international markets was critical for most SOE managers, but obtaining market information and developing marketing strategies were important for almost all small-business owners. Small-scale entrepreneurs lacked information on almost all aspects of business start-up and operation, but especially information and know-how about marketing their goods and services. As a result of the dominance of large, vertically-integrated state monopolies during the Communist era, Czechoslovakia did not develop a system of wholesaling, making it difficult for small business owners to find marketing channels for their goods during the transitional period.

Both small businesses and SOEs had limited access to credit during the transition. Even by 1992, the State Investment Bank would only make short-term loans to small business for operating expenses; it would not make loans for capital investment unless the entrepreneur could provide 100 percent collateral. Because property rights were not completely restored, it was difficult for most people starting a business to find adequate capital. Most commercial banks would not make capital investment loans to small-scale entrepreneurs except in special circumstances and, again, only with substantial collateral.

About 45 percent of the respondents in the survey reported that they obtained capital exclusively from their own savings or from family and friends, 36 percent reported receiving bank loans that partially capitalized their business, but most of the small businesses also drew heavily on the owners' personal savings. Only 3 percent of the companies surveyed, primarily SOEs, received some form of financial assistance from the government.

By 1992 no special programs had yet been established for small businesses, except provision of loans at about 1 percent below the standard rate for those that provided 100 percent collateral. In mid-1991, State Investment Bank rates ranged from 19 percent for one-year loans to 24 percent for four-year loans. Although these rates were lowered marginally in July, the cost of credit for small businesses remained high. Some regional attempts were made to provide credit for small enterprises through private sources. For example, the Bank of Bohemia was opened in April 1991 by a Czech emigre from Canada with $10 million obtained from Czech trade unions and other sources to provide loans to small enterprises. The Bank's owners were seeking up to $70 million in additional funds from individual savings deposits.[39] Demand for credit so far outpaced supply, however, that most small business owners had to continue to finance their operations with personal resources.

Even if they had funds available, neither state nor commercial bankers felt qualified to assess proposals from small business owners, who in any case did not generally have the capacity to prepare the types of business plans or financial statements that the banks could evaluate. Two years after the Velvet Revolution, Czechoslovakia still did not have a guarantee program to secure the loans of small businesses, and the banks were reluctant to change their lending policies unless guarantees could be provided. There was still no legal basis for bank liens, and no effective institutional basis for making credit decisions.

Although many new small businesses did not need large amounts of start-up capital, they did need loans to expand and to cover accounts receivable. Privatizing state enterprises needed large amounts of capital to repair and maintain deteriorating physical plant, to replace obsolete equipment and to obtain new technology. Because limited amounts of capital were available from state or commercial banks in Czechoslovakia, privatizing SOEs had to rely on foreign investment or loans from foreign banks.

Additional problems arose from the fact that neither the State Investment Bank nor commercial banks had rapid and reliable payment mechanisms. In 1991 it took four to six weeks to clear checks for payment and it often took up to three months to transfer funds internationally. Thus, banks were also seeking foreign partners or connections to improve their operations as well as to expand their capital resources.

Business Planning and Operations

Even if they could identify a market and obtain sufficient capital to begin their businesses, entrepreneurs and SOE managers reported problems with developing business plans, managing their financial and accounting activities, and obtaining modern equipment. Obtaining inputs and supplies, skilled labor and adequate physical space for operations also concerned many of the respondents.

Although SOE managers were often technically skilled, most lacked the capacity to operate in a market economy. They had worked in an environment that for over forty years rewarded them for obedience, conformity and meeting planned targets. Most were not used to taking risks or responsibility for decisions. They did not know how to identify competitive opportunities, to assess or hedge against risk, to mobilize and invest capital to create market advantages, to use information systems for business operations, or to value the assets and liabilities of their companies.

Managers of SOEs were also unfamiliar with cash flow management and standard systems of accounting. Traditional Soviet accounting principles were useless in dealing with international companies after the Communist regime fell, but many SOEs did not change until Parliament passed a law requiring them to adopt Western European accounting standards in 1992.

The large backlog of housing demand, slow construction and lack of building maintenance during the Communist regime left little space for business operations for those wishing to start up or expand their operations. In cities, Soviet-style large-scale apartment buildings had insufficient space for living and virtually no space for commercial activities, inhibiting the start-up of home-based small production activities as well as small trade and service businesses. Some successful private vending operations appeared on the streets in 1990, and office and production space was beginning to be made available as leasing of excess space became more common in 1991. But in cities like Prague the rents for commercial and production space rose rapidly due to scarcity, and most small businesses simply could not afford them. Office rents were reported to start at about $80 per square meter in the central areas of Prague, compared to $55 in Warsaw and $45 in Budapest.[40]

The space problems were exacerbated by irregularities in the implementation of the property restitution and small privatization laws. Many of the properties—groceries, restaurants, retail shops, and services—were supposed to be auctioned in the first round only to Czechoslovakian resident citizens. However, foreign investors found residents to bid for them, a widespread practice that inflated the costs of property beyond the financial means of most small entrepreneurs. Although foreign investors would have to wait two years before the property could be officially transferred, the pervasiveness of foreign-backed bidders made it impossible for residents with only small amounts of capital to compete fairly. The Ministry of Privatization was aware of the irregularities but officials dismissed complaints by arguing that "our job is to put capital to work. We are not concerned with how they [bidders] obtained capital."[41]

Uncertainties in the Business Environment

Changing government policies and the uncertainty accompanying those changes were serious problems affecting more than 58 percent of the respondents. About half of those responding also anticipated the high cost of raw materials as a problem in the future and 44 percent identified the low quality of raw materials and inputs as a serious difficulty. About one-third of the respondents saw the high cost of government rules and regulations and inadequate telecommunications as problems that they would have to face over the next five years. These problems were followed in frequency by the high cost of transportation and difficulties of obtaining licenses or permits to do business.

Even when entrepreneurs could find adequate space, they were often unable to acquire the equipment and services necessary to allow them to operate efficiently. In 1991 it still took at least two months to obtain a telephone in Prague even if a business owner could afford to pay up to $600 in bribes on top of the official cost of about $66.[42] After the equipment was installed, the business owner had to cope with an extremely inefficient domestic telephone system plagued by busy lines and long delays in completing calls. Ironically, foreign calls could often be placed faster than domestic calls. But at busy periods of the day, a long distance call from Prague to New York usually required a wait of up to 30 minutes. (However, even this was substantially better than the 24-hour waits common in Moscow.)

Business owners had to pay substantial taxes and social benefits for employees and adhere to both old regulations and new government restrictions that raised the cost of doing business. In 1990, the Federal Assembly imposed a 22 percent turnover tax on all businesses that sold goods and a profit tax ranging from about 15 percent for profits of more than 65,000 crowns (about $2200) to 55 percent for profits of more than 500,000 crowns ($17,000). The Federal budget in 1991 sought 54 percent of its revenues from the turnover tax and another 25 percent from enterprise duties.[43]

Companies had to make heavy contributions for social security, sick pay, health, unemployment and other benefits for employees to support the strong "safety net" of social programs established under the socialist regime, many of which were kept in place to reduce social tensions during the transition period. Social security and benefits taxes of 50 percent on employee wages were particularly difficult requirements for small businesses to meet. As a result, small business owners were generally reluctant to hire employees.

Although it was relatively easy for small businesses to obtain licenses by applying to the municipal government office, larger businesses had to register through the courts, which could be more complex. Also, state-owned enterprises had to receive permission to privatize, and some divisions or branches of larger enterprises were denied approval. The delaying tactics of the large number of holdover officials (*nomenklatura*) from the previous regime still in the government during the transition period made it difficult for some potential entrepreneurs to receive permits to establish new businesses.[44] Finally, entrepreneurs had to overcome the challenge posed by the deep suspicion in Czechoslovakia of those who purchased small businesses under the law that sold these shops to the highest bidder. The bidding process gave no preference to existing employees. Many shop workers complained that the only people who had the capital to buy these businesses were black marketeers (many of whom were accused of being gypsies and foreign workers) and corrupt former officials and *nomenklatura*.

Some small business owners complained that immediately after the 1989 revolution, government officials were able to start side-businesses while they worked for the government, taking advantage of inside information, contacts and in some cases illegal payments to get a head start in various sectors. Only when their businesses were established did some of these officials leave the government; others remained in public employment while engaging in sideline activities. All of these factors, along with the socialist ideology that prevailed for forty years condemning the accumulation of individual wealth, initially created suspicion and outright hostility toward entrepreneurs, and especially the most successful ones.

Creating Institutions for Private Sector Development

During the early transitional period from 1989 to 1992, the government gave its attention almost exclusively to macro-economic reforms and largely ignored the micro-economic issues affecting small-business owners and enterprise managers. Federal Finance Minister Klaus objected strongly to dealing with micro-economic issues until after the macro-economic reforms were in place. Focusing on micro-economic concerns, he insisted, "is a trap because, all other things being equal, shifting the locus of decisionmaking to micro-economic agents without changing the basic characteristics of the system brings more problems than solutions."[45]

But reformers may have underestimated the importance of creating support institutions for small-business owners in tandem with macro-economic reforms. A large gap quickly developed during the transitional period between new economic conditions and the capabilities of potential entrepreneurs and existing managers to respond to them. As noted earlier, small-scale entrepreneurs and managers of privatizing SOEs faced myriad problems in establishing and expanding their businesses during the transition. Some of those problems will be addressed by reforms now under way or under consideration by the government—for example, changes in the tax law, the development of new accounting standards, and changes in laws affecting business operations. But many others will require more serious attention by the government, international financial and technical assistance, and considerable self-help on the part of Czech and Slovak entrepreneurs and business managers.

Need for Small Business Assistance Programs

In order to achieve the goals of the economic reforms and to accelerate privatization and private enterprise development, the Czech and Slovak Republics will have to develop an institutional base to strengthen emerging businesses and to stimulate entrepreneurial activity. A first priority must be to meet the immediate needs of small-scale entrepreneurs and managers of privatizing SOEs for management and technical assistance. The types of business assistance needs that were identified in interviews with owners and managers are summarized in Table 5.5. Among the most urgent needs are:[46]

Table 5.5
Management and Technical Needs of Small Businesses

o How to start and organize a small business

o How to prepare a business plan for domestic and foreign financing and investment

o How to establish contact with foreign investors, and gain access to foreign markets and technology

o How to negotiate joint venture or licensing contracts

o How to gain access to information on Czechoslovakian legal and financial rules and an understanding of how they affect business

o How to deal with foreign markets (e.g. customs regulations, prices, tariffs, transportation costs)

o How to access Western data banks for contacts and market information

o How and where to obtain credit and venture capital

o How to obtain information on new technologies, especially computer and related MIS techniques

o How to improve quality and efficiency of production

o How to gain access to adequate physical space for business operations

o How to deal with the banking system and establish creditworthiness in the absence of adequate collateral

o How to do market research

o How to train, motivate and improve the skills of employees

Source: D. Rondinelli, S. Dougherty and J. VanSant, *Management and Technical Assistance Needs of Small Businesses in Czechoslovakia* (Washington, DC: Central European Small Business Enterprise Development Commission, 1991).

1. *Access to information about the business formation process, business systems, practices and procedures, and markets.* Small-business owners and managers of privatizing SOEs identified a critical need for current, accurate information to support the business development process, including information on the legal system and requirements for property ownership, joint venture management, international marketing opportunities, export processes, and capital resources. These needs were not being met during the transition, and entrepreneurs wanted private or non-profit organizations to create business development centers that could: maintain accurate, current information on the legal system and business requirements; develop a core reference and business resource library; identify and access appropriate business database services; prepare useful short materials for use by business owners and those planning to go into business; and maintain information on international markets and foreign business interests.

2. *Practical counseling and consulting services.* As the rate of new business start-ups increased and as more firms were privatized in Czechoslovakia, the urgent need for professional business counseling services became more apparent. Survey respondents pointed out that these services will be critical to reducing the risk of business failures and improving business growth and development. They will also be the most difficult to provide because of the absence of a pool of trained business professionals in the Czech and Slovak Republics.

3. *Broad-scale business ownership and management training.* Although widespread training is needed in both the Czech and Slovak Republics, the number of qualified trainers is limited. The survey of 48 business owners and managers revealed that less than half (48 percent) of the respondents' companies had ever obtained outside management training or technical assistance. Respondents suggested that consideration be given to developing a training center that would offer comprehensive business management training programs. This would start with a specially designed pre-business planning process that would include a series of several short workshops and related workbook materials to help individuals think through the business start-up process. Training modules could then be developed for a more diverse range of typical small business management issues as planning, marketing, record-keeping, advertising, promotion, and distribution. Once developed, these training packages could be offered through a variety of organizations and institutions across the country.

The survey also revealed a strong need in the CSFR for training of trainers. A training center must begin by developing a core staff to train other resource personnel, including school teachers from secondary schools, faculty from universities, and business managers. Staff trainers would become first-line trainers, help plan and organize training events in larger companies, and supervise external resource personnel.

Those business owners and managers interviewed saw an urgent need for training materials translated in the Czech and Slovak languages. During the Communist regime none of the universities offered small-business training programs and thus they did not develop indigenous training materials. Much of the training material now being used must be translated from small-business development literature in the United States and Western Europe. But respondents felt that indigenous materials must be created quickly. This process is taking place on a small scale in various organizations such as the Center for Democracy and Free Enterprise, the Prague School of Economics, the U.S. Business School and other organizations. However, the need far outstrips the supply of such materials, and any serious small-business development program must make this task a high priority.

4. *Business development facilities.* During the transition period, commercial space for business (retail, wholesale, manufacturing and service) was extremely scarce. With the privatization of real estate this condition should improve, although limited availability of capital will impede the rate of new commercial development, and major renovations of existing properties will be slow. The new business formation processes may be slowed simply because of the lack of space for business start-ups.

A partial solution would be to establish a "business service facility" program that would develop a network of small- to mid-sized business incubators in the Czech and Slovak Republics. These incubators would provide space and shared services to start-up firms in a few key regional centers such as Plzen, Brno, and Bratislava. If these facilities were developed as an integral part of a comprehensive small-business development program, they could also house the information-resource function and other core services of the program. These facilities would also provide a laboratory setting for the trainers and business development specialists who will be needed to serve as the staff of the program. Finally, these facilities could provide highly visible models of successful private enterprise in their communities.

No systematic effort is now being made in either the Czech Lands or

Slovakia to meet the above needs. The government has limited revenues because of the recession and the decline in exports, and has limited administrative and technical capacity to create or support such programs. In any case, small-scale entrepreneurs distrust programs sponsored by the government and prefer to obtain assistance from Czech and Slovak non-government organizations such as the Chamber of Commerce and Association of Entrepreneurs or from new programs being supported by foreign aid. Many entrepreneurs and managers have expressed a willingness to pay for appropriate services, but the institutional structure is not yet in place to extend these services widely throughout the country.[47]

Establishing Business Management Programs in the Formal Education System

An additional requirement for effective reform is expanding knowledge of how a market-oriented economy works and how businesses operate within it. Although Czechoslovakia had a long tradition of crafts, manufacturing and trade, the republics now lack experience with private enterprise and the institutional infrastructure to educate entrepreneurs and managers. The Deputy Minister of Foreign Affairs has pointed out that "the four-decades-long isolation and enforced predominance of Marxist doctrines entirely prevented the country from accumulating the critical mass of management and business know-how. There are no domestic centers that are ready to disseminate [principles of] market economy-based business management."[48]

Few managers or business owners in the Czech and Slovak Republics have been formally educated in corporate or small-business management, or even in the basics of market economics. Intensive programs are needed to change the curricula of elementary and secondary schools that focused on Marxist social and economic theory and political indoctrination during the Communist regime. Continuing education programs are needed for elementary and secondary school teachers, to expose them to the principles and operation of market economies and democratic governments. Special attention must be given to secondary vocational schools that offer apprenticeship training. The introduction of courses on small enterprise development can have a strong impact in providing opportunities for many of the graduates of these technical and vocational schools, who are unlikely to find good opportunities for employment in privatizing SOEs, to start their own businesses.

A nation-wide program of business and market economics education is needed especially in colleges and universities. Czechoslovakia's former Deputy Foreign Minister noted that among the areas in which training and education are most urgently needed are: (1) privatization and market economy operations; (2) management functions; (3) management tools, including total quality management, project management, information technology management and management of information systems; and (4) human resources management and development.[49]

Conclusion

In sum, the success of economic reforms in the Czech Lands and Slovakia will depend on privatizing the large state-owned enterprises that now dominate the manufacturing sector and on developing a critical mass of small- and medium-scale enterprises that can generate employment. An institutional structure will be needed for providing small-scale enterprises and privatizing SOEs with management and technical assistance quickly, re-orienting the educational system to provide a better and more pervasive understanding of how market economies and democratic governments operate, and developing within colleges and universities the capacity to educate the next generation of managers and entrepreneurs in business administration.

Foreign aid agencies and international assistance organizations could play an important role in helping to create and strengthen the institutional infrastructure for small business promotion in both states by providing grants to public and private organizations engaged in small-business assistance or promotion. Creating a stronger organizational structure for small-business promotion in the Czech Lands and Slovakia is a prerequisite to providing other types of business assistance effectively and will be critical in accelerating the transition from a command- to a market-oriented economy.

Notes

1. Portions of this chapter were reprinted with permission, from Dennis A. Rondinelli, "Developing Private Enterprise in the Czech and Slovak Federal Republic: The Challenge of Economic Reform," *The Columbia Journal of World Business* 26, no. 3 (1991): 27–36. Copyright 1991.

2. See Alice Teichova, *The Czechoslovak Economy, 1918–1980* (London: Routledge, 1988).

3. World Bank, *Czechoslovakia: Transition to a Market Economy* (Washington: The World Bank, 1991).

4. Cited in Gerald A. McDermott and Michal Mejstrik, "The Role of Small Firms in the Industrial Development and Transformation of Czechoslovakia," manuscript, Prague, Charles University Center for Economic Research and Graduate Education, 1991.

5. Ibid.

6. Michal Mejstrik and James Burger, "Privatization in Practice: Czechoslovakia's Experience," manuscript, Prague, Charles University Center for Economic Research and Graduate Education, 1992.

7. See Peter Martin, "Privatization: A Balance Sheet," *Report on Eastern Europe* 2, no. 5 (February 1, 1991): 7–11.

8. See "Investment Level Much Higher than Expected, Central Bank Says," *Eastern Europe Reporter* 1, no. 2 (November 11, 1991): 71–72.

9. Mejstrik and Burger, "Privatization," 24.

10. Joshua Charap and Karel Dyba, "Economic Transformation in Czechoslovakia," *Osteuropa-Wirtschaft* 36, no. 1 (March 1991): 35–46.

11. World Bank, *Czechoslovakia: Transition*.

12. See Vaclav Klaus, "A Perspective on Economic Transition in Czechoslovakia and Eastern Europe," *Proceedings of the World Bank Annual Conference on Development Economics 1990* (Washington: World Bank, 1991): 13–18.

13. Ibid., 13.

14. See Dennis A. Rondinelli, "Developing Private Enterprise in the Czech and Slovak Federal Republic: The Challenge of Economic Reform," *The Columbia Journal of World Business* XXVI, no. 3 (1991): 26–37.

15. Jiri Pehe, "Czechoslovakia: The Instability of Transition," *Report on Eastern Europe* 2, no. 1 (January 4, 1991): 11–16.

16. Anthony Robinson, "Czechs Hang 'For Sale' Sign on 50 of Republic's Key Companies," *Financial Times* (June 14, 1991): 2.

17. Mejstrik and Burger, 18–20.

18. Jiri Havel and Eugen Kukla, "Privatization and Investment Funds in Czechoslovakia," *RFE/RL Research Report* 1, no. 17 (April 1992): 37–41.

19. "New Law Allows Foreign Branches; Sets Rules for New Banks, Subsidiaries," *Eastern Europe Reporter* 2, no. 5 (March 2, 1992): 164–166.

20. "Accounting: New Law Adopts EC Standards," *Eastern Europe Reporter* 2, no. 1 (January 6, 1992): 10.

21. Jiri Pehe, "Divisions of the Communist Party of Czechoslovakia," *Report on Eastern Europe* 2, no. 30 (July 26, 1991): 10–13.

22. George Essaides, "Prospects for Profits: Czechoslovakia Through 1993," *Business International* (February 25, 1991): pp. 68–69.

23. See Jan Vanous, "Recent Czechoslovak Economic Performance," *PlanEcon Report* VII, nos. 40–41 (November 8, 1991): 1–44.

24. Kamil Janacek, "Survey of Major Trends in 1991," *RFE/RL Research Report* 1, no. 12 (March 20, 1992): 31–32.

25. See Harold Horstmeyer, "Economic Downturn Less Severe for Czechs Shifting to Market Controls," *The Journal of Commerce* (June 18, 1991): 4A.

26. Peter Martin, "Economic Reform and Slovakia," 6–13.

27. The Economist Intelligence Unit, *Czechoslovakia Country Report*, no. 2 (1992): 19.

28. Ibid., p. 9.

29. See "Slovakia Receiving Scant Notice from Investors, Statistics Show," *Eastern European Reporter* 2, no. 2 (January 20, 1992): 51.

30. Jan Obrman, "President Havel's Diminishing Political Influence," *RFE/RL Research Report* 1, no. 11 (March 13, 1992): 18–23.

31. "Parliament Inspires Little Confidence," *RFE/RL Research Report* 1, no. 11 (March 13, 1992): 74.

32. The Economist Intelligence Unit, *Czechoslovakia: Country Report*, no. 1 (1991).

33. Jiri Pehe, "Czechoslovakia: The Agenda for 1991," *Report on Eastern Europe* 2, no. 3 (January 18, 1991): 11–16.

34. Leslie Colitt and Anthony Robinson, "Heavy Going Slows the Pace of Race to Reform Czechoslovakia's Economy," *Financial Times* (March 26, 1991): 2.

35. "New Labor Pact Opens Investment Doors," *The Journal of Commerce* (March 26, 1991): 8A.

36. Gail E. Schares, "Czechoslovakia: Reluctant Reform," *Business Week Special Report* (April 15, 1991): 55.

37. See Havel and Kukla, "Privatization and Investment Funds," for a detailed discussion of the potential weaknesses in the voucher scheme.

38. The study was carried out in January and April 1991 by a team from the Kenan Institute of Private Enterprise of the Kenan-Flagler Business School, University of North Carolina at Chapel Hill, with assistance from the University of North Carolina Small Business Technology and Development Center, and the Center for International Development of the Research Triangle Institute. The American members worked closely with Czechoslovakian counterparts in the Center for Democracy and Free Enterprise in Prague, and Dum Techniky in Plzen. Members of the team interviewed more than 65 people in Czechoslovakia from government, educational institutions, banks, large industries undergoing privatization, and small businesses about the technical and management needs of small businesses and entrepreneurs and about the institutional capacity in Czechoslovakia to provide small business development programs. A more detailed survey of 48 business owners and managers was done to determine their technical and management needs. Results are reported in Dennis A. Rondinelli, Scott Daugherty and Jerry VanSant, *Management and Technical Assistance Needs of Small Businesses in Czechoslovakia* (Washington, D.C.: Central European Small Business Enterprise Development Commission, 1991).

39. Gail E. Schares et al., "Reawakening: A Market Economy Takes Root in Eastern Europe," *Business Week* (April 15, 1991): 46–50.

40. See "East European Statistics: Looking for Clues," *The Economist* (August 10, 1991): 58–59.

41. Quoted in Laura Pitter, "Auction Prices Prohibitive," *Prognosis* (March 1991): 3.

42. "East European Statistics: Looking for Clues," 59.

43. Peter Martin, "The 1991 Budget: Hard Times Ahead," *Report on Eastern Europe* 2, no. 9 (March 1, 1991): 12–16.

44. See Jiri Pehe, "Building a State Based on the Rule of Law," *Report on Eastern Europe* 2, no. 9 (March 1, 1991): 7–11.

45. Klaus, 16.

46. See Rondinelli, Daugherty, and VanSant, *Management and Technical Assistance*, 15–18.

47. Ibid. 37–40.

48. Zdenko Pirek, "Czechoslovakia's Needs in Training in Market Economics and in Business Management," manuscript prepared for delivery at White House Conference on "Economics in Transition: Management Training and Market Economics Education in Central and Eastern Europe," Washington, D. C., February 26–27, 1991.

49. Ibid., 3–4.

6

The Growth of Small Enterprise and the Private Sector in Yugoslavia

*Evan Kraft**

Yugoslavia held a unique position among the Communist countries. In 1948, only four years after taking power, the Yugoslav Communists broke with Stalin and the Soviet Communists. For the next four decades, the Communists of Yugoslavia remained outside the Soviet bloc, pursuing a foreign policy of non-alignment. The Yugoslav Communists used this position to gain generous aid from the West, while maintaining fairly good relations with the East after their rapprochement with the Soviets in 1956.

The role of the private enterprise in Yugoslavia was shaped by Yugoslavia's unorthodox approach to socialism. The Yugoslavs were the first practitioners of "reform socialism," groping their way toward a new economic model that involved decentralization of the planning mechanism in the years 1950–52.[1] At the same time, Yugoslavia instituted worker self-management (an organizational structure which nominally put rank-and-file workers in charge) in the factories. Yugoslav ideologists considered this a decisive break with Soviet "state socialist" practice, and began to refer to their system as "socialist self-management" to distinguish it from the Soviet model.

Even more important for the fate of the private sector was the Yugoslav retreat from the gung-ho collectivization of agriculture of the first years of Yugoslav socialism. In 1948, Stalin had denounced the Yugoslav party for failing to behave like true Communists, and the Yugoslav party's

*The author wishes to thank the International Research and Exchanges Board for supporting his research in Yugoslavia in 1990, and to acknowledge the help of Milan Vodopivec in preparing this chapter, as well as the many useful comments of the editor. Any remaining errors are the author's responsibility.

response had been to speed up collectivization in 1949. However, by 1951, the Yugoslav Communists had realized their mistake. The party had endangered the peasant base it had relied on in the struggle against the Nazis, a base that it continued to need in the struggle with the Soviets. The retreat from collectivization was on, and soon private farming accounted for the bulk of Yugoslavia's agricultural production.[2]

Hand in hand with this capitulation to private agriculture came a toleration—however grudging—of small private enterprise. The limits were strict—private business could have no more than ten employees, and the taxes and regulations imposed were heavy—but Yugoslavia clearly was going to put up with some small private enterprise.

Over the years, this grudging toleration proved fairly stable. Sometimes, ideological campaigns or harassment by zealous local party or government officials would imperil small private business; at other points, reformers would point to the need for more small private ownership to enhance the provision of consumer goods and services. The net result was the survival, at very low levels, of a private sector. Yugoslavia thus followed "Aaslund's Law" of private sector survival, in a manner quite similar to Poland. (See Chapter 2 of this volume for a description of Aaslund's Law and its application to the Polish case.)

Finally, in the early 1980s, it appeared that the reformers had won out. Encouragement of small business, even small private business, now seemed to be fashionable in official documents and rhetoric. But the rhetoric of the 1980s was not matched by reality. Following Tito's death, the Yugoslav Communist Party entered a period of collective leadership characterized by growing fragmentation along regional and ideological lines. Although a thorough-going "Long-Term Program for Economic Stabilization" was approved by both the League of Communists (LCY) and the Federal Assembly in 1982, conservative forces within the LCY succeeded in limiting the implementation of reforms in subsequent years.

Because of the political stalemate brought about by the conservatives' foot-dragging, the achievements of the 1980s were very limited when it came to small enterprise. The rate of growth of small enterprise in both the social[3] and private sectors was modest indeed. Only in 1988, with Yugoslavia facing runaway inflation, a stubbornly high foreign debt and falling living standards, did a consensus emerge within the Party to make decisive changes in the economic system. With the policy changes of 1988–90, small enterprise, and especially small private enterprise, began to flower again in Yugoslavia. Private enterprises seemed to sprout everywhere, especially in the nooks and crannies left vacant by the social sector. But the overall contribution of the private sector to national income and employment remained modest through early 1991.

In this chapter, the private sector is examined as a part of the small and medium enterprise (SME) sector in Yugoslavia. The SME sector provides fertile soil for the reemergence of the private sector, since socially-controlled enterprises' lack of flexibility and efficiency are most manifest in small and medium firms. In addition, small and medium firms are more easily privatized than large firms. Thus, the SME sector both needs private firms, and is the sector where private firms will most readily appear.

The Private Sector Under Yugoslav Socialism:
Private Production and Ownership Patterns

The cornerstone of legal private-sector production in socialist Yugoslavia was private agriculture. As late as 1965, individual agriculture accounted for 56% of sales and procurement of agricultural goods. While that percentage gradually fell to 44% in 1989, private agriculture remained a major part of the Yugoslav scene.[4]

Another element of private production under Yugoslav socialism was the private crafts. In 1955, these employed 192,221 people (including owners), or some 9.6% of the employed. By 1988, however, this number had only grown to 283,711, or a mere 4.2% of persons employed. All told, the private sector, excluding agriculture and construction, employed some 364,875 workers in 1987. Major areas of craftwork in 1988 included the production of metal parts and electrical products, as well as the more traditional areas of wood, textile and leather product manufacture.[5]

Also of great importance to social welfare—but difficult to document statistically—were the "grey" and "black" economies. People supplemented their incomes, or even supported themselves, from activities such as watching the neighbors' children and performing services at home (often with tools borrowed from the factory). A favorite way to repair one's car in Yugoslavia was to rent a car, remove any desired parts, and return the car to the rental company.

These "grey market" activities could be supplemented with "black market" activities such as illegally buying and selling hard currency, or actually stealing tools or materials from social enterprises. While these activities were illegal, they were widely practiced and infrequently prosecuted. For example, buying and selling hard currency on a small scale was near universal in the mid-1980s, and carried virtually no threat of punishment. In addition, it was not illegal to work on one's own account. Thus Yugoslavia differed substantially from the traditional Soviet practices of prosecuting people for "parasitism" or "profiteering," and of severely limiting opportunities for making income "on the side."

Only the crudest estimates of the size of these grey and black market activities exists. Miroslav Glas's survey research in Slovenia found that supplementary income accounted for only 3.14% of total income of urban worker families. However, this income was distributed in a highly unequal fashion. In 10% of the families surveyed, such income amounted to 10% of total income.[6] Furthermore, such income tended to be concentrated among the wealthier families. The main types of work were agricultural services; the construction of houses, apartments and weekend houses; and the repair of cars, machines and appliances. In a more permissive environment for small business, much of this work (excluding agricultural services) could easily have been undertaken by small firms or independent contractors. In part, therefore, the grey market served to provide services that normally would have been provided by small, fully legal firms.

Like private production, private ownership also continued to exist under Yugoslav socialism. Private home ownership was perhaps the most important form of private ownership. In 1954, 64% of housing was privately owned. This percentage fell in the latter part of the 1950s, as social sector housing boomed. But social sector housing reached 50,330 units in 1966, and then fell in absolute terms for almost a decade, surpassing its previous level only in 1974. By that time, 62% of housing was privately owned. The percentage then rose all the way to 74% in 1989.[7] These percentages of private home ownership were relatively high by the standards of socialist countries, especially in the 1950s and 1960s, and can be considered an important element of Yugoslav socialism's higher living standards relative to many of the Soviet-bloc countries in that period.

An important underpinning of this high level of private ownership was the Yugoslav experience in Western Europe. With the opening of Yugoslavia's borders in 1965, Yugoslav workers flooded into the West. Many stayed only long enough to build up a nest egg, then returned. Prevented from investing their money in existing social-sector ventures, and limited by the many constraints on private enterprise, many former "guestworkers" ended up putting their money into building themselves housing.

To summarize, under traditional Yugoslav socialism, the private sector accounted for nearly half of the country's agricultural output, but a much more modest share of craft production, and a rather limited fraction of manufacturing and trade. If the grey and black markets were added in, however, the private sector was probably an important part of urban income generation as well. Private home ownership and open borders also contributed to making Yugoslav socialism a very different model from that practiced elsewhere.

Doing Business Under Yugoslav Socialism

Despite a comparatively non-restrictive policy environment, the life of a private business person under Yugoslav socialism was not easy. The obstacles in his or her way were as much created by anti-business attitudes of the population or by local officials as by formal legal restrictions, but in any case, the net result was an often unfriendly environment for private business relative to that common in the West.

Although some private enterprise was grudgingly tolerated in socialist Yugoslavia, many people felt that making money was essentially immoral. Sociologist Josip Zupanov has described Yugoslavia's "egalitarian syndrome,"[8] arguing that this stress on equality was a product of the peasant social structure that gradually died out in the years of Yugoslav socialism. Nonetheless, it may have contributed to popular mistrust of private entrepreneurs, and made the population more willing to accept bureaucratic accusations that entrepreneurs were cheating the public.

The key obstacle to the private entrepreneurs, however, was not the local population but the local politician. Officials of the Commune, the lowest level of government in Yugoslavia, often exacted punitive levels of taxation. Furthermore, they controlled the allocation of commercial real estate. Getting a good retail spot in a major city required connections with the top party or government leadership of the city. (This same phenomenon was later seen in other Central and East European countries as their private sectors began to expand.) Thus, private restaurants often found it more practical to locate in suburbs or on the outskirts of town. Local officials could also make the process of registering a new private business a Kafka-esque affair. Paperwork mysteriously would multiply and delays would build up. The entrepreneur thus needed great stamina to survive even the start-up phase of business.

This political resistance to small business had several roots. For one thing, local officials often had an ideological axe to grind: they hadn't fought in the Partisan War in order to allow capitalists to take over their city! Also, given officials' ability to control commercial real estate and business licensing, the potential for "rent-seeking" through bribery was not at all trivial. Finally, local officials were protective of the social sector, which they viewed to a certain extent as their own property that had to be shielded from competition from the private sector.

Another key obstacle to private sector expansion was the private sector's difficulty obtaining credit from social sector banks. These, after all, were closely tied to the same local and republic-level politicians who were making the private business people sweat over real estate and licenses. Private banks were non-existent, so the only alternative was to assemble all necessary finance from relatives, partners, or other private backers. The consequence of limited credit availability, naturally, was limited growth potential for small business.

While the legal limit on employees certainly had a crucial role in limiting the private sector, this set of procedural and operational restrictions also kept private enterprise from growing in socialist Yugoslavia. Red tape proved highly effective in slowing down private business, and was very difficult to remove when the political winds changed in favor of private business.

In sum, the Yugoslav private sector was stymied to a great extent by the bureaucracy. Yet, the bureaucracy had its own substitute for the private sector—the small-scale social sector—which we turn to now.

Social Sector SMEs: A Substitute for the Private Sector?

Self-Management, Decisionmaking and the Effectiveness
of Social Sector SMEs

Social sector SMEs were socialist Yugoslavia's answer to private enterprise. For this reason, to understand the past role and possible future shape of private enterprise in Yugoslavia, it is useful to look at the small and medium enterprise (SME) sector of the economy, both social (i.e., collectively- or state-run) and private.

Advocates of worker self-management hoped that Yugoslav firms in which workers were legally in charge would prove more dynamic and more productive than either state-owned firms of the Soviet type or Western capitalist firms. This hope was not without some basis: recent literature suggests that worker participation in management can have positive effects on productivity.[9] (Some examples of participation are Japanese quality circles, worker-owned firms in the United States, and the Mondragon co-operatives of Spain.) The main theoretical reasons for such productivity gain are (1) that workers may have the best knowledge of how the detailed work process they are involved in can be streamlined; (2) that workers may simply work harder if they feel they are being consulted; and (3) that incentive schemes based on productivity can be facilitated by worker involvement.

However, it seems that Yugoslav self-management did not realize these potential gains of participation very well.[10] A key problem seems to have been overlapping lines of authority. While workers' councils were legally supposed to be the ultimate decisionmakers in Yugoslav enterprises, management bodies in fact had a crucial role both in day-to-day decisions and in long-run planning. Management had two advantages: first, managers ran the enterprise every day; and second, managers had better ties to the local Communist Party, local banks and local political officials.

The problem was not so much that managers had considerable power, but that neither managers nor workers were able to take action on their own. Decisionmaking became an excruciatingly complex process, involving getting ideas through a host of different bodies. Worse yet, after such decisions were made, no one person or body had clear responsibility for implementing them.[11]

These general problems with self-management in Yugoslavia help explain why small firms did not thrive in the social sector. As Ljubomir Madzar, a well-known economist from Belgrade puts it, "the social sector, with its notorious inadequacy in decisionmaking capacity, is at a clear disadvantage" in running small firms.[12]

As a consequence of the social sector's lack of the decisionmaking capacity needed to run small firms, the social sector showed a strong bias toward large firms. This bias was probably reinforced by the traditional Marxist view that technological development inexorably creates economies of scale, as well as the pragmatic reality that it is easier for political authorities to control a few large firms than a myriad of small firms.

Table 6.1 illustrates this, showing the size distribution of all firms in Yugoslavia in 1986. What is striking in the table is the bi-modal distribution. There are really two main clumps of firms: those employing 1–15 workers, and those employing 61–500 workers. The first group is by far the largest, accounting for 90.81% of all firms, but only 6.8% of employment and 4.4% of national income. The second group, by contrast, accounts for only 6.7% of the firms, but employs 54.8% of all workers and produces 58.4% of national income.

The really strange part here is the gap from 15–60 workers. Yugoslav economists Tea Petrin and Ales Vahcic have called this the "black hole."[13] Such a gap, according to Petrin and Vahcic, is not found in market economies. It indicates strong systemic impediments to the growth of small and medium firms. If small firms from the 1–15 employees category grew normally, we would expect to see quite a few firms with 15–30 employees, as well as significant numbers of 30–60 and so on.

The "black hole" can be partly explained by the legal prohibition of private enterprises with more than ten workers, and the various operational restrictions on private enterprise discussed above. These factors keep private enterprise from filling the hole. But it must also reflect some obstacles in the social sector as well. Apparently what happens is that small social sector enterprises either stagnate or merge with larger firms, thereby jumping over the intermediate range from 15 to 100 workers. Thus, in part, the "black hole" was caused by the social sector's bias toward larger firms.

Structural Gaps in the SME Sector

In addition to the gap in the size distribution of firms, there are gaps in the sectoral distribution of small firms. SMEs are notably absent from certain key areas of the Yugoslav economy, such as manufacturing and trade. This can be seen from the sectoral breakdown of SME production.

Table 6.1
Distribution of Enterprises, Employment and National Income
According to Number of Workers, 1986

	TOTAL	1-15	16-29	30-60	61-125	126-250	251-500	501-1000	1001-2000	2000+
Enterprises										
Total	270278	245405	2257	4092	5917	5976	4183	1890	461	92
Social	27685	2812	2257	4092	5917	5976	4188	1890	461	92
SME	2511	533	333	457	616	435	117	15	5	-
Private[a]	242593	242593	-	-	-	-	-	-	-	-
Percent[b]		90.81	0.84	1.51	2.19	2.21	1.55	0.70	0.17	0.03
Employment										
Total	5835441	396773	50320	181319	534438	1074543	1461627	1270320	602101	264000
Social	5461669	23001	50320	181319	534438	1074543	1461627	1270320	602101	264000
SME	217326	4006	7426	20155	55174	75166	39241	8789	7369	-
Private[a]	373772	373772	-	-	-	-	-	-	-	-
Percent[b]		6.80	0.86	3.11	9.16	18.41	25.05	21.77	10.32	4.52
National income (billion dinars)										
Total	18340.7	802.3	175.9	624.9	1855.3	3654.3	4758.6	3950.4	1683.5	835.4
Social	17656.0	117.6	175.9	624.9	1855.3	3654.3	4758.6	3950.4	1683.5	835.4
SME	620.8	39.0	29.9	65.6	156.5	194.8	89.4	23.1	22.7	-
Private[a]	684.7	684.7	-	-	-	-	-	-	-	-
Percent[b]		4.37	0.96	3.41	10.12	19.92	25.95	21.54	9.18	4.55

[a]Private sector enterprises have been legally constrained to employ no more than ten workers.
[b]Column total as percent of grand total.
Note: Data include all productive and some non-productive activities; in the private sector, construction is excluded.
Source: Internal material of the Federal Statistical Office, Belgrade: "Communication Number 16" 1988.

The statistics available of SMEs are based on the definition of SMEs in the Social Compact of 1980. This compact, which was intended to promote SME development, defined small and medium enterprises as those with less than 200 workers (125 workers in Slovenia) in either the social or private sector. In addition, all enterprises classified as crafts, those operating in less developed regions, those performing auxiliary functions for a parent organization, and those performing services for and by organizations of the handicapped, could be considered small and medium enterprises. Privately-owned farms, however, were not included in the definition of SMEs.

Table 6.2 shows the shares of SMEs in national income in various sectors in 1986. SMEs were important players in three areas: crafts, construction, and manufacturing. The first area included the production of metal parts and electrical products, as well as the more traditional areas of wood, textile and leather product manufacture. The second area reflected the existence of small building firms, both in the social and private sector. The third area reflected the existence of significant numbers of smaller social-sector manufacturing enterprises. (The figure for manufacturing, however, is probably inflated by the legal inclusion of larger manufacturing enterprises in less developed regions in the Social Compact of 1980.)

Table 6.2 also shows that private SMEs were congregated mainly in arts and crafts, followed by construction, transport and communications, and catering and tourism. Transport and communications mainly includes such occupations as taxi drivers and boat operators; catering and tourism include private restaurants and people renting rooms to tourists. The biggest hole in the private enterprise sectoral distribution occurs in manufacturing, where the private SME sector had no representation whatsoever. This suggests that manufacturing, along with trade, where the private sector share was a tiny 0.2%, could be a key target of post-reform private sector expansion.

The Consequences of the Black Hole

What were the consequences of these holes and gaps in Yugoslavia's industrial structure? Let us examine three problem areas: entry and exit, retail and service provision, and employment.

Flexibility is a key to adaptation to new production, technologies and tastes. The Yugoslav economy should have been more flexible than the Soviet. In contrast to the first country of socialism, Yugoslavia had dismantled the central plan, decentralized economic decisionmaking to local governments and enterprises, empowered workers to make important decisions, and unleashed market forces to a degree.

In fact, the Yugoslav economy does appear to have been significantly

Table 6.2
The Composition of the SMEs by Output Shares, 1986

	Share of SMEs in Output of Sector	Share in Total National SME Output
Total Economy		
SME social sector	2.7	46.3
SME private	3.1	53.7
Total SMEs	5.7	100.0
Manufacturing		
SME social sector	2.3	17.0
SME private sector	0.0	0.0
SMEs-manufacturing	2.3	17.0
Agriculture		
SME social sector	0.0	0.1
SME private sector	0.0	0.0
SMEs-agriculture	0.1	0.1
Construction		
SME social sector	9.1	11.0
SME private sector	8.6	10.5
SMEs-construction	17.7	21.5
Transport and Communications		
SME social sector	0.1	0.1
SME private sector	6.6	8.3
SMEs-trans. and com.	6.7	8.4
Trade (Distribution)		
SME social sector	0.6	1.7
SME private sector	0.2	0.7
SMEs-trade	0.8	2.4
Catering and Tourism		
SME social sector	0.0	0.0
SME private sector	13.5	7.2
SMEs-cater. and tour.	13.5	7.2
Arts and Crafts		
SME social sector	25.3	16.1
SME private sector	42.4	27.0
SMEs-arts and crafts	67.7	43.1

(Table continued on next page)

Table 6.2 (continued)

	Share of SMEs in Output of Sector	Share in Total National SME Output
Public Utilities		
SME social sector	0.6	0.1
SME private sector	0.0	0.0
SMEs-public utilities	0.6	0.1
Other Productive Services		
SME social sector	0.3	0.2
SME private sector	0.0	0.0
SMEs-other prod. serv.	0.3	0.2

Source: Internal material of Federal Statistical Office of SFR Yugoslavia.

more flexible than Soviet-type economies. Nonetheless, the Yugoslav economy displayed many of the same types of rigidities and weaknesses, albeit to a somewhat lesser degree.

A crucial aspect of this rigidity was the limited level of entry and exit. In dynamic, innovative economies, new firms arise and old ones die at a significant rate. New firms tend to be the bearers of new products, technologies and organizational methods, although very often the best of these are snapped up by larger firms after proving themselves viable. (For a discussion of factors influencing entry and exit behavior in the Russian context, see Chapter 7.)

The data in Table 6.3 document the level of entry and exit in Yugoslavia for the mid-1980s. For example, in 1987, new enterprises accounted for 2.4% of the previous total. Since much of that figure is made up by reorganizations of existing enterprises, it is more revealing to look at newly activated enterprises. These amounted to only 0.8% of the existing total. By way of comparison, in the United States in the same year, new incorporations amounted to some 11.4% of the total of existing businesses.[14]

The U.S. figure is probably among the highest in the world, given the developed infrastructure, networks of venture capital and high level of wealth of Americans. Yugoslavia, therefore, should not be expected to equal the American level. Still, the tiny rate of new firm formation underscores the difficulties faced by would-be entrepreneurs in Yugoslavia, difficulties that may have been than in other socialist countries such as Hungary and China which encouraged private enterprise formation in the 1980s.

At the same time, exits were also at a low level. Exits-through-reorganization probably is not a very good indicator of exit; very often, this kind of exit meant the consolidation of Basic Organizations of Associated

Table 6.3
Entries and Exits of Enterprises, Social Sector, 1983-87[a]

	1984	1985	1986	1987
New Enterprises	829	803	785	760
In Formation	92	92	122	176
Activated	233	249	297	252
Completed Construction	19	63	79	59
Immediate Activation	214	186	218	193
Reorganizations	504	462	366	332
Exit				
Bankruptcies Started	32	67	69	98
Bankruptcies Completed	65	79	62	43
Exits via Reorganization	1029	1393	1545	1903
Memo Items				
Total No. of Enterprises	32883	32863	32093	31333
Failure rate per 10,000	19.8	24.2	21.5	13.7
U.S. failure rate	107.0	115.0	120.0	102.0

[a]The data pertain to activities 1-11 according to the Yugoslav
"Unified Classification of Activities" of 1976, corresponding
closely to a so-called economic sphere. The data are furnished by
enterprises reporting changes of their legal or organizational
status. Under "New enterprises in formation" are presented only
those starting with the formation that year; the overall number
of enterprises in formation is likely to be bigger, since the
process of formation may last more than a year. Similar remarks
apply to "Bankruptcies started". New enterprises activated
immediately (no reported period of construction) could be founded
by enterprises in formation starting as temporary basic
organizations. Reorganizations include all kinds of merges and
splitting.
Sources: "Organizations and Communities," Statistical Bulletin
1421, 1545, 1588, 1688, Federal Statistical Office of SFR
Yugoslavia. U.S. data are from Economic Report of the President
(Washington, DC: USGPO, 1992): 404.

Labor, which are subdivisions of a larger entity. (See below.) Such consolidations may have little effect on the firm's product line or technology.

The key figure on exits, then, is bankruptcies completed. The Memo Item "Failure Rate" gives the number of firms completing bankruptcy per 10,000 firms. If we compare this to the Memo Item "U.S. failure rate," we find that Yugoslav firms failed roughly 4 to 7 times less frequently than American firms in the years in question. We can conclude that the threat of bankruptcy to an existing firm in 1987 in Yugoslavia was relatively low.

The weak enforcement of bankruptcy had far-reaching consequences for economic performance. Aware that they were very unlikely to go out of business, Yugoslav firms could remain somewhat indifferent to the needs of their customers. Lack of profitability could be papered over with various types of indirect government subsidies. Very likely, this freedom from bankruptcy played a big part in limiting the productivity and competitiveness of Yugoslav firms.[15]

Another important weakness of the Yugoslav economy was the limited development of retail and service activities. Compared to the United States, Yugoslavia had a low ratio of retailing to wholesaling. In Belgrade in 1982, there were almost as many wholesale organizations (168) as retail organizations (179).[16] By contrast, in the United States in the same year, there were 1,425,000 retail establishments, as compared to 435,100 wholesale establishments, a ratio of greater than 3 retail to 1 wholesale establishment.[17] Also, if one compares the number of workers in retail to the number in wholesale, in Yugoslavia the ratio was 2.29 in 1987, and in the U.S., the ratio was 3.18 in the same year. Interestingly enough, the Yugoslav figure represented a substantial improvement from the level of 1955, which had been 1.89.[18]

These figures do not indicate a country that is totally without provision for consumers. The long lines for food and other items, so widespread in the Soviet Union, were not seen in Yugoslavia from the mid-1950s on. Nonetheless, shopping was still somewhat difficult, service was indifferent, and choice limited.

Furthermore, services such as repair services were very hard to come by. Since the social sector offered virtually no repair services to private individuals, Yugoslavs fell back on the private sector or the grey market. Finding a *majstor* (skilled worker) to fix a broken window or door, for example, could be a major undertaking involving all the connections one could muster. The price of the service would very often be steep indeed. Under these circumstances, it was easy for a repairperson to take payment, start the job, and leave without finishing.

Most often, such services were organized through the informal economy. Even the formal service sector operated according to the same principles, however. When I entered a radio repair shop on the biggest street in Belgrade in 1987, the proprietor was shocked that a customer had come in merely because he had seen the sign outside. The repairman could scarcely understand why someone would come to him without having a "connection" to him.

A final problem associated with the limited presence of small and medium enterprises in Yugoslavia was high unemployment. Although it varied dramatically by region, unemployment was a significant problem in Yugoslav socialism. During the 1980s, registered unemployment rose steadily from 11.9% in 1980 to 14.9% in 1989. Since many Yugoslavs do not bother to register for the very modest unemployment benefits available, this figure understates actual unemployment levels considerably.

In many market economies, the small and medium enterprise sector comprised a key area of employment growth in the 1980s.[19] However, in Yugoslavia employment in the small private sector was highly limited, amounting to only 5.3% of employment in 1987. Hence it seems fair to say that part of Yugoslavia's unemployment problem can be attributed to its failure to promote small and medium enterprise.

To summarize, Yugoslavia's relative lack of private firms and SMEs led to low levels of economic flexibility, limited exit and entry, inadequate emphasis on retail, and unnecessarily high unemployment. The next section examines what Yugoslavia tried to do about all of this in the 1980s.

Small and Medium Enterprise:
Promotion and Stagnation in the 1980s

Yugoslav economists and political officials were not unaware of the consequences of the limited size of the small and medium enterprise sector. In 1980, a social compact for the development of small and medium enterprises was signed at the federal level. The compact was designed to identify and aid the SME sector.

What were the consequences of the social compact? Unfortunately, small and medium enterprise appear to have had a fairly disappointing experience in the years after the compact. Overall, there were only 7.3% more SMEs in 1987 than 1982.

Considerable regional variations were contained in this aggregate figure, however. Croatia in particular experienced a substantial growth in SMEs, with the 1987 figure being some 32.3% higher than the 1982. Probably a large number of these were enterprises offering services to tourists on the Adriatic coast. By contrast, Slovenia had an 11.4% decline in SMEs in the same period.

The story is rather similar if we look at national income rather than number of firms. Social sector SMEs experienced a modest 7.9% growth in real income over the period, while the private sector SMEs experienced a 6.1% fall. As the rest of the economy grew, the share of social sector SME income in total national income rose modestly, from 2.4% of national income in 1982, and 2.7% in 1987, while private sector SMEs lost share, from 3.3% of national income to only 3.1% in 1987.

SME employment trends provided a welcome, but modest, positive element. As shown in Table 6.4, SMEs expanded their share of employment in the whole economy from 8.1% in 1982 to 8.9% in 1987. Social sector SME employment rose 15.0% in the period, and private sector SME employment rose an impressive 31.8%. By contrast, overall employment

Table 6.4
Employment -- SME Sector Compared to Overall Economy,
1982-1987

	1982	1983	1984	1985	1986	1987
Total	6295555	6426113	6570651	6738394	6935508	7080000[a]
SME-social sector	191692	195762	193041	199204	217326	220036
SME-private sector	315669	329226	346208	360667	373772	416215
Total SMEs	507361	524988	539249	559871	591098	636251

Employment Shares (percent)

	1982	1983	1984	1985	1986	1987
Total SMEs	8.1	8.2	8.2	8.3	8.5	8.9
SME-social sector	3.0	3.0	2.9	3.0	3.1	3.1
SME-private sector	5.0	5.1	5.3	5.4	5.4	5.8

Total Percent Growth of
Employment 1982-1987

Total	12
SME-social section	15
SME-private section	32
Total SMEs	25

[a]Estimate

Sources: *Statistical Yearbook of SFR Yugoslavia*, various issues; Communication No. 397-1983, 16-1988, 313-1988; *Statistical Bulletin* 1457, 1526, 1661; Federal Statistical Office of SFR Yugoslavia.

increased only 12.5%. Hence it appears that SMEs did play a positive role in expanding employment, although perhaps not by as much as they might have in a more favorable environment.

Typically, small enterprises offer opportunities for very rapid growth. At the same time, however, much higher percentages of small businesses fail in market economies than larger ones. To judge the success of a group of small, therefore, one would like to find out whether growth or failure predominates.

One technique for doing this is the "survivor test." This test follows a selected group of SMEs over a period of years. The test aims at evaluating whether the given group of SMEs continues to survive and expand, or whether it contracts as member firms fail. In order to make this evaluation, let us examine Table 6.5, which shows the share of Slovenia's gross material product (a national output measure) accounted for by a selected group of Slovenian SMEs. The group's share falls through 1984, then rises in 1985 and 1986. This indicates a significant amount of resilience on the part of the SMEs; enough of them survive and expand that, four years down the line, their share of Slovenian output actually rises. That is to say that, once founded, this set of SMEs was relatively hardy.

To summarize, neither the number of SMEs nor the income produced by SMEs showed substantial increases during the years after the signing of the social compact. SMEs did, however, provide important employment growth at a time when larger enterprises were not expanding vigorously at all. Moreover, they seemed to survive rather well once established.

Table 6.5
Survivor Test Applied to Slovenian Social Sector SMEs[a]

Year	Output Share of Selected Social Sector SMEs in Total GMP (%)
1980	2.35
1981	2.34
1982	2.31
1983	2.22
1984	2.11
1985	2.13
1986	2.17

[a]Only the population of SMEs that was continuously in existence in the period of 1980-86 is taken into account (252 enterprises).
Source: Internal material of the Statistical Office of SR Slovenia.

Small and Medium Enterprise
in the Reform Process, 1988–90

Liberalization and Legal Reform After the "May Measures"

In May 1988, with inflation running at figures well over 200% annually, and a foreign debt near $20 billion, Yugoslavia's leaders agreed on a package of measures to stabilize the economy. It was not the first stabilization and reform package of the decade. In fact, it was the fifth package introduced by Prime Minister Branko Mikulic, who was only two years into his four-year term. But the "May measures" were in fact a dramatic change from previous policy in Yugoslavia. For one thing, the "measures" accompanied a stand-by agreement for new credits from the International Monetary Fund, something Yugoslavia had not had since 1985. Also, the "measures" contained a reasonably coherent orthodox anti-inflation policy relying on a combination of price liberalization and tight monetary and fiscal policies. But, most important, the reform package reflected a political consensus for dramatic changes in the legal infrastructure of the Yugoslav economy.

It may seem paradoxical that Yugoslavia, the first Communist country to break away from the Soviets, was not at the forefront of the wave of reform that swept much of the Communist world in the 1980s. With Tito having died in 1980, the conditions might have been thought to be ripe for basic changes. However, the Communist leadership remained split. Key members of the collective presidency vetoed any significant changes in ownership relations as late as 1987. Branko Mikulic, prime minister from 1986 to 1989, later commented that two members of the presidency, "thinking they were Marx and Lenin themselves," refused to allow him to introduce crucial innovations such as allowing companies to issue stock and expanding the limits on private ownership.[20] These top leaders had significant support in the party apparatus and rank and file in their home republics.

The "May measures" broke the political stalemate, leading to widespread liberalization of the Yugoslav economy. Most prices were freed from government control. Import quotas were removed in most cases. The exchange rate of the dinar was allowed to float freely.

Even though inflation continued to accelerate, these liberalizing measures were maintained. And, in January 1989, a new "Law on Enterprises" was passed that dramatically transformed the organization of the Yugoslav economy.

The "Law on Enterprises" broke with the previous system in almost all major respects. In contrast to previous legislation, which enshrined social or self-managed enterprises as the main property form, while grudgingly allowing co-operatives and individually-owned private business, the

"Law on Enterprises" laid the basis for various property forms to coexist: state, social, private, co-operative and mixed. It also opened up a multitude of new forms of enterprise: public enterprises owned by governments, joint-stock companies, limited liability companies, limited partnerships, and companies with unlimited joint liability of their members.

The "Law on Enterprises" was a veritable Magna Carta of a mixed economy. While neither the law itself nor subsequent legislation could be considered free of major ambiguities, it formed the basis for a flowering of new types of enterprise. During 1989, the "Law on the Circulation and Disposal of Social Capital" specified that socially-owned enterprises could be sold, with the proceeds going into a republic-level fund for development; the "Law on Securities" allowed equity shares to be issued; and a "Banking Law" allowed banks to be turned from non-profitmaking institutions into joint-stock and limited-liability banks. Additional legislation simplified the registration of enterprises in courts, clarified and strengthened bankruptcy procedures, allowed 100% foreign-owned companies, and forced the Yugoslav bureaucracy to either accept or reject the registration of foreign ventures within 30 days of application.

The Federal Agency for Development and Restructuring

In addition to changing the laws, the government of Prime Minister Ante Markovic, who had succeeded Mikulic in April 1989, sought to promote small and private business by setting up a Federal Agency for Development and Restructuring in 1990. The Agency, it was stressed, would not be a permanent part of the state bureaucracy. Instead, it would be a short-term, task-oriented body that would help get the restructuring process going, and in particular would lay great emphasis on creating the infrastructure for new small enterprises.[21]

The Agency's director, Dr. Ales Vahcic, emphasized that its mission was to dynamize the economy by creating competition and raising the technological level of business. To do this, it would be necessary to create entrepreneurship, establish sources of risk capital, and create the conditions for bringing in foreign capital.

The main obstacles, according to Vahcic, were (1) a lack of all sorts of information and expertise, including basic knowledge of finance, marketing and bookkeeping; (2) extremely limited banking services, particularly for venture capital; (3) problems in communication, including weaknesses in postal and telephone service, along with the extremely high cost of crucial machines such as faxes and cars; and (4) difficulty finding business space, coupled with ambiguities concerning property rights over buildings and other immovable property. (In this regard, Yugoslavia clearly shared many of the institutional problems common throughout Central and Eastern Europe at this time. See Chapter 5.)

The Agency's strategy for overcoming these problems had two major components: (1) fostering horizontal links among enterprises on a voluntary basis to blend cooperation with competition; and (2) promoting leading entrepreneurial firms.

To accomplish the first goal, the Agency looked to service centers to provide advice on technology, finance, and bookkeeping, to make connections between the universities and business, and to allow the joint use of equipment by various businesses. Tea Petrin, the Agency's co-director, cited the case of the Slovenian furniture industry, which was in the process of building a network of firms to help finance common projects and create an environment in which the whole industry could prosper.

Incubators were to be the key instrument for the second goal. Incubators had developed in the United States as ways of fostering new, entrepreneurial firms. According to a recent study, incubators "provide affordable space, shared support services, and business development assistance in an environment conducive to enterprise creation, survival and early-stage growth."[22]

While only ten incubators could be identified in the United States before 1980, some 385 existed in 1990. Firms participating in incubators are estimated to have an average of nine employees upon "graduation," and perhaps as many as 86% of the firms in incubators "graduate" and establish themselves in their own business space. Some U.S. incubators were developed by local governments as ways to create jobs and revitalize urban areas; others revolve around universities, whose scientific and engineering personnel develop marketable products and services for the new ventures. Still others are private, for-profit ventures aiming either at real-estate appreciation, as the tenants prosper, or the support and supervision of start-ups in which the entrepreneur has invested venture capital.

The first Yugoslav incubators were started in 1988 in universities with the aim of developing new technologies. The Agency's intention was to get large enterprises involved in the incubators, since these enterprises had the necessary excess capacity (especially space) for new projects.

Both Drs. Petrin and Vahcic put the work of the Agency in the context of a strategy of flexible specialization.[23] They looked to an economy dominated not by large industrial corporations making uniform, mass-market goods, but consisting mainly of flexible, small firms that could adapt their production to specific customer requirements and seize niche markets. They saw their work as creating industrial regions in which networks of small firms could create external economies of scale. That is, the presence of a large number of flexible, small firms in a given region would allow the region to produce cheaply, without creating large-scale enterprises. Petrin and Vahcic cited Italy's Emilia-Romana, Denmark's

Jutland, Sweden's Smaland, and Germany's Baden-Württemburg as ex-. amples of regions successfully following such an approach.

A final goal of the Agency was to seek external financial help for enterprise development. The European Free Trade Area (EFTA) countries had promised some $20 million. World Bank funding was to be sought as well.

It is difficult to say how much of the success of small business in 1990 (described below) can be attributed to the Federal Agency. The Agency's leaders were both able economists and skilled promoters; they may have done a better job at marketing the Agency then at building small industry. But at least the Agency can be credited with producing a vision of methods for the promotion of small business, and appearing to be energetically attempting to carry through that vision.

The Expansion of the Private Sector, 1988–90

Legal changes beginning in 1988, along with the work of the Federal Agency, led to a dramatic transformation of the Yugoslav economic landscape. By the end of October 1990, 37,866 private enterprises were registered. These firms constituted 74.2% of all enterprises.[24]

These private enterprises were mainly of two types: simple private enterprises and limited-liability companies. Simple private enterprises, owned by a single entrepreneur and subject to unlimited liability, numbered 23,222, or 61.4% of the total of private enterprises. Limited liability companies numbered 14,209, or 37.5% of all private enterprises.

However, not all of these enterprises actually functioned. The 37,866 figure refers merely to enterprises registered. A Yugoslav business magazine estimated that about 41% of the new firms were in operation by September 1990. In addition, under the new laws, it would have been possible for the new private enterprises to be large enterprises, rather than SMEs. However, according to the business magazine *Privredni Pregled*, the average size of the new enterprise was 2.5 employees, so it seems doubtful that many very large private enterprises have been founded.[25]

Most of the new private enterprises were in fact totally new. Even though the legal basis for privatization of existing enterprises was in place, the actual procedure to be followed remained fairly unclear. What few privatizations of previously existing social sector firms did occur involved "spontaneous privatization"—the transfer of the enterprise to its managers, usually at a ridiculously low price without a public sale. Naturally, this type of privatization provoked considerable public outcry, and was curbed fairly quickly. Thus, as was true in Poland (see Chapter 2), the indigenous private sector was the main force for expansion of private enterprise in the reforming Yugoslavia.

Sectoral and Geographic Distribution of New Enterprises

It is quite clear that there was a major flowering of new organizations in general, and private firms in particular, in 1989 and 1990. Let us now address the nature of the firms founded during this period, and their location.

Table 6.6 shows the sectoral breakdown of new enterprises in 1989. The largest number of new firms—1231—appeared in the retail sector, where they were greatly needed. Following that were financial and other services with 1027, and manufacturing and mining with 621 new firms, respectively.

The data in Table 6.6 refer to all enterprises, both private and social. Hence it is unclear what the specific role of private enterprise was in the burst of new firms in 1989. However, the data in Table 6.7, which refer to 1990, make the issue clearer. As was true for new enterprises in general, the three main sectors of private enterprise expansion are trade, financial and other services, and industry.

The expansion in private trade was one of the most visible changes in Yugoslavia in 1990. Often, the new firms were small stores such as grocery stores. For example, when I was living in Zagreb in 1990, the socially-owned grocery store in my apartment building found its local monopoly challenged by a private store not 50 feet away. The new store had a slightly different product assortment, some price differences (some lower and some higher), and longer hours.

The pattern was repeated throughout Zagreb. A city that had never heard of health food was now treated to three different health food stores (only one of which, a well-established and well-run store blessed with

Table 6.6
New Enterprises by Sector, 1989

	In Formation	New	Reorganizations
Total	139	3750	125
Industry	33	621	50
Agriculture	7	143	27
Construction	15	242	9
Trade	24	1231	8
Catering & Tourism	7	155	2
Crafts	12	215	3
Finance	31	1027	13
Other[a]	10	116	13

[a]Forestry, waterworks, transport and communications and communal services.
Source: Federal Statistical Office of Yugoslavia, "Organizations and Communities," 1989.

Table 6.7
Private Enterprise by Sector, 1990

	Enterprises	Percent of Sector Total
Total	37866	74.2%
Industry	4765	54.9
Agriculture	542	29.0
Construction	1549	54.2
Transportation & Communication	743	59.6
Trade	19572	91.4
Catering & Tourism	1500	71.3
Crafts	1493	71.0
Financial Services	6819	80.3
Education and Culture	697	68.7
Health & Social Protection	43	28.1
Other[a]	143	19.8

[a]Forestry, waterworks and housing and communal services.
Source: Federal Statistical Office, Communication Number 407,
"Enterprises in Yugoslavia," November 29, 1990.

crowds hankering after its baked goods, seemed destined to last). Other shops, including clothing stores, seemed to make their appearance daily.

The expansion in financial and other services was also obvious to the naked eye. Banks competed for customers, even taking television time for advertising. However, appearances were probably deceiving; there is little evidence that these private sector banks actually did much business.

Furthermore, the new private banks that did function may not have been exactly what reformers had been hoping for. One Zagreb banker, Ibrahim Dedic of Promdei Bank, emphasized in a magazine interview how he insisted on prompt repayment of loans. "(T)hat is the Western system. I give them my money, invest my capital and I want them to return it however they have to." Dedic adds, with disarming candor, "I don't do anything dishonest and I don't want anything that isn't mine. Our people have the authority to collect the debt with the use of force. The truth is, we are not allowed to injure the debtor severely, we can't kill him, but we could for example hold him under water . . ."[26]

Just as Mr. Dedic found his niche in the previously neglected realm of financial services, significant numbers of more conventional entrepreneurs moved into industrial pursuits. The expansion in private enterprises in industry was to be expected from our finding above that the private sector simply did not exist in industry before 1989. It seems especially impressive, therefore, that 4765 of the 8684 firms registered in industry in November 1990 were private firms. However, there is strong reason to suspect that the impact of these firms in employment and income terms was not nearly so great as the share of total firms would indicate.

The spread of private enterprise occurred in all of Yugoslavia's six constituent republics, as is seen in Table 6.8. There was some variation in the rate of constitution of new private enterprises, however. In the Republic of Bosnia-Hercegovina, private enterprises were only 53.6% of the total, and in the Autonomous Province of Vojvodina, only 58.1% of the total, as compared to a Yugoslav-wide rate of 74.2%.

Undoubtedly, the spread of private enterprise depended considerably on the extent of private savings in a given area. Foreign investment could supplement this, but in practice the two most likely sources of funds for private enterprise had to be the savings built up by former party officials and managers, and the savings of Yugoslavs living abroad. Most likely, the first group put their money into spontaneous privatization of existing social enterprises. While there are no figures to document the second group's actions, anecdotes about Americans of Croatian descent opening hotels and other businesses suggest that the expatriate community responded to the new opportunities in Yugoslavia as well. Given the considerable accumulated wealth of at least some members of the expatriate communities, it seems safe to expect that overseas Yugoslavs played a significant role in the rise of the private sector in 1989–90.

What we can document is the number of foreign ventures in Yugoslavia. Joint ventures actually have a long history in socialist Yugoslavia. The first joint venture law was written in 1967. However, the early law did not allow foreigners an equity share in the joint venture, and limited the foreign partner to a minority role.[27] In these respects, the law on foreign investment of 1989 represented a major step forward, increasing the permitted foreign ownership to 100%, and allowing equity holdings in joint foreign-domestic ventures. By November 1990, foreign-owned and

Table 6.8
Private and Foreign Firms
As a Percentage of Total Firms by Region, 1990

	Private Firms	Foreign Firms
Yugoslavia	74.2%	2.1%
Bosnia-Herzegovina	53.8	0.0
Montenegro	78.2	0.0
Croatia	73.5	2.8
Macedonia	76.2	1.0
Slovenia	87.4	2.0
Serbia	72.7	2.7
Serbia without the autonomous provinces	75.9	3.2
Vojvodina	58.1	1.8
Kosovo	80.4	0.3

Source: Federal Statistical Office, Communication Number 407, "Enterprises in Yugoslavia," November 29, 1990.

joint foreign-domestic enterprises accounted for 2.1% of total enterprises in Yugoslavia. The regional figures varied from a flat zero in Bosnia-Hercegovina and Montenegro, to 3.2% in Serbia proper (without the autonomous provinces of Kosovo and Vojvodina). Croatia came in second place with 2.8%, closely followed by Slovenia at 2.7%.

The political instability of the federal Yugoslav government, however, especially from the middle of 1990 on, precluded any truly massive inflow of foreign capital. As early as April 1990, it was clear that the major auto companies would bypass Yugoslavia. *Fiat*, although still professing some interest in the maker of the *Yugo*-car, *Crvena Zastava*, appeared unwilling to conclude a deal for *Zastava's* truck division. *Renault* and *Volkswagen* simply refused offers by Yugoslav partners to make joint investments and to increase equity shares.[28] Unfortunately, these examples were fairly typical of the treatment Yugoslavia got from foreign investors in 1990 and 1991.

Developments in the agricultural sector during the reform years were of little more promise. Debate on lifting the legal maximum on landholdings proceeded slowly. Meanwhile, the large, social-sector farms remained well-entrenched and politically powerful. Further change continued to hinge on lifting the legal limit on private landholding, but the civil war in Yugoslavia ensued before action was taken.

To summarize, Yugoslavia experienced an impressive flowering of private enterprise in the years 1989 and 1990. The new firms were concentrated above all in trade, finance and other services, and industry. However, the contribution of these new enterprises to employment and national income is not as dramatic as their numbers would indicate. Further improvement waits upon the growth and development of the newly-founded private firms, and/or the widespread privatization of existing social sector firms. Yugoslavia made important strides in the years 1988–90, but it had a long way to go before the "black hole" could be filled, retail trade brought up to the needs and demands of consumers, and unemployment reduced to acceptable levels.

After the Civil War?

The outbreak of war in late June 1991 marked the effective end of the Yugoslav federation. In fact, in the months leading up to the war, Yugoslavia's republics had increasingly ignored federal policy. Thus, separate republic-level privatization laws, for example, were written, each displaying a different balance between state and private ownership.

At the time this article is being written, Slovenia, Croatia and Bosnia-Hercegovina have been recognized as independent states by the countries of the European Community, and Macedonia has stated its intention to seek recognition as well.

It is therefore extremely difficult to make any intelligent statements about the future development of private enterprise, and SMEs, in the successor states to Yugoslavia. It may well be that the role of the state sector will be strengthened in the short term. Most of the republics had provisions in their privatization laws that social property would revert to state property if it was not privatized within one to two years. This might seem like a strong incentive to worker collectives to go private. Unfortunately, however, privatization involves "buying" the firm by paying into a republican fund for development. Few collectives appear to be in strong enough financial shape to do this. If collectives fail to privatize themselves voluntarily, and cannot find outside buyers, much of the economy would end up in state hands by late 1992 to mid-1993. Such an outcome seems especially likely in Croatia, where the government has shown a predilection for nationalization as a way to "protect Croatian property."

What remains of private enterprise and SMEs then? War damage will take a heavy toll on these businesses. Property losses were estimated at $16 billion to $20 billion in Croatia alone; damage in Bosnia continued apace as these lines were written. The story of Steve Lovric, an American of Croatian heritage who invested his life savings of $300,000 in a body shop in the Adriatic coast town of Drnis, may be typical. Serbian forces chased him and his family from the business, later carting off some $200,000 worth of pneumatic fender-fixing tools.[29]

The damage, however, will not be limited to the areas where the war was actually fought. The general economic crisis will hit private enterprises and SMEs in all the successor states heavily. While there no doubt will be many opportunities to make fortunes via war-time black marketeering, provisioning troops, and serving UN peacekeepers, more fortunes will be lost than gained.

When peace is restored, there will be much ground to make up. Many people will have lost their savings in failed private businesses. It remains to be seen whether private enterprise is a delicate flower which, once crushed, does not return with the same beauty, or whether it proves a hardy weed that pokes its head up again and again despite all attempts to eradicate it.

Notes

1. An eyewitness account of the genesis of the self-management concept is found in Milovan Djilas, *The Unperfect Society* (New York: Harcourt Brace and Jovanovich, 1969), 220–222. See also Dennison Rusinow, *The Yugoslav Experiment*

(Berkeley: University of California Press, 1977), Chapters 1–3 for an excellent account of the origins of the Yugoslav model.

2. Branko Horvat, *The Yugoslav Economic System* (White Plains: International Arts and Sciences Press, 1976), 110–112.

3. According to Yugoslav legal theory, enterprises were owned by society and managed by the collective of workers employed in the enterprise. To distinguish this ownership form from the Soviet variant, the Yugoslav enterprise is said to be under social ownership (as opposed to state ownership in the USSR). For this reason, this chapter refers to social ownership or the social sector when speaking about Yugoslav non-private enterprises.

4. Federal Statistical Office, *Statistical Yearbook of SFRY* (Belgrade: Federal Statistical Office, 1990), 236.

5. Ibid., 284.

6. Miroslav Glas, "Characteristics of the Complex Division of Personal Income and Other Income of Urban Worker Families in Slovenia," *Jugoslovensko Bankarstvo* (February 1987): 39–55. (in Serbo-Croatian)

7. Federal Statistical Office, *Statistical Yearbook of SFRY*, 294.

8. Josip Zupanov, "Economic Aspirations and Social Norms of Equality" in *Self-Management and Social Power* (Zagreb: Globus, 1990). (in Serbo-Croatian)

9. Allan Blinder, ed., *Paying for Productivity* (Washington: The Brookings Institution, 1990.)

10. Milan Vodopivec, "The Labor Market and the Transition of Socialist Economies," *Comparative Economic Studies* 33, no. 2 (1991): 157.

11. Evan Kraft, "Yugoslavia 1986–88: Transition to Crisis" in *Crisis and Reform in Eastern Europe*, edited by Andrew Arato and Ferenc Feher, 457–459 (Englewood, NJ: Transactions, 1991).

12. Ljubomir Madzar, "Restructuring Property Relations in Yugoslavia," manuscript, Belgrade, February 1990, 26.

13. Ales Vahcic and Tea Petrin, "Financial System for Restructuring the Yugoslav Economy" in *Financial Reform in Socialist Economies*, edited by Ales Vahcic and Tea Petrin, 157 (Washington: The World Bank, 1989).

14. *Economic Report of the President* (Washington: United States Government Printing Office, February 1992), 404.

15. Evan Kraft and Milan Vodopivec, "How Soft Are the Budget Constraints on Yugoslav Firms?," *Journal of Comparative Economics* (forthcoming, 1992). For the theory of the soft-budget constraint, see Janos Kornai, *The Economics of Shortage* (New York: North Holland, 1982).

16. Jovan Todorovic, Stipe Lovreta, Nikola Malenkovic, Nikola Stevanovic, Nevenka Subotic, *The Self-Managed Organization of Associated Labor in the Function of Increasing Business Efficiency in Serbia* (Belgrade: Economics Faculty of Belgrade, Scientific-Research Center, 1984), 105. (in Serbo-Croatian)

17. Bureau of the Census, *Statistical Abstract of the United States* (Washington: Bureau of the Census, 1990), 779.

18. Federal Statistical Office, *Statistical Yearbook of SFRY*, 326.

19. David Storey, *Are Small Firms the Answer to Unemployment?* (London: The Employment Institute, 1987.)

20. Branko Mikulic, "Our problems are nobody's fault but our own," *Borba* (May 16, 1990): 7. (in Serbo-Croatian)

21. Ales Vahcic, Tea Petrin and Iztok Kremser, seminar presentation on the work of the Federal Agency for Development and Restructuring, Zagreb, July 9, 1990.

22. David N. Allen and Richard McCluskey, "Structure, Policy, Services and Performance in the Business Incubator Industry," *Entrepreneurship Theory and Practice* 15, no. 2 (Winter 1990): 61. A similar business development strategy for Czech and Slovak firms is described in Dennis A. Rondinelli, Chapter 5, this volume.

23. The idea of flexible specialization is developed in Charles Sable and Michael Piore, *The Second Industrial Divide* (New York: Basic Books, 1984).

24. Federal Statistical Office, *Communication #407: Enterprises in Yugoslavia* (Belgrade: Federal Statistical Office, November 29, 1990), 2.

25. Cited in Milica Uvalic, "Property Reforms in Yugoslavia," *Most* 3 (1991): 46.

26. Ramiz Mehulic, "They follow me and eavesdrop," *Danas* (March 10, 1992): 18–19. (in Serbo-Croatian) For related discussion of financial market difficulties in the economies in transformation, see Chapter 8 of this volume, and Perry L. Patterson, "Capital Markets and Financial Markets in Economies in Transition," *American Journal of Agricultural Economics* (December 1992): 1170–73.

27. Patrick Artisien, *Joint Ventures in Yugoslav Industry* (Brookfield, Vermont: Gower, 1985), 34–38.

28. Slobodan Pejovic, "Capital Passes Over Yugoslavia," *Ekonomska Politika*, no. 1984 (April 9, 1990): 11. (in Serbo-Croatian)

29. Blaine Harden, "Yugoslavia's Civil War Robs American of Dream, Savings," *Washington Post* (February 8, 1992): A17.

PART TWO

The Environment
for Private Enterprise

7

Competition Under the Laws Governing Soviet Producer Cooperatives During Perestroika

Michael A. Murphy

Introduction

During the era of *perestroika*, the Soviet government loosened its control over the economy and permitted the development of various forms of private enterprise. One of the consequences of this policy shift was the emergence and growth of a sector of producer cooperatives. Cooperative forms of production existed in Imperial Russia and occupied an important position in the trade and light manufacturing sectors of the economy during Lenin's New Economic Policy. As the foundations of the centrally-planned economy were laid, however, cooperative producers were either eliminated or brought under the control of the state administrative apparatus. Beginning in 1986, the Soviet government set out to revive this sector, envisioning a role for newly-established and independent cooperatives in a variety of activities including the provision of consumer goods and services, construction, and the recycling of industrial byproducts and waste.

The cooperative sector grew substantially over the next several years. By early 1991 the number of cooperatives selling goods and services in the USSR had risen to around 255,000, and these businesses employed close to 6.5 million people in the production of goods and services worth an estimated 42 billion rubles.[1] The cooperative sector's output mix was varied and constantly evolving, but production was largely concentrated in the areas of construction, consumer goods manufacture, and the provision of scientific, technical and engineering services to the state sector. These businesses also tended to be relatively small in size (employing an average of twenty-five people) and tended to be located in larger cities and in the European republics.[2] The development of this sector eventually slowed under *perestroika,* and the reported number of operating cooperatives levelled off in 1990–91. This seems to have resulted from a slowdown in the rate of new cooperative creation (in the face of mounting political and economic uncertainty in the country) as well as the enactment of laws permitting the creation of small private businesses. Many cooperatives subsequently reorganized themselves as small businesses in order to avail themselves of tax breaks granted to these, and thus continued to function as part of the growing fully private sector.

As the cooperative sector developed, its operations (and fortunes) grew to become closely intertwined with those of the state sector. Cooperatives were often affiliated with state enterprise sponsors, which provided access to production facilities and inputs. A substantial share of the cooperative sector's output was also sold to the state. Indeed, by late 1990, more than eighty percent of all cooperatives were attached to state enterprises and their activities accounted for about eighty percent of the cooperative sector's output.[3] This dependence arose first from the cooperatives' need to secure inputs and to protect themselves from political opposition. State enterprise managers, however, established cooperatives within their factories once they discovered that they could make use of these to circumvent various state controls on enterprise operations and earn higher incomes for themselves and their workers in the process.[4]

As the cooperative sector grew, its activities generated substantial debate, and political and government authorities alternately waxed and waned in their support of these businesses. The Soviet press carried innumerable articles scrutinizing and analyzing this sector's activities, and public opinion polls indicated that there was substantial popular discontent with cooperative prices and incomes and alleged corruption and ties to organized crime. It is, of course, difficult to determine precisely what to make of all this. Official statistics from this period at best provide flawed measures of the number of cooperatives and their sales, the prices they charged, incomes earned by their members and the amount of corruption which accompanied their development. Moreover, much of the data on these businesses was generated by journalists, researchers and government authorities who were positioned on various sides of the ongoing Soviet political debates over these matters and were not always disinterested observers.[5]

The Soviet government's new policies toward cooperative enterprise introduced competition into some areas of the Soviet economy during this period. This occurred, however, despite the fact that the laws governing cooperative enterprise significantly restrained the competitive process which resulted. In particular, state controls directly limited cooperative access to inputs and some lines of business, and handicapped these businesses' ability to compete with each other and their state-sector rivals. *Perestroika*-era Soviet laws and regulations governing cooperative enterprise also frustrated the competitive process by limiting cooperative formation. These barriers contributed to high cooperative prices and generated and protected cooperative profits which helped to sustain the high incomes earned in this sector and contributed to the official corruption which fed on these businesses. The nature of the leasing arrangements by which cooperatives acquired their capital inputs from the state also weakened cooperative investment incentives, as did other constraints on cooperative activity.

In sum, cooperative-sector regulation under *perestroika* encouraged a variety of suboptimal enterprise behaviors. It remains to be seen whether enterprise regulation in the Soviet successor states will prove substantially better in producing a genuinely competitive private-sector environment. However, as we shall see, the *perestroika* era provided numerous examples of policies which post-Soviet governments should avoid.

The Legal Foundations of Cooperative Enterprise

A number of federal statutes played an important role in establishing the legal foundations of cooperative business activity in the Soviet Union during *perestroika*. The earliest piece of legislation of consequence was the "Law on Individual Labor Activity," which was passed in late 1986 and which contained provisions pertaining to the establishment of small scale cooperatives for supplying the population with goods and services.[6] This law—in combination with a number of other laws and decrees—regulated the establishment and conduct of producer cooperatives until the "Law on Cooperatives in the USSR" was enacted on May 26, 1988.[7] This statute was a codification of previous federal legislation in this area and was amended on October 16, 1989 and on June 6, 1990.[8] Further amendments under post-Soviet governments seem likely, but the Law provides an interesting case study of a legal attempt to promote market efficiency, while preserving substantial state control.

Basic Cooperative Property Rights

A cooperative is an organization of individuals established for the purpose of engaging in some form of business activity. Cooperatives can be formed for diverse purposes, and the Law on Cooperatives recognized this and differentiated between producer and consumer cooperatives. Thus, a production cooperative (*proizvodstvennyi kooperativ*) was to produce and sell goods and services to buyers outside the cooperative while a consumer cooperative (*potrebitelskii kooperativ*) would contract for goods which it would then distribute to its members.

Articles 5–16 of the Law on Cooperatives granted formal property rights and protections to producer cooperatives which were far-reaching in comparison to those granted to state-owned enterprises during *pere-stroika*. Indeed, these rights and guarantees were similar to those afforded to partnerships in the United States under the Uniform Partnership Act.[9] Since a cooperative was a collection of individuals, any property of the cooperative was considered by the Law to be the jointly-owned property of those individuals. The Law permitted cooperatives to own assets in the form of buildings, machinery, goods in progress and financial capital contributed by members and purchasers of shares in the cooperative. Cooperatives were also permitted by the Law to jointly-own assets with state enterprises, associations and other organizations. A cooperative could sell, lease and lend its property to other entities and could participate in joint ventures with other cooperatives and state entities.

The Law on Cooperatives also attempted to create inalienable private property rights for these businesses. Article 8 of the Law formally granted to cooperatives state protection of their assets and permitted confiscation of cooperative property only by decision of a court or *arbitrazh* body. The Law further forbade state bodies from interfering in the activities of cooperatives and permitted a cooperative to petition the Soviet courts to rescind any directives issued by government officials in contravention of this article. More importantly, cooperatives were permitted to sue for damages resulting from the illegal actions of government bodies as well as damages resulting from breach of contract by other cooperatives.

While the above provisions would seem to establish clear property rights for the cooperative, numerous additional provisions clearly diminished those rights. Article 5, for example, called on cooperatives to take an active role in the "economic and social development" of the country, to help maximize national production "under socialism," and to operate in a manner which recognized the interests of society in addition to the interests of the cooperative's members.[10] To ensure the representation of these interests in the cooperative, the Law formally recognized and empowered other stakeholders in the cooperatives. Article 6 stipulated that a cooperative's decisionmaking process must allow for the participation not only of the cooperative's members but also of any employees, Communist Party, Komsomol, trade union or other organizations active within the cooperative. Similarly, the cooperative was called upon to protect and improve the quality of any land it used and to protect its physical surroundings in accordance with existing environmental laws of the USSR and its republics.

Article 11 of the Law enumerated rules governing the creation and registration of new cooperatives. It stipulated first that a cooperative must have three or more members before it could be registered. These members must agree on a charter (*ustav*) which would describe "the object and purpose" of the cooperative's activities, members' rights and responsibilities, management structure, initial capital investments, and the distribution of income and profits generated by the cooperative's activities. This statute was to be registered with and approved by the local *soviet* (council) of people's deputies. Although Article 11 permitted local officials to refuse to register a cooperative's statute, they could do so only when this statute was in violation of existing laws. In this fashion the Law sought to help cooperatives overcome the opposition of any antagonistic local authorities. The Law also permitted the members of a cooperative to amend its statute, subject again to approval of the local *soviet*.

Articles 12–14 governed membership in cooperatives and the rights and responsibilities of cooperative members. The members of the cooperative were called on to elect a chairman in a general meeting at which each member would have one vote irrespective of the size of his or her contribution to the cooperative's capital pool. Cooperative members were also to decide collectively on rules governing membership, income and profit distribution and work plans for the business. Outside employees of the cooperative were permitted to participate in general meetings of the cooperative although they could not cast votes at these meetings. The Law permitted an individual to be a member in more than one producer cooperative when that individual had one of these cooperatives as his or her primary place of employment. State-sector employees were permitted by the Law to be members of only one producer cooperative and could work there only in their spare time.

Cooperative Finance and Taxation

The Law on Cooperatives stated that producer cooperatives were financially independent of the state and provided formal guarantees of that financial independence. This guarantee took the form of a prohibition against government confiscation of cooperative moneys.[11] Cooperatives were also held responsible by the Law for their own financial viability and were thus denied access to the state subsidies so routinely provided to Soviet state enterprises. The initial capitalization of a cooperative consisted of the financial contributions of its founding members. This pool could be augmented by borrowings from state and cooperative banks as well as from other (unaffiliated) individuals and organizations. The Law permitted newly-formed cooperatives to receive credits from state banks on "preferential terms," but required these borrowers to pay interest on their borrowings and to repay the principal. Such requirements differed markedly from the pre-*perestroika* Soviet government's credit policies in the state sector. Cooperatives were also able to borrow from cooperative and private banks during this period and utilized these sources of capital for short-term credits.

For long-term borrowing, cooperatives were permitted by the Law to sell a form of equity called "shares" to other cooperatives and state organizations as well as to employees who were not members of the cooperative. These shares carried a fixed face value which was to be determined by the issuing cooperative and paid a dividend which was also to be set by the issuer.[12] Shares were non-tradable during this period and were to be secured by the cooperative's assets. As such, these shares more closely resembled secured debt as opposed to the equity shares which their name suggested. Under the Law, issuance of shares by a cooperative was contingent upon approval by state financial authorities, who were to assess the cooperative's ability to make the payments required by the issued shares. Article 22 of the Law additionally stipulated that the total value of a cooperative's outstanding shares should not exceed its annual income.

The Law on Cooperatives included vaguely-described procedures for determining when a cooperative was financially insolvent and subject to liquidation. State banking authorities were authorized (under Article 23) to request the local *soviet* to liquidate a cooperative which "repeatedly" failed to meet its payment obligations. The Law, however, nowhere defined the term "repeated failure," and was silent on whether shareholders were similarly empowered to make the same request of the authorities should a cooperative fail to make a dividend payment. Other legislation established procedures governing the payment of creditors in the event of cooperative bankruptcy. Upon liquidation, the physical assets of the cooperative were to be sold (at negotiated prices) by local authorities. The proceeds from this sale were to be combined with any financial reserves of the cooperative and used to cover any claims outstanding against it. Any remaining funds were to be apportioned among the cooperative's members.

While operating, a cooperative was held liable by Article 17 of the Law for damages caused by its failure to fulfill its previously-assumed contractual obligations to its customers. Under bankruptcy, however, the liability of a producer cooperative was limited (under Article 43) to the value of its financial and physical assets plus any additional amount above this as determined by a vote of the cooperative members themselves.[13] The cooperative was required, however, to state in its statute the amount of liability which its members were willing to assume. By comparison, partners in firms operating under the Uniform Partnership Act in the United States typically are required to assume unlimited liability for their firm's actions.

Article 21 of the Law addressed cooperative taxation and stated that taxes would be levied on the cooperative's income (profits) as well as on the personal incomes of its members and employees. The cooperative's corporate income tax base was defined (in a February 1989 Edict of the

Presidium of the USSR Supreme Soviet) as being equal to revenue minus expenditures on material inputs, payments for services rendered by outside organizations, depreciation allowances, leasing expenditures, interest payments on bank credits, and transportation expenses.[14] Thus the cooperative's corporate income tax base was essentially equivalent to gross value added. The actual determination of the tax rates for this cooperative value added tax was left to the discretion of the union republics by the February edict. The union republics were free to vary these rates in accordance with factors as the type of business of the cooperative, the "needs of the population," the amount of contract labor hired by the cooperative, and the incomes of the cooperative's members. The local *soviet* with which a cooperative was registered was also permitted to grant tax breaks (in the form of a period of tax exemption or reduced tax rates) if it so desired. A great deal of variability in tax rates across republics and different lines of business resulted from this.[15] It should also be noted that the personal incomes of self-employed individuals and cooperative members were subject to taxation with the highest marginal tax rate weighing in at 50%.[16] Article 21 of the Law on Cooperatives itself additionally stipulated that if a cooperative sold its goods and services at centrally-set prices, then the tax rate on the personal incomes of the cooperative's members and employees would be equal to the lower (flat) rate levied on the incomes of employees of state enterprises and organizations.

Cooperative Contracting for Inputs and Sales

Article 17 of the Law stated that producer cooperatives were free to choose their contractual partners and to sign contracts with state and public entities as well as other cooperatives. The Law also provided guarantees against state intrusion into cooperative contractual relations and allowed a cooperative which was subject to such unwarranted intrusions to sue the interfering individuals and agencies.

Despite the presence in the Law of these provisions directed at granting freedom of contract to cooperatives, the Law nevertheless placed many restrictions on cooperative contracting for inputs and sales. As was noted above, each producer cooperative was required to draw up a charter describing the business activities of the cooperative and to register this document with local authorities. Business activities outside of the activities described in the statute were, however, prohibited by paragraph 2 of Article 8 which stated that, "The use of cooperative property for purposes unrelated to its statutory tasks is prohibited."[17] While the Law permitted statute amendments, these had to comply with existing federal and local laws. Such a determination was not always straightforward during this period.

During *perestroika*, government authorities at all levels enacted legislation which placed direct controls on cooperative entry into a number of business areas. For example, a USSR Council of Ministers' resolution dated December 29, 1988 prohibited the cooperatives from engaging in the production of votive candles, wine, vodka, firearms and ammunition, the distribution and/or showing of foreign films, the operation of gambling establishments, the provision of most types of medical assistance, and the organization of general education schools. The Council of Ministers' resolution also listed other activities which the cooperatives could engage in only under contract with state enterprises and institutions which were themselves already engaged in these activities and which would serve as prime contractors. It additionally empowered the union republics to likewise ban other types of cooperative activity in their territories and to specify other business ventures which cooperatives could undertake only under contract with state organizations.

The Law on Cooperatives also permitted state administrative authorities to exercise a great deal of control over prices charged by the producer cooperatives. Article 19 of the Law stated that prices charged by cooperatives should "be established taking into account the mutual interests of cooperatives and of consumers and the economy as a whole in promoting the development of economic cost accounting and self-financing."[18] During *perestroika*, Soviet laws placed prices into three different categories: centrally-controlled prices, negotiated (i.e., contractually determined) prices, and free prices.[19] Centrally-controlled prices were set in the traditional manner (i.e., they were basically equal to accounting cost plus some profit margin) by various price-setting authorities in the government.[20] Negotiated (contract) prices were determined by bargaining between the buyer and seller within a framework determined by the state.[21] Free prices were confined in this period largely to what were deemed new products, certain sales of agricultural products, and sales of goods and services tailored to the unique demands of the buyer.

Article 19 of the Law (as well as other legislation) specified the category into which the price charged by a cooperative seller would fall. This determination was based on whether the buyer was a state or a private entity and whether or not the seller's source of inputs was the state. If the cooperative seller was producing goods which were not considered new or unique, then whenever some state entity (such as a state enterprise, association, or retail store) was the purchaser, the price was to be either controlled or negotiated. When the state was the source of inputs for goods sold to non-state entities (such as other cooperatives or the public), the state could also extend its controls over those prices placing them in either the controlled or negotiated categories. When a cooperative sold goods or services to non-state entities and acquired its inputs from private sources, then it was permitted to charge free prices. If the good or service sold was determined to be new or unique, then the cooperative could set its own price. It should also be noted in this regard that state pricing restraints were routinely violated during the inflation which accompanied the early part of *perestroika*.[22] In February 1989 the Council of Ministers responded to this and adopted a resolution aimed at tightening price discipline in the state and cooperative sectors of the economy.[23] One part of this strategy was to empower local *soviet* executive committees to establish price ceilings and maximum price markups for cooperatives selling goods and services to the public.

The producer cooperatives likewise faced controls on their contracting for inputs during *perestroika*. While the Law permitted cooperatives to employ non-members as workers, it also simultaneously permitted local *soviets* to regulate the ratio of non-member workers to member-employees. These regulations were designed to constrain the extent to which cooperatives employed outside labor and thus exploited it in the traditional Marxist sense. In addition to these controls on outside labor, the Law also required that the cooperative pay its employees wages which were at least as great as the state-mandated minimum wages for comparable work at state enterprises. Likewise, the cooperative was required to provide to its members and employees pension, vacation, and health care benefits comparable to those offered by the state sector.

The Law on Cooperatives (along with other legislative acts) also constrained cooperative acquisition of land and buildings. During the era of *perestroika*, all land in the Soviet Union formally remained the property of the state, and cooperatives, individuals or other entities were prohibited from owning it. Under these conditions, cooperatives needing land or buildings had to locate government or state enterprise authorities who were willing to lease these to them. For reasons discussed below, this was no easy task. In fact, obtaining these facilities was so difficult that many cooperatives—which were already registered with authorities—were unable to commence operations because of a lack of facilities. This is reflected in official statistics from this period which show a persistent and substantial disparity between the number of registered and operating cooperatives.[24]

Cooperatives seeking to acquire machinery and material inputs from state sources encountered legal complications here as well. The Law on Cooperatives permitted cooperatives to lease or purchase inputs from state sources, but other legislation mandated that these sales of machinery and other materials to the cooperative sector occur at prices which were substantially higher than those charged by the state wholesale trade network to state enterprises.[25] There were, however, other direct controls placed on cooperative input purchases by the Law on Cooperatives. For example, Article 27 of the Law permitted local *soviet* authorities to draw up lists of goods and products which could not be sold to cooperatives by state stores in their jurisdictions.

Economic Implications of the Legal and Regulatory Structure

Although Soviet laws governing cooperative enterprise permitted the creation of many such businesses, these same laws simultaneously constrained competition between the cooperative and state sectors as well as within the cooperative sector itself. The above survey of these laws has already identified some of these constraints. In this section of the essay I will more formally analyze these and their economic implications.

Entry Conditions and the Cooperative Laws

From their studies of the process of competition, economists have concluded that certain factors—termed barriers to entry—can impede the flow of resources into markets. These barriers are said to be present when economic rents accrue to incumbent (pre-existing) producers and arise from product differentiation advantages, sunk costs generated by relationship-specific, unrecoverable investments, and cost advantages enjoyed by incumbent firms.[26] The very nature of the business environment facing the cooperatives during *perestroika* guaranteed that these firms would not face some of the entry barriers which firms operating in market economies sometimes do. Patents, for example, are one common source of barriers to entry in market economies. Throughout most of the era of *perestroika*, however, Soviet patents (called inventors' certificates) were non-exclusionary in nature and could not bar rival producers from competing with enterprises already using the patented technology.

Incumbent firms in market economies often find themselves in the position of having secured a certain amount of loyalty from their customers by virtue of having established reputations for providing high-quality goods and services. Under such conditions, potential entrants into these markets may find it necessary to employ various business strategies (e.g., advertising and price discounts) to draw customers away from the incumbents; these conditions place would-be entrants at a competitive disadvantage vis-a-vis incumbent producers. One would not expect, however, that Soviet state-owned enterprises enjoyed such incumbency advantages since they generally had reputations for delivering low quality goods and services to their customers and did not engage in advertising aimed at building name recognition and reputation.

These considerations notwithstanding, cooperative producers encountered a diverse array of entry barriers. Entry into a number of different types of business was precluded or controlled by the December 1988 Council of Ministers' resolution, which placed a number of business niches out of bounds to the cooperatives and empowered lower government authorities to add to this list. Numerous press accounts from this period described the activities of local government authorities aimed at preventing cooperative creation and/or driving them out of business once they were established. The volume of such reports suggests that such state actions were quite common.[27] The impact of this resolution was perhaps most significant in the cooperative health care sector, which was virtually wiped out.

Soviet (and other) observers were quick to note at the time that many of the prohibitions in the Council of Ministers' resolution seemed designed to protect economic interests being challenged at that time by the producer cooperatives. For example, the prohibition against production of votive candles seemed designed to protect the Orthodox Church's monopoly in this area, the prohibitions against cooperative medical practices seemed to be aimed at protecting the bribe incomes of individuals employed by the state health-care network, and the controls on alcohol production would have protected the state's significant turnover tax receipts from this product.[28] Indeed it would seem that many of these measures were directed at protecting rents earned by incumbent producers and thus constituted barriers to cooperative entry.

These examples illustrate how dependent the cooperatives were on the support of political and government authorities. This dependence was manifested in other ways as well. As was noted earlier, party and government authorities (who controlled access to land and buildings) were in a position to—in effect—issue operating permits to cooperatives in much the same manner as city authorities sometimes issue medallions to taxi operators in the United States. The cooperatives' excess demand for business startups (equal to the difference between the numbers of registered and operating cooperatives) demonstrates that Soviet authorities were not providing enough operating permits (in the form of land and buildings) to the cooperative sector for its operations. Soviet officials exploited this situation by either extracting bribes from cooperatives seeking operating facilities or by accepting memberships in cooperative partnerships which provided the officials with incomes but required little in the way of work. Operating permits of this nature are valuable only when they protect their holders from future competition by generating incumbency rents, i.e., only when they create entry barriers.

Cooperative competition was also constrained by bottlenecks in the supply of inputs. Throughout *perestroika*, the state administrative apparatus continued to exercise effective control over the production activities of its enterprises through the state contracting system. While the *perestroika*-era contract system introduced some flexibility into the extraordinarily rigid system it supplanted, it nevertheless accounted for nearly all of the output of state enterprises via its use of (compulsory) government contracts.[29] The Law on Cooperatives mandated that the producer cooperatives be granted access to the state wholesale trade network on an equal footing with state enterprises, but this never occurred. Instead, not only did cooperatives find it difficult to obtain material inputs from the state, but they faced higher prices (than those charged to state enterprises) on those inputs made available to them. This state-administered input supply bottleneck and the attendant price differentials provided state enterprises with cost and input availability advantages relative to their would-be cooperative competitors which arose not from state sector superiority in production efficiency but rather from the incumbent position which state enterprises occupied in the input distribution system.[30]

As was noted earlier, producer cooperatives were quite dependent upon state enterprises for their supplies of capital and other material inputs. While these vertical ties between the two sectors provided the cooperatives with much-needed access to inputs, the structure of these contractual relationships limited cooperative entry. As was noted earlier, the December 1988 Council of Ministers' resolution listed a number of business activities which could only be carried out by the cooperatives under contract to state enterprises and permitted lower government authorities to draw up similar lists. Restrictions of this sort weakened the bargaining power of cooperatives forced into these sub-contracting relationships by preventing them from negotiating direct sales of their produce to final buyers. Under such circumstances, state enterprises were in a position to expropriate some portion of the profits which would otherwise have gone to the cooperative seller. In this manner, these restrictions created and protected incumbency rents for state enterprises and thus constituted barriers to cooperative entry.

Business Conduct Under the Cooperative Laws: Pricing, Investment and Product Choice

During *perestroika*, nominal prices charged by cooperatives selling to the public tended to be higher than those charged by state enterprises and organizations.[31] Several factors can be identified which contributed to this. Substantial entry barriers permit firms which are protected by these to exercise some degree of market power and set price above marginal cost. To the extent that some cooperatives enjoyed such protection—by virtue of their access to scarce inputs, political protection, etc.—these contributed to the higher prices charged by these firms. As was noted earlier, however, cooperatives typically paid higher prices than did state entities for state-delivered inputs. Cooperatives also used their own cooperative sources of supply (such as farmers' markets), which often were higher priced than state sources. These higher input costs no doubt drove up cooperative prices relative to state sector prices.

The cooperatives' choices about which product segments of their markets to enter (when the market under consideration encompassed diverse product qualities and characteristics) also affected the prices they charged. Tirole has demonstrated that when firms compete on both price and product quality, the firm which chooses the higher quality product will charge a higher price in equilibrium.[32] When an incumbent firm already occupies the lower quality market niche, the entrant's profit-maximizing strategy is to enter into the higher-quality product market segment and to charge a price higher than the incumbent. It is reasonable to assume that most state sector enterprises were mired in the low quality segments of their markets for many consumer goods and services during this period. Thus one would have expected producer cooperatives to enter higher quality market niches and to charge higher prices as a result.

One would also expect that the investment risks encountered by cooperatives also had an effect on the prices they charged. When risk-averse investors are presented with investment opportunities, they will take into account both the expected return on their investments as well as the variability of the distribution of possible returns. Risk aversion impels the investor to demand a higher expected rate of return on his investment as compensation for the greater variability of the return. Thus if investors are choosing between two competing projects which are subject to similar degrees of variability in their returns, the project with the higher expected return will be preferred. One might expect that considerations of these sorts generated a bias in cooperative creation towards higher price and higher profit types of business endeavors in order to compensate investors for their risk bearing.

One of the more significant risks encountered by the cooperative businesses arose from the possibility of a government policy reversal towards private enterprise. As Litwack has argued, the government was unable during this time to demonstrate an irrevocable commitment to *perestroika*.[33] This lack of commitment and the resulting climate of uncertainty about future government policies which it generated would have raised concerns in the minds of cooperative investors about possible future regulatory restraints on cooperatives, legal harassment, and state confiscation of assets. Such fears could only weaken incentives to invest in appropriable assets or to engage in activities which might later be perceived as being criminal. As cooperative investors assigned higher probabilities to future policy reversals which would lower the returns on their assets, they no doubt reduced their investments in appropriable assets.[34,35] The irony of this situation is that the likelihood of future governmental policy reversals was perhaps itself partly a function of how well the cooperative sector performed. A thriving cooperative sector which catered to the public's demands at low prices would have won substantial popular support and therefore would have been better able to protect itself politically.

The usual sources of risks of failure which threaten business startups in market capitalist economies also faced cooperative entrepreneurs. While those risks were limited perhaps by substantial pent-up consumer demand, other risks arose from such factors as the arbitrary enforcement of regulatory rules which were used by authorities to shut down cooperatives which operated in the gray zone of Soviet law. While business-specific risks could not be eliminated altogether, they could have been mitigated by lifting the sanctions against speculation in capital goods. These laws served to prohibit the sorts of activities which were necessary to develop secondary markets in capital goods. When entry into a market is risky, investors will naturally be concerned about recovering their investments should the venture fail. The greater the extent to which up-front investments are sunk, the greater will be the losses imposed upon investors in the event of failure. Some of the costs of business startups (e.g., licensing fees, advertising expenditures) are intrinsically unrecoverable. When there exist re-sale markets for the physical capital assets of businesses, however, some portion of the investments in these assets is recoverable. Soviet laws forbidding speculation during this time prevented the development of such markets and thereby increased the investment returns required by cooperative ventures to compensate for these risks.

Performance: Static and Dynamic Efficiency and Corruption

The Soviet laws governing cooperative enterprise during *perestroika* constrained the ability of this sector to compete with established state-sector enterprises, as we have seen. In addition, these laws supported monopoly power within the cooperative sector itself. For this reason, it would seem that these laws generated allocative inefficiencies *within* the cooperative sector. An analysis of the welfare effects of these laws which ended with the inefficiencies associated with monopoly would, however, be deficient. Standard partial-equilibrium analyses of the welfare implications of monopoly identify an allocative inefficiency arising from the fact that the monopolist fails to exhaust all gains from trade when it sells its output at a price above marginal cost. Such an argument, however, proceeds from an assumption that the monopolist is in place, and is problematic in this context for that reason. It is instead more appropriate to compare social welfare in the pre-cooperative state with that in the state which arose after the creation of the cooperatives. Thus even though the cooperative laws may have been responsible for creating and sustaining very imperfectly competitive environments, social welfare was no doubt increased by the creation of these businesses.

In this more complete consideration of the welfare implications of the cooperative laws, one would consider the increase in consumer welfare arising from improvements in product quality and the availability of goods and services resulting from the creation of the cooperatives and cooperative rents. Yet even if one takes such factors into consideration, the analysis will still be incomplete if it fails to consider the effects which competition between the cooperative and state sectors over resources had on the performance of the state sector and the economy as a whole. Competition between these two sectors may have directly worsened the performance of the state sector as resources were bid away from state production by cooperatives. It is of course possible that competition between the cooperatives and the state sector forced state enterprises to marginally improve their performance and/or caused state adminis- trators to adjust the controls which they exercised over the economy. The interaction between these two sectors during this period was compli- cated and much debated in the Soviet press, and the issue of whether or not cooperative competition improved or degraded the performance of the state sector is beyond the scope of this chapter.

While a thorough assessment of the effects of the cooperative legal climate on the technological progressivity (i.e., dynamic efficiency) of the cooperative sector is impossible, it does seem to be the case that the nature of the vertical contractual ties between the state and cooperative sectors restrained this progress. As was noted earlier, cooperatives typically relied on long-term leases with the state for access to the state sector's plant and equipment. Under contractual arrangements of this form, the cooperative lessee and the state (enterprise) lessor both had limited prop- erty rights in the production assets in question.

When assets have multiple owner-users with different rates of risk aversion and/or time preference, however, it is difficult to contractually stipulate and enforce both parties' investments in the maintenance and improvement of these assets. This, in turn, creates incentives for the two parties to free ride on each other's investments and can result in econom- ically inefficient underinvestment in actions which would benefit both parties. Reliance on long-term leasing arrangements additionally pro- vides the lessor with the chance to behave opportunistically (at the time of lease renewal) and adjust the lessor's rent so as to expropriate the prof- its generated by the lessee's investments.[36] This possibility only further weakens the lessee's incentives to make appropriable investments. Under such contractual arrangements, weakened investment incentives would have adversely affected dynamic efficiency.

During the era of *perestroika*, the Soviet press carried many articles linking the producer cooperatives to crime and corruption. Part of this linkage no doubt owed to the fact that it was—practically speaking—virtually impossible for cooperatives to go about their business without somehow running afoul of ambiguously-written Soviet laws governing price-setting and speculation. The attendant corruption is also not surprising; the laws governing cooperative enterprise seem to have been well suited for promoting various types of corrupt practices. For example, as was noted earlier the laws governing cooperative enterprise permitted cooperatives to choose their level of liability and register it in their charter. Some cooperative members took advantage of this and borrowed money from the state (at concessionary interest rates) and absconded with it rather than investing it. Mandating higher liability levels for cooperative members (as the state ultimately did) certainly would have helped curtail this form of corruption.

This legal framework further invited bribe payments to authorities since the laws governing cooperative creation provided government and political authorities with the ability to control the creation of cooperatives and the flow of resources to them. Individuals who could affect the distribution of chronically scarce resources in the state sector were in positions to extract some of the rents which cooperatives could derive from the use of state-supplied inputs. In such a setting, however, the use of bribe payments to these officials may have actually improved social welfare to some extent. Officials who were administering the allocation of such resources no doubt lacked the ability to determine which of the competing (private-sector) claims on these resources would have best served the population's interests. To the extent that bribe size provides a signal which is positively related to the increase in social welfare (i.e., the increase in consumer and producer surplus) generated by the business undertaking, then using these payments as a guide to resource allocation could have been welfare-enhancing.[37] When considered in their entirety, this official corruption may also have worked to sustain the reform process. Rumer has argued that the involvement of the *nomenklatura* elite in the process of cooperative formation tied the fortunes of this important group to the fate of Gorbachev's reforms and thus guaranteed this group's continued political support of the process.[38]

The fact that such corruption accompanied the development of cooperative business during this period itself says something about how well-suited these laws were to the task of fostering vigorous competition in the cooperative sector. Political and government authorities are able to exact tribute from businesses only when there exist barriers to entry under the control of these authorities. When entry is truly free to all firms seeking to establish themselves, firms will not be required to make such payments nor could they possible benefit from them. Similarly, firms which earn no economic profits (as when they sell in competitive markets) are unable to make such payments. The mere existence of payoffs to government and party officials during this period is itself further evidence that the legal structure governing cooperatives established a very imperfect form of competition in this sector.

Summary and Conclusions

Perestroika failed to give birth to the socialist market which its architects had hoped would supplant the traditional bureaucratic mechanism for guiding economic activity. In particular, Gorbachev's reforms failed to create a vigorously competitive cooperative private sector, despite initial expectations on the part of many that this sector would lead the way in revitalizing the economy. The economic, political and legal environment in which cooperative businesses carried on their operations was simply incapable of supporting truly free competition.

The *perestroika* chapter in Soviet economic history is nevertheless an interesting and instructive one for the way in which it illustrates the problems inherent in the *de novo* establishment of private enterprise laws and traditions. The Soviet government permitted the creation of cooperative businesses with the enactment of a relatively few pieces of legislation. The task of sensibly regulating the activities of this sector, however, proved to be much more difficult in that it required restraint on the part of an administrative apparatus accustomed to heavy-handed management of every aspect of the economy's operations. Ericson has argued that the move to a true market system could not occur within the Soviet-type system configured and designed solely for the purpose of central planning; the entire apparatus had to be dismantled before real economic transformation could take place.[39] The experience of the cooperative sector during this period demonstrates that this system could not adapt itself to new property institutions.

One would expect that the cooperative businesses developed in the Soviet Union during the era of *perestroika* will play an important role in the Russian economy as it moves toward a market system. Such an expectation seems justified first on the grounds that this sector provided and still provides a home to many Russian entrepreneurs and that these businesses have shown themselves to be quite innovative in the past. Other forms of firm organization, however, will no doubt continue to dominate the Russian economic landscape in terms of their share of total output, as was the case during the era of *perestroika*. This domination is also to be expected based upon an examination of the statistical record from market economies. This record suggests that while cooperatives and partnerships are a useful means of organizing firms providing many types of services, proprietorships and corporations are more important forms of firm organization in aggregate terms. The development in Russia of these other organizational structures is now underway. It remains unclear, however whether these new Russian private enterprises will regulated in a manner substantially different from that which governed *perestroika*-era cooperatives.[40] In that regard, the failures of Gorbachev-era regulation of cooperatives remain important lessons, even in the post-Soviet period.

Notes

1. *Ekonomika SSSR v 1 polugodii 1991 goda*, 30 (July 1991) supplement, 1–3.

2. For a survey of Soviet statistics describing the dimensions and locations of cooperative production see Anthony Jones and William Moskoff, *Ko-ops: the Rebirth of Entrepreneurship in the Soviet Union* (Bloomington, IN: Indiana University Press, 1991).

3. "Ekonomika SSSR v 1990 godu," *Ekonomika i zhizn'*, (January 5, 1991): 9–13.

4. For a discussion of these issues see Simon Johnson and Heidi Kroll, "Managerial Strategies for Spontaneous Privatization," *Soviet Economy* 7, no. 4 (1991): 281–316, and Michael Burawoy and Kathryn Hendley, "Strategies of Adaptation: A Soviet Enterprise Under Perestroika and Privatization," *Berkeley-Duke Occasional Papers on the Second Economy in the USSR*, no. 29 (June 1991).

5. A thorough survey of this complex and interesting public debate—and the political battles accompanying it—can be found in Jones and Moskoff, *Ko-ops*.

6. "Zakon Soiuza Sovetskikh Sotsialisticheskikh Respublik. Ob individual'noi trudovoi deiatel'nosti," *Pravda* (November 21, 1986).

7. "Zakon Soiuza Sovetskikh Sotsialisticheskikh Respublik o kooperatsii v SSSR," *Ekonomicheskaia gazeta*, no. 24 (June 1988).

8. See "Zakon Soiuza Sovetskikh Sotsialisticheskikh Respublik o vnesenii izmenenii i dopolnenii v Zakon SSSR 'O kooperatsii v SSSR,'" *Ekonomicheskaia gazeta*, no. 44 (October 1989): 3; and "Zakon Soiuza Sovetskikh Sotsialisticheskikh Respublik o vnesenii izmenenii i dopolnenii v Zakon SSSR 'O kooperatsii v SSSR,'" *Izvestiia* (June 25, 1990). A translation of the latter can be found in "Amended Law on Cooperatives Published," *Foreign Broadcast Information Service Daily Reports: Soviet Union* (July 12, 1990): 42–47.

9. The Uniform Partnership Act is the legal statute which governs the formation and operations of partnerships in the United States. See L. Smith and G. Roberson, *Business Law*, 3rd edition (St. Paul, Minnesota: West Publishing Co., 1971), Appendix B, 119–128.

10. All quotations in this paper drawn from the Law can be found in its translation "Law on Cooperatives in the USSR," *Soviet Statutes and Decisions* 26 (Winter 1989-90): 46.

11. State enterprises lacked such protection during this era.

12. The issuing cooperative was permitted to adjust these dividend payments.

13. Later legislation stipulated that the members of a cooperative must each

individually assume a financial liability of an amount no less than one year's income. See the July 1990 amended version of Article 43 of the Law in "Amended Law on Cooperatives Published," *Foreign Broadcast Information Service Daily Reports: Soviet Union* (July 12, 1990): 47.

14. See "On Taxation of the Income of Cooperatives," *Soviet Statutes and Decisions* 26 (Spring 1990): 69–70.

15. See *Sotsialisticheskaia Industriia* (July 28, 1989): 3.

16. See the Decree of the Presidium of the USSR Supreme Soviet "On the Draft Law of the USSR on Amendment of Individual Income Tax Procedures and Rates," *Soviet Statutes and Decisions* 26 (Spring 1990): 62–67.

17. "Law on Cooperatives in the USSR," 48.

18. Ibid., 60. Emphasis mine.

19. For an explanation of these pricing methodologies see Alexei Klishin, "Economic Reform and Contract Law," *Columbia Journal of Transnational Law* 28 (1990): 253–262.

20. It should be noted, however, that there was a great deal of variability in this practice and that many of these prices remained fixed for very long periods of time.

21. In many instances these prices were determined by the ministries superior to the enterprise(s) involved in the transaction. See Klishin, "Economic Reform and Contract Law," 257.

22. For example, a 1989 audit of 12,000 cooperatives found that nearly 25% of these were violating price regulations in force at the time. *Ekonomika i zhizn'*, no. 17 (1990): 18.

23. See the translation of the resolution entitled "On Measures to Eliminate Shortcomings in the Existing Practice of Price Formation," published in "Controlling Prices: Some New Measures," *Current Digest of the Soviet Press* 41, no. 5 (1989): 10.

24. For example, while there were 250,500 cooperatives registered nationwide as of January 1, 1990, 40,000 (i.e., fifteen percent of the total) were not operation at the time. Forty-three percent of the 135,600 cooperatives registered as of January 1, 1989 were not in operation. See Jones and Moskoff, *Ko-ops*, 16–17 for these statistics and a discussion of them.

25. See "On the Procedure for Payment for Goods and Services by Cooperatives and Citizens Engaged in Individual Economic (Labor) Activity," *Soviet Statutes and Decisions* 26 (Spring 1990): 24–30. A cursory examination of the coefficients listed in these tables and used to determine the markup paid by cooperatives over (wholesale and wholesale plus turnover tax) prices charged to state enterprises suggests that these coefficients are higher for goods and commodities for which one might expect that the cooperatives would have significant demand.

26. See Richard Gilbert, "Mobility Barriers and the Value of Incumbency," in *Handbook of Industrial Organization*, edited by R. Schmalensee and R. Willig, vol. 1, pp. 475-536 (Amsterdam: North-Holland, 1989). As Gilbert states on page 478, a barrier to entry is "the additional profit that a firm can earn as a sole consequence of being established in an industry." Entry barriers are absent when the market in question is perfectly contestable.

27. See Jones and Moskoff, *Ko-ops,* for a survey of the Soviet press describing this opposition.

28. The resolution's restraints on health care cooperatives were preceded by an earlier campaign against health care cooperatives waged by the Ministry of Public Health. This began in October 1988 when the Ministry issued regulations barring state health care facilities from renting equipment to cooperatives when it was not in use. The Ministry's regulations were attacked in the pages of *Izvestiia* by one of that paper's writers as designed to protect the bribe incomes of individuals employed by the state health-care network. For a summary of this debate and the Ministry's policies towards these cooperatives see M. Jacobs, "Are the Restrictions on Medical Cooperatives Justified?" *Radio Liberty: Report on the USSR* 1, no. 13 (1989): 9–12.

29. This situation changed in 1989 as a result of a centrally-mandated reduction in the percentage of enterprise output accounted for by state contracts. Prior to this, approximately ninety percent of manufacturing production was accounted for by state contracts. For further discussion of this, see L. Abalkin, "Perestroika ekonomiki: sovetskaia tochka zreniia," *Voprosy ekonomiki* 4 (April 1989): 3–10.

30. For a formal analysis of how access to bottlenecked inputs permits firms which control these to extract incumbency rents see S. Salop and D. Scheffman, "Raising Rivals' Costs," *American Economic Review, Papers and Proceedings* 73 (May 1983): 267–271.

31. Despite these disparities in nominal prices, it is not clear that cooperative prices were higher than state prices when these are properly defined. State sector prices remained under various forms of control during this period and were often set below market clearing levels. Under such circumstances, the price which the buyer paid in the state sector included queuing costs and bribe payments in addition to the nominal price charged for the good.

32. See J. Tirole, *The Theory of Industrial Organization* (Cambridge, MA: MIT Press, 1988), Chapter 7.

33. See John M. Litwack, "Discretionary Behaviour and Soviet Economic Reform," *Soviet Studies* 43 (1991): 255–279; and John M. Litwack, "Legality and Market Reform in Soviet-Type Economies," *Journal of Economic Perspectives* 5, no. 4 (Fall 1991): 77–90.

34. Such concerns afflicted not only Soviet entrepreneurs but those operating in other reforming socialist countries as well. When asked why he still used fifty-year old equipment despite the fact that his pork smoking and packing business was flourishing, one Polish entrepreneur responded, "I don't want expensive machines. If the situation changes, I'll get stuck with them." Barry Newman, "Poland's Farmers Put the Screws to Leaders by Holding Back Crops," *The Wall Street Journal* (October 25, 1989): 1.

35. Concerns about future policy shifts would also affect the savings and consumption behavior of cooperative members and introduce a bias against accumulating assets which could easily be seized in the future (such as rubles in bank accounts) and in favor of current consumption. This may be reflected in the discovery by a *Time* magazine reporter examining the relatively lavish lifestyles led

by some of the more prosperous cooperative members that many of these individuals saved none of their incomes. See Ann Blackman, "A Taste of the Luxe Life," *Time* (April 10, 1989): 82.

36. For a discussion of long-term contract governance and the incentive problems it engenders, see O. Williamson, *The Economic Institutions of Capitalism* (New York: The Free Press, 1985).

37. One can perhaps think of the sale of political patronage in this context as similar to an auction of the resource to the highest bidder. If the amount of the bid is positively related to the size of the surplus generated by the use of the resource, then such auctions will be efficiency enhancing. This argument requires, of course, that all bidders have equal access to the seller and understand the rules of the game.

38. B. Rumer, "New Capitalists in the USSR," *Challenge* (May-June 1991): 19–22.

39. Richard Ericson, "The Classical Soviet-Type Economy: Nature of the System and Implications for Reform," *Journal of Economic Perspectives* 5, no. 4 (1991): 11–28.

40. John Tedstrom, Chapter 3, suggests that old Soviet habits may die hard.

8

Banking and Financial Reform in a Mixed Economy: The Case of Hungary

David L. Bartlett

One of the most important components of Hungary's New Economic Mechanism (NEM) was the creation in 1987 of a two-tiered banking system, composed on one level of the National Bank of Hungary and on the other of five commercial banks. The central aim of the banking reform was to improve flows of credit to Hungarian enterprises. Under the previous monobanking system—where both macroeconomic policy and commercial lending roles were filled by one institution—allocation of credit to enterprises was monopolized by the National Bank, whose policies were guided by the imperatives of plan fulfillment and not economic efficiency. The designers of the two-tiered system expected that the new banks, organized as Western-type shareholding companies, would base their lending decisions on standards of creditworthiness, profitability, and other business-type criteria.

Subsequent to the dramatic political upheavals throughout the region, Poland, Czechoslovakia, and other former socialist countries have followed Hungary's lead and set up two-tiered banking systems of their own. Hungary's experiment with commercial banking is therefore of great interest to other countries undergoing the transition from plan to market. This chapter evaluates the impact of the Hungarian banking reform on patterns of credit allocation and illuminates some of the broader problems likely to complicate the establishment of Western-type financial systems in Eastern Europe.

The Socialist Monobanking System

The socialist monobanking system dates back to the early Stalinist period in the Soviet Union. In the late 1920s and early 1930s, the functions of currency issue and credit allocation, which in capitalist economies are separated between central banks and commercial banks, were fused within the Soviet State Bank. The purpose of the Soviet monobanking system, which was subsequently adopted by China and Eastern Europe, was to centralize control of money and credit. However, the Soviet State Bank and the other socialist central banks proved unable effectively to control financial flows in the planned economies. It was precisely the weakness of financial control under the monobanking system which prompted Hungarian reformers to create a two-tiered system in the 1980s.

The Monobank and Central Economic Planning

The Soviet monobank was part and parcel of the system of central economic planning. Indeed, central planning would not have been possible without a monobank. For central planners to assert command over the allocation of resources in the economy, they needed to "deactivize" money, to minimize the possibilities for banks and enterprises to use credit for purposes not specified in the national plan. To this end, the Soviet authorities undertook a series of measures between 1927 and 1932 aimed at centralizing control of credit. They transferred all short-term credit operations from commercial banks to the State Bank, abolished bills of exchange and other forms of inter-enterprise credit, reorganized the various investment banks into four specialized banks with carefully defined long-term crediting functions, and established a clearing system that placed the financial accounts of state enterprises under the supervision of the State Bank.[1]

Principles of Financial Control

Control of credit under the monobanking system is based on two principles. The first is the separation of working capital (short-term financing of the current operations of enterprises) and fixed capital (long-term financing of investment in plant and equipment). This arrangement deprives credit of any role in fixed capital investments. These are to be financed entirely by budgetary grants allocated through the investment banks, leaving the central bank responsible for financing the working capital requirements of enterprises through allocations of short-term credit. In this scheme, socialist enterprises are prevented from diverting credit earmarked for working capital expenses to fixed capital investment and vice versa.

The second principle is the separation of the economy into cash and non-cash circuits. In the cash circuit, comprised chiefly of households, money plays essentially the same role as in capitalist economies. Households are free to dispose of their disposable income as they wish. They may retain it in liquid forms, deposit it in a bank, or use it to purchase commodities of their choice. In the non-cash or transfer circuit, composed of state enterprises, money is "passive." With minor exceptions, enterprises are not permitted to hold cash. All of their financial resources are held in accounts controlled by the central bank. Wage payments, purchases and sales of capital goods, fixed capital investments, depreciation, tax payments, and all other types of transactions are recorded by the bank as adjustments in those accounts. By monitoring the flow of funds in and out of the accounts, the central bank can in theory ascertain whether or not enterprises are fulfilling the requirements of the plan. Financial flows in the enterprise sector become the counterpart of physical processes specified in the plan, with deviations showing up as imbalances in the accounts supervised by the bank.[2]

The central bank's role in this system is strictly that of a monitor, not a policymaker. Divergences from the physical plan show up as irregularities in the financial accounts of state enterprises. The bank detects and reports these deficiencies to superior organizations in the economic administration; the latter then determine what corrective measures are needed. Such measures include financial sanctions applied by the bank to the offending enterprise—blocking of certain accounts, contraction of credit, interest rate penalties, increased tax payments, and reduction or elimination of managerial bonuses. In theory, corrective action can even go as far as the liquidation of the enterprise in question.[3]

Control of Working Capital

The system of control of working capital in the planned economies is designed to eliminate the possibilities for state enterprises to use their working capital assets for purposes inconsistent with the plan. The state budget allocates seed capital to enterprises, generally the minimal level of funds needed to carry out ordinary, day-to-day operations. The central bank then advances credits to cover any expenses which exceed this base level, namely those arising from seasonal fluctuations in working capital requirements, payments problems, or other unanticipated hitches in the execution of the plan. By attaching these credits to specific components of working capital assets and requiring quick repayment, the center seeks to ensure that the recipients of bank credits use them for the intended purposes.[4]

In theory, the elastic adjustment of the credit stock to above-normative working capital requirements would not present a problem if the central bank were able to compel enterprises to use the credits for the intended purposes. But in reality, the bank cannot do so. Technical constraints on the bank's oversight capability prevent it from detecting many financial irregularities in the enterprise sector. And even if the bank detects and reports infractions committed by enterprises, the central planners are very reluctant to impose penalties: sanctions would disrupt the operations of the enterprise in question, and hence its ability to meet production goals. Enterprises faced with financial penalties are also likely to withhold payments due to their suppliers. This creates liquidity problems for the suppliers, which in turn fall into payments arrears to their own creditors, and so on down the chain of transactions. Thus, the application of financial discipline on weak enterprises merely has the effect of drawing other enterprises, many of which are innocent of any mismanagement, into a cycle of mutual indebtedness.

In this scenario, the expedient course of action for the planning authorities is to prevail upon the central bank to extend special bridging credits or other financial favors to the guilty enterprises. Inefficient enterprises, anticipating that the bank will eventually provide whatever liquidity they need to sustain their day-to-day activities, are thereby deprived of any incentive to cut costs and improve productivity.[5]

The end result is that the socialist monobank, far from promoting financial control in the planned economies, serves instead to finance inefficiency at the microeconomic level and to generate excessive monetary growth at the macroeconomic level, as the total supply of working capital credit expands more or less automatically to meet the demand of the enterprise sector.[6]

Control of Fixed Capital

The rationale behind the decision in the early 1930s to finance fixed capital investment entirely through non-repayable budgetary grants was twofold. First, it would maximize central control of what was widely regarded as the most vital element in the long-term development of the socialist economy. By divorcing bank credit from the fixed capital sphere, the central authorities could control investment directly through planned disbursements of budgetary funds. Second, this arrangement would serve to avoid the cyclical movements in investment that are endemic to capitalist economies. The sharp fluctuations in investment in the Western economies are primarily a function of the high sensitivity of capitalist firms to profitability and to the general business climate. Socialist theorists reasoned that one of the great advantages of central planning would be its capacity to avoid these kinds of wave-like fluctuations in investment behavior. Central planners would be far less sensitive to short-term movements in the economy and more attentive to long-term development goals. Thus, by placing control of fixed capital investment entirely with the central planning apparatus, the socialist countries could pursue a steady and sustained growth of the capital stock.[7]

The actual course of events in the socialist countries dashed these hopes, as investment cycles plagued Soviet planners throughout the pre-war period. Likewise, the East European economies exhibited sharp oscillations in fixed capital investment throughout the postwar period.[8]

Reforms of the Hungarian Banking System

Hungary's New Economic Mechanism, launched in 1968, saw no fundamental changes in the monobanking system described above. The National Bank of Hungary retained responsibility for both the functions of currency issue and credit allocation. The 1968 reform and subsequent phases of NEM *did* bolster the Bank's authority to use differential interest rates and attach performance criteria to credits issued to state enterprises. But in practice, the National Bank remained a very subordinate actor within the system of economic administration, and thus lacked the political muscle to resist pressure from the central planning organs to supply state enterprises with easy credit lines.

This state of affairs continued up to the 1987 banking reform. As part of the preparation for the transition to the two-tiered system, in the mid-1980s the National Bank was separated into currency issue and credit allocation divisions. The former was charged with regulating the aggregate supply of money in the economy; the latter was in turn separated into several directorates organized by branch sector, operating under global targets set by the issuing division.

But this administrative reshuffling within the Bank did little to alter the substance of Hungarian financial policy. Loan officers in the credit directorates retained close ties to the branch sectors under their jurisdictions, and continued the longstanding tradition of supplying state enterprises with whatever liquidity they needed to fulfill the expectations of the central planners.[9]

Patterns of inefficient credit allocation persisted even when externally-imposed economic austerity compelled the Hungarian authorities to contract the aggregate supply of liquidity to the state sector. For example, in the early 1980s the authorities enacted sharp reductions of fixed capital investment in the state sector as part of an IMF-supervised stabilization program. Measured in terms of its impact on aggregate investment activity, the program *was* a success: by 1984, total fixed capital investment was 30 percent below the level of 1978.[10] However, within this diminished aggregate pool of investment finance, the distribution of fixed capital credits among Hungarian enterprises remained as inefficient as ever, as the largest and least profitable state enterprises continued to receive the lion's share of fixed capital and to undertake the bulk of investment projects.[11]

Theoretical Rationale of the Two-Tiered System

By the early 1980s, a number of influential Hungarian economists had concluded that a radical reform of the banking system was essential to overcome these problems. They argued that the monobanking system was incapable of simultaneously discharging the functions of monetary control and credit allocation. Indeed, in the context of central economic planning, the two functions operate at cross-purposes. So long as the National Bank is obliged to provide the state sector with an elastic supply of credit, it cannot regulate monetary aggregates. Proponents of the reform argued that effective monetary control and efficient capital allocation could only come about through a devolution of the crediting function to commercial banks. Organized as profit-seeking shareholding companies and legally protected from administrative interference in their lending decisions, such banks could be expected to disburse credit on the basis of efficiency criteria. The National Bank, freed from its obligation to supply credit directly to state enterprises, would then be able to operate as a real central bank, concentrating on regulation of aggregate liquidity in the economy through reserve requirements, interest rate policy, and other Western-type instruments of monetary control.[12]

In January 1987, the new system began operations, as the National Bank ceased all direct credit relations with Hungarian enterprises by transferring its entire loan portfolio to five commercial banks.

Credit Allocation Under the Two-Tiered System

The expectation of the designers of the 1987 reform was that the incentive structure guiding the activities of the new commercial banks would differ fundamentally from that of the previous credit divisions of the National Bank. The shareholders, interested above all in maximizing returns on their investments of capital, would direct the managers of the banks to pursue lending policies consistent with that objective. Since the most profitable enterprises presumably represented the best credit risks, the banks would redirect the flow of capital from weak to strong enterprises.

We now ask whether or not the banking reform achieved this objective. In particular, how did the introduction of joint stock ownership into the banking system affect patterns of credit allocation to Hungarian enterprises? As shown below, the performance of the two-tiered system was mixed. On the one hand, flows of credit *between* different sectors proved marginally more efficient than before. On the other hand, flows *within* sectors continued to exhibit some of the same inefficiencies which plagued the monobanking system, as the new banks persisted with the old habit of channeling credit to poorly performing enterprises.

This was not a consequence of the irrationality of the new banks. The reform *did* succeed in reorienting bank managers in the direction desired by the designers of the two-tiered system; namely, towards protection of the assets of the shareholders. But ironically, it was precisely their concern for the interests of the shareholders which induced the banks to sustain credit lines to poorly performing enterprises. When they began operations in 1987, the banks inherited a large number of dubious enterprise loans accumulated under the previous monobanking system. Seeking to avoid extensive loan writeoffs which would compromise the value of their portfolios, the banks extended fresh credits to weak clients, thereby enabling those enterprises to sustain payments on the old loans. Thus, the paradoxical result of the introduction of joint stock ownership into the commercial banking sector in Hungary was to reproduce the same patterns of intra-sectoral credit allocation which obtained before the reform.

Credit Flows to Hungarian Enterprises, 1986–87

Table 8.1 shows the percentile shares of bank credit allocated to the eight principal branches of the Hungarian state sector in 1986, the last year of the monobanking system, and 1987, the first year of the two-tiered system. While the data do not reveal any dramatic shift in credit flows, they do suggest that capital allocation moved in the general direction which the designers of the reform had desired. The two chief loss-making sectors, mining and metallurgy, both lost credit shares. The main

Table 8.1
Allocation of Bank Credit
Within the Hungarian State Sector, 1986-87[a]

Sector	1986		1987	
	Sectoral Allocation	% of Total	Sectoral Allocation	% of Total
Mining	18,550	16.1%	17,859	15.7%
Electrical Energy	18,208	7.1	8,298	7.3
Metallurgy	12,374	10.8	10,720	9.4
Machinery	25,505	22.2	24,246	21.3
Construction	216	0.2	182	0.2
Chemicals	34,101	29.6	36,774	32.3
Light Industry	16,069	14.0	15,782	13.9
Other	53	0.05	69	0.06
Total	115,076	100.00	113,930	100.00

[a]Figures are in millions of forints. Totals include both working and fixed capital credits issued to state sector.
<u>Source</u>: Hungarian Ministry of Industry

winner was chemicals, by and large the most successful industry in the Hungarian state sector. The chemicals sector was a cornerstone of the long-term strategy for industrial development that the Hungarian government was pursuing with the assistance of the World Bank. Thus, the expansion of credit to chemicals was consistent with both the particular financial interests of the shareholders of the banks and the broader interests of the national economy.

Intra-Sectoral Credit Flows: The Case of Chemicals

But while the sector-level data indicate a generally favorable outcome in the first year of the reform, the allocation of credit *within* specific sectors shows that a number of old problems persisted amidst the transition to the two-tiered system.

Some of these problems were associated with the showcase chemicals industry. While the chemicals sector as a whole was the leading performer in the Hungarian economy, it was also a very heterogeneous industry, with the financial indices of individual enterprises exhibiting a high degree of variation. And so once the decision was taken to increase their lending to the chemicals sector, the relevant creditors faced the task of discriminating between highly diverse enterprises that presented applications for credit.

Performing that task required the kinds of sophisticated credit evaluation procedures which were almost wholly alien to Hungary and the other socialist countries. As one of the conditions for Hungary's admittance into the IMF and World Bank in the early 1980s, the National Bank agreed to adopt the international standards of loan analysis established by the latter organization: return on capital, debt-service ratio, liquidity (ratio of liquid assets to current liabilities), and leverage (ratio of outstanding debt to book value of capital). However, loan officers in the National Bank paid little heed to these standards, persisting with their longstanding practice of allocating credit on the simple basis of enterprise demand.

This problem continued with the transition to the two-tiered system in 1987, despite the fact that loan officers in the new commercial banks were now operating under an incentive structure which presumably demanded close attention to the World Bank's lending criteria. A high percentage of the staff of the banks came from the National Bank. Indeed, many of them had transferred directly from the counterpart branch offices of the Bank's credit division, bringing with them the same habits and organizational ethos which characterized their previous jobs. Under the best of circumstances, it would take a considerable amount of time to root out the culture of the socialist banking system and to train a cadre of Hungarian bankers familiar with modern credit analysis techniques.

The dubious quality of the balance sheet information supplied to the banks by Hungarian enterprises further complicated the task of evaluating credit applications. Accounting procedures in Hungary remained extremely antiquated at the time of the banking reform. In particular, the financial indices of state enterprises only accounted for nominal (non-inflation-adjusted) values, thus preventing loan officers from ascertaining the effects of inflation and depreciation on the value of the assets of applicants.

Despite these constraints, loan officers at the Hungarian Credit Bank, which took over the bulk of the National Bank's chemicals portfolio, made a credible attempt to apply the World Bank's criteria in their lending decisions during the first year of the reform. The results of these efforts were mixed. Among the biggest recipients of bank credit were chemical companies with relatively high leverage and low liquidity ratios, financial indices which would ordinarily indicate long-term debt servicing problems. At the same time, several of the strongest, and presumably most creditworthy, enterprises in the sector incurred losses in credit share.[13]

But while the deficiencies of the Hungarian accounting system doubtlessly complicated the task of assessing the relative creditworthiness of chemical enterprises, they were not the decisive factor shaping general patterns of credit allocation under the two-tiered system. Credit flows in another major sector of the Hungarian economy, mining, showed that the absence of requisite information was not a satisfactory explanation of the behavior of the new commercial banks. In that particular case, the banks continued to channel credit towards enterprises well-known to be running losses.

Intra-Sectoral Credit Flows: The Case of Mining

As Table 8.1 demonstrates, the aggregate supply of credit to the Hungarian mining industry as a whole decreased during the first year of the two-tiered banking system, consistent with the general aims of the reform. However, credit flows within that sector revealed some problems. Here, the patterns of credit allocation were precisely the reverse of what one would expect of a bank intent on applying exacting standards of risk analysis. Of Hungary's eight mining companies, two received increases in credit in 1987. Not only were these the least profitable enterprises in the sector; they were the only ones that incurred absolute losses during the year. To make matters even more perplexing, these credit increases came at the expense of the six mining companies that managed to generate positive rates of return, with the biggest reductions applied to the three most profitable enterprises.[14]

The unavailability of the technical skills and information necessary to evaluate the financial status of credit applicants from the mining sector cannot explain why the creditor in question, the Budapest Bank, elected to implement this lending strategy. The problems of that sector were of long standing, and it did not require sophisticated asset valuation techniques for loan officers in the Bank to determine that credits issued to certain mining companies would be highly risky.

This raises the following question. If the absence of an effective system of loan analysis doesn't explain the seemingly irrational patterns of credit allocation within the mining sector, what does?

Political Interference in Commercial Bank Activities

One possible explanation of the persistence of economically irrational credit policies under the two-tiered system is political intervention in the lending policies of the commercial banks. Lossmaking sectors like coal and metallurgy had powerful political patrons in the Central Committee of the Communist Party, local Party committees, the Ministry of Industry, and other state institutions. At the same time, the putative legal independence of the new banks did not free them from direct and indirect political influence by those actors.

The most important mode of political intervention in commercial bank activities was utilization of the Hungarian state's voting power as principal shareholder in the new banks. The state's possession of majority ownership of all five of the banks created the possibility that the two-tiered system would merely reproduce the same patterns of inefficient credit allocation as obtained under the monobanking system. The joint stock form, intended as a means of inculcating business-like behavior in the banking sector, would serve instead as yet another medium of transmission of the preferences of central planners.

An earlier experiment with commercial banking, the 1965 reform in Yugoslavia, had well illustrated the dangers attendant to the introduction of joint stock ownership in socialist economies. There, local enterprises together with their patrons in communal-level Party and government organizations became the principal capital subscribers in the new commercial banks, with highly adverse consequences for the Yugoslav economy.[15]

The reform of the banking system in Hungary was undertaken under rather different circumstances. Hungary was free of the sorts of ethnic, national, and developmental cleavages which underlay the local biases of the Yugoslav commercial banks. Hungarian state enterprises also remained far more closely tied to the central planning apparatus than their Yugoslav counterparts. The relevant issue in the Hungarian case was whether the distribution of equity ownership would place the banks under the sway of *central* political interests, to the detriment of economic rationality.

It was obviously no coincidence that the Hungarian state enjoyed majority equity ownership of the new banks from the time of their establishment in 1987. This raises two questions. First, what were the Hungarian state's objectives *vis-à-vis* the commercial banking sector? And second, to what extent was it able to use its majority voting power to achieve those objectives?

The Hungarian State and the Commercial Banks

The case of the Hungarian Credit Bank, the largest of the new commercial banks, illustrates the interests and activities of the state as equity owner. When the Credit Bank began operations on January 1, 1987, the Hungarian state owned 76 percent of its registered capital, with the remaining shares distributed among some 850 state enterprises, cooperatives, local governmental organizations, and other institutional investors. Subsequent stock issues to non-state investors resulted in the reduction of the state's share to 51 percent.

The composition of the Board of Directors testified to the state's highly visible role in the Credit Bank. The Chairman of the Board and Chief Executive Officer was Sandor Demjan, formerly the head of the *Skala* cooperative. Of the remaining eighteen seats on the Board, thirteen were allocated to senior officials from the government and state administration, one to the managing director of a major insurance company, and four to the managing directors of large state enterprises. Each of the latter was a client of the Credit Bank.[16]

Evidence for political influence on specific lending decisions taken by the management of the Credit Bank is suggestive, but not conclusive. One of the four big state enterprises whose managing director had a seat on the Board received an exceptionally generous increase in its credit line during the first year of the banking reform. This individual, moreover, was coincidentally a member of the Politburo of the ruling Communist Party.

While it obviously did not damage that particular enterprise's bargaining position to have such a well-connected chief, it is not clear that her presence on the Board of Directors was a key factor in the decision to expand the Bank's exposure to the enterprise. Irrespective of how large the state's ownership share or how heavy the representation of Party and state officials on the boards of the commercial banks, the joint stock form itself was ill-suited as a medium for those actors to influence individual lending decisions. The assembly of shareholders met only infrequently; and during those meetings, its sphere of decisionmaking extended only to matters of general corporate strategy (i.e., appointment of the management, determination of the size of the annual dividend, endorsement of the main business policy of the bank, approval of the annual report) and not to specific crediting decisions.

Of course, this did not prevent political authorities from attempting to interfere in the latter type of decisions. But such attempts came not through the formal legal mechanisms of the joint stock company, but rather through the very same informal channels which existed prior to the banking reform. These channels were part of what Laszlo Antal calls the "plan bargaining" system that emerged in Hungary after 1968. Deprived of the authority to impose legally binding directives on state enterprises, central planners devised indirect mechanisms for influencing microeconomic decisions. The most important of these techniques was to extract concessions from state enterprises in exchange for favorable regulatory treatment.

The key to the plan bargaining system was the mutual dependence of state enterprises and central authorities. The former controlled the labor and capital needed to achieve production goals vital to the center; the latter controlled the financial levers (taxation, wage and price regulations, import licensing, etc.) vital to the operation of the enterprises. Bargaining typically focused on the regulatory arrangements necessary to permit individual enterprises to meet convertible currency export targets. And so, for example, ministerial officials dissatisfied with the export production of a particular enterprise would bring pressure to bear on the managing director; the director would agree to ramp up production in exchange for a special export subsidy, a tax exemption, or some other regulatory exception.[17]

The same mutual dependence which animated the behavior of state enterprises and central planners under the plan bargaining system characterized the relationship between the commercial banks and state regulators under the two-tiered banking system. The banks possessed primary control over credit allocation, which afforded them considerable influence over the working and fixed capital accounts of state enterprises, which in turn gave them indirect leverage over the latter's ability to fulfill production goals vital to the central authorities. The state meanwhile exercised control over a range of regulations integral to the operation of the banks: taxation, capital financing, reserve requirements, interest rates, rediscounting of bills of exchange, and refinancing credit.

Let us consider a hypothetical, but probably not atypical, example. A senior official from the Ministry of Finance would make a telephone call to a division chief in one of the commercial banks to inquire as to the status of a loan application from a coal mining enterprise. The bank manager would reply that the enterprise in question was a lossmaker; approval of the loan was therefore a risky proposition. The ministerial official would then suggest that the expeditious approval of the loan might help to persuade the Finance Ministry's tax auditors to overlook certain irregularities in the bank's balance sheet.

In this sense, the introduction of the joint stock form into the commercial banking sector did not add anything new to the Hungarian state's repertoire of informal mechanisms of influencing microeconomic decisionmaking. The under-the-table bargaining, the exchanging of microeconomic concessions for regulatory exceptions, continued in a political-economic environment still characterized by a strong emphasis on physical production goals and a low degree of regulatory normativity.

In short, insofar as specific lending decisions were concerned, joint stock ownership did not constitute a new medium of political influence over the banks, as the institutional framework of the joint stock company did not readily permit this. But at the same time, joint stock ownership did not prevent the central authorities from doing what they had been doing all along: extracting concessions out of legally autonomous microeconomic agents by promising favorable regulatory treatment.

The State and Bank Dividends

What *was* new for the Hungarian state was the opportunity to exercise its prerogatives as majority shareholder and cast its vote on the annual dividends of the commercial banks. This, unlike lending decisions, was under the formal purview of the Board and the general assembly of shareholders.

The state's behavior in this regard was interesting and illuminating. In March 1988, the shareholders of the Hungarian Credit Bank assembled for their annual meeting. For Demjan and the other senior managers of the Credit Bank, it was a matter of pride and prestige that Hungary's biggest commercial bank should pay the highest dividend in the banking sector. Within that general guideline, the Board of Directors offered the shareholders three alternatives: 12, 14, and 17 percent. The assembly then took a vote.

Despite the fact that five other state ministries as well as the National Planning Office were included on the Board, the Ministry of Finance was formally designated as the state's representative as shareholder in the Credit Bank. The Finance Ministry did not, however, come to the shareholders' meeting as a unified actor. The Ministry dispatched three officials to vote on the state's behalf: the head of the Office of Banking Supervision, which was responsible for regulating the capital financing and asset accumulation activities of the commercial banks; the director of the National Refloatation Committee, which was charged with managing the restructuring and liquidation of Hungary's lossmaking enterprises; and the chief of the Finance Ministry's budget department.

These three officials came from different divisions within the Ministry of Finance, and brought with them differing perspectives concerning the Hungarian Credit Bank's dividend policy. The representative from the

Office of Banking Supervision preferred a low dividend. A high dividend, he believed, would endanger the long-term financial stability of the new banks. The head of the Refloatation Committee also preferred a low dividend, but for different reasons: a low dividend would leave the Credit Bank with larger reserves for writing off non-performing loans, and thereby facilitate the restructuring of lossmaking state enterprises. By contrast, the Finance Ministry's budget chief preferred a high dividend. His primary concern was the maximization of short-term returns on the state's investment in the bank, which would provide an immediate infusion of cash into the state's hard-pressed treasury and help to reduce Hungary's burgeoning budget deficit. In fact, this official was sufficiently enthused about the prospect of utilizing the state's equity portfolio as a revenue source that he proposed the creation of a special regulation which would enable the Ministry of Finance to receive its bank dividend *before* the shareholders' meeting.[18]

The conflicting views of the Finance Ministry's representatives demonstrated that the Hungarian state's incentives as equity owner of the commercial banks were highly ambiguous, and in certain respects contradictory. Predictably, the budgetary authorities exhibited a strong preference for maximizing short-term income flows from the state's equity portfolio. Yet other officials whose primary concern was regulation of the financial balances of the new banks and disposal of the non-performing loans in their portfolios preferred dividend policies aimed at preserving the long-term stability of the banking sector.

In short, it was impossible to ascribe to the state any single, coherent set of preferences concerning commercial banking policy. The Hungarian state approached its role as equity owner as a deeply divided political actor.

Conflict Between the State and the Banks

That the Hungarian political authorities were unable to present a united front had important implications for their relationship with the commercial banks. In particular, it strongly affected the conflict between the banks and the state over the disposition of the enormous backlog of bad loans in the former's portfolios.

At the time of the start-up of the two-tiered system in 1987, the National Bank of Hungary transferred its entire portfolio of enterprise loans to the commercial banks. A significant portion of the loans, accumulated over many years during the pre-reform period and amounting to tens of billions of forints, was owed by enterprises in metallurgy, mining, and other lossmaking sectors. Inclusion of these highly uncertain assets in the balance sheets of the new banks immediately placed them in a precarious position. Especially vulnerable was the Budapest Bank, which was saddled with the accounts of the mining sector as well as Ganz-Mavag, the giant railroad company which had the dubious distinction of being the single biggest lossmaker in the Hungarian economy. Together, the outstanding debts of the coal mines and Ganz-Mavag exceeded the Budapest Bank's entire registered capital.

Although it was widely understood that the principal on most of the bad loans stood little chance of ever being paid back, the managers of the Budapest Bank and the other commercial banks were extremely reluctant formally to declare them in default. Their position was that the new banks had not issued the loans in the first place—that the National Bank had—and that they couldn't ask the shareholders to take the full financial hit for writing off a huge backlog of loans which had accumulated over the years as a consequence of the imprudence of policymakers in the Party and state administration. The bank managers further argued that the political authorities were pressuring them to write down their loan portfolios at the same time as the state itself was sustaining the flow of enterprise subsidies which stood at the core of the problems of the loss-making sectors. Until the center terminated budgetary support of those sectors and demonstrated a firm resolve to implement an industrial restructuring program, those problems would not go away. Poorly performing enterprises would continue to generate losses, more loans would become non-performing, and the banks would be faced with the necessity of making repeated loan writeoffs. And so from the banks' perspective, the Hungarian state was pressuring them to accept responsibility for its own mistakes while continuing the very same soft financial policies that encouraged inefficiency in mining, metallurgy, and other lossmaking sectors in the first place.

The state's position was that the banks' assumption of the old loan portfolio was a regrettable but nevertheless unavoidable consequence of the transition from the monobanking system to the two-tiered system. Budgetary pressures precluded any possibility of the state itself absorbing the losses. Moreover, the unnaturally high profits of the banks during their first year of operation, which were less a result of the skill and brilliance of the bank management than of the undiminished willingness of cost-insensitive state enterprises to pay exorbitant interest rates on commercial credit, left them well-positioned to build up their loss reserves and gradually write off their non-performing assets.

What makes this conflict particularly interesting is the fact that the banks presented their case against the state in the context of a defense of the interests of their shareholders, when the state itself was the majority shareholder. This underscored the contradictory position of the Hungar-

ian state *vis-à-vis* the commercial banking sphere. As executors of budgetary and industrial restructuring policies, the political authorities had a
strong interest in (1) persuading the banks to write off non-performing
loans, and thereby relieving pressure on the state budget to cover the
losses; and (2) compelling the banks to assume primary responsibility for
restructuring the lossmaking sectors, and thereby shifting the blame for
the socioeconomic fallout of industrial restructuring away from the Party
and state.

But as majority shareholders in the banks, the state authorities had an
equally strong interest in *opposing* those very same measures. That is, for
the banks themselves to assume the entire burden of disposing of the bad
loans would not only reduce current profits, and hence deprive the shareholders of justification for voting themselves high dividends. It might
also undermine the long-term financial stability of the banks, and thus
reduce the resale value of the equity shares which the state owned.

The result of the introduction of joint stock ownership into the commercial banking sector in Hungary was thus to heighten the bargaining
power of the bank management while concomitantly reducing that of the
state, which held the majority of shares. The managers of the banks could
present a united front on the issue of loan writeoffs and restructuring,
their resistance to political pressure based on the quite justifiable premise
of defense of shareholder interests.

By contrast, the dual role of the state left it deeply divided on those
very same issues. As shareholder, it could not unequivocally support
loan writeoffs, poorly coordinated restructuring programs, and other
measures that threatened the long-term security of its equity shares in the
banks. As policymaker, the state sought to coerce the banks to take
precisely these measures, and thereby divest itself of the political and
economic costs of disposing of the old loan stock and restructuring Hungarian industry.

But here joint stock ownership placed sharp limits on the range of
coercive devices available to the state. The authorities could use their regulatory powers to force the banks to set aside a specified portion of retained earnings to create reserve funds for loan writeoffs. They could also
revise the legal code which governed the loan classification system in
such a way as to make it more difficult for bank managers to continue to
report dubious loans as performing assets. However, they had no authority to compel bank managers involuntarily to declare specific loans in
default. The joint stock form gave the banks a solid legal foundation for
resisting the state's attempts to compel them to take such steps. This is
in fact precisely what the two banks most exposed to the lossmaking
sectors, the Budapest Bank and the Hungarian Credit Bank, elected to
do.[19]

Consequences of the Loan Portfolio Problem for Credit Flows

Therein resides the main explanation for the decision of the Hungarian commercial banks to sustain credit lines to coal mines and other state enterprises well-known to be running losses. Until their conflict with the central authorities over the loan portfolio problem was resolved, the prudent course of action for the banks was to sustain credit flows to loss-makers. Fresh credits would keep those enterprises sufficiently liquid to enable them to make payments on old loans, and thus allow the banks to continue to report those loans as performing assets.

The bank managers held to this strategy even as the National Bank of Hungary was reducing the aggregate supply of money to the commercial banking sector. While the aim of this monetary squeeze was to force the banks to reallocate capital from their poorly performing clients to their strongest ones, both the Budapest Bank and the Hungarian Credit Bank did just the opposite. They cut credit lines to their strong performers and increased them to their lossmakers, reasoning that it was precisely the latter which were least able to tolerate the liquidity crunch, and whose debt servicing capability was in greatest need of support through the issuance of new loans.

The Paradox of Joint Stock Ownership

The persistence of inefficient credit flows under the two-tiered system was thus not merely a consequence of the absence of modern accounting procedures and effective mechanisms of asset valuation. Nor was it a simple manifestation of the tendency of the new banks to replicate the mindset and procedures of the old monobanking system. The introduction of joint stock ownership *did* represent a significant departure from the situation which obtained before 1987. The incentive structure under which the managers of the commercial banks operated *was* fundamentally different from the one which guided the behavior of loan officers in the previous credit division of the National Bank. The bank managers genuinely regarded themselves as primarily responsible to the shareholders, and they adopted lending policies designed above all to preserve the value of the banks' equity capital.

But ironically, it was precisely the managers' preoccupation with protecting shareholder interests that induced them to make lending decisions which were, from a purely economic perspective, irrational. The peculiar circumstances which attended the transition to the two-tiered system, whereby the new banks assumed responsibility for a vast portfolio of bad loans accumulated over many years by the National Bank of Hungary, created strong incentives for the managers to sustain credit flows to weak clients in order to avert massive loan writeoffs which might sharply reduce profits and undermine the long-term value of the banks' equity capital. Far from a reflection of the banks' vulnerability to political influence, such lending policies were logical and prudent given prevailing circumstances; the bank managers could legitimately claim that they were defending the interests of the shareholders.

That the main shareholder was the Hungarian state does not constitute evidence for the politically-motivated use of the joint stock form to subvert lending decisions. On the contrary, the fact that the state was the majority shareholder left the political authorities in a *weak* bargaining position. While the bank managers could base their lending policies on the clear and unambiguous grounds of defense of shareholder interests, the position of the political leadership was contradictory. As shareholder, it had a manifest interest in preserving the value of its equity investments in the banks; as executor of national economic policy, it had an equally strong interest in pressuring the banks to take precisely those measures that endangered the equity capital of the banks, namely writing off large numbers of non-performing loans.

In the face of the center's equivocal bargaining position, the banks succeeded in resisting pressure to write down their portfolios. By supplying their weak clients with just enough credit to allow them to service their debts, the bank managers could continue legally to claim the bad loans as performing assets. Therein resides the main explanation for the persistence of inefficient patterns of credit allocation under the two-tiered banking system.

Recent Developments in Hungarian Banking

Several recent developments in economic reform policy have proved of special significance to the Hungarian banking system:

1. an expansion of the political authority of the National Bank of Hungary which has enabled it to sustain a very tight monetary policy,
2. changes in the Hungarian accounting laws which require both banks and enterprises to adopt Western-type procedures of financial reporting, and
3. initiation of an ambitious privatization program which lays the foundation for a fundamental transformation of ownership relations in the Hungarian economy.

However, while these measures succeeded in altering the economic environment in which the commercial banks operate, they have not resolved the specific problem discussed in the present chapter, the disposition of the backlog of bad loans accumulated during the pre-1987 period. With the banks and the Hungarian state authorities still deadlocked over that matter, the former have persisted with their policy of channelling credit towards the weakest enterprises in their portfolios.

Expansion of the National Bank's Political Authority

The most important recent development in the Hungarian banking system is the transformation of the National Bank, long subordinated to the fiscal organs of the state administration, into a Western-type central bank capable of regulating the money supply. This has endowed the Bank with the political wherewithal to implement a highly restrictive monetary policy. The consequence for the commercial banks has been a contraction of the supply of refinancing credit from the National Bank, their chief source of liquidity. Whereas previously, the banks had high confidence that the monetary authorities would ultimately yield to political pressure to ease off liquidity squeezes, they now face the problem of how to allocate a sharply diminished supply of credit.[20]

Reforms of the Hungarian Accounting System

As noted earlier, the deficiencies of the Hungarian accounting system have impeded the banks' ability to evaluate the balance sheets of debtor enterprises, and hence to apply rigorous standards of efficiency in their credit decisions. In 1987, the central authorities drafted a law that required Hungarian state enterprises to adopt double-sided balance sheets, following standard accounting practice in the West. But this did little to improve the quality of the financial indices reported by enterprises. State enterprises still lacked any concept of cash flow, any sense of the relationship between assets and liabilities. Beyond this, the utility of enterprise balance sheets as an instrument of credit analysis was greatly undermined by the high level of state subsidization. Commercial banks could not make confident judgments about the creditworthiness of heavily subsidized enterprises, as subsidies transformed what would otherwise be lossmakers into profitable enterprises.[21]

In 1989, the authorities began a comprehensive reform of the Hungarian accounting system. The new accounting laws propose the following:

1. The assets and liabilities of enterprises and banks, heretofore reported as nominal values, will be adjusted to reflect present values;
2. Certain income-producing items previously treated solely as liabilities, such as leases, will now be reported on both sides of the balance sheet;

3. Enterprises and banks will be subjected to stricter regulations concerning the classification and writing off of dubious assets.[22]

But while modernization of the accounting system and deep subsidy cuts are prerequisites to proper evaluation of the balance sheets of debtor enterprises, commercial banks face other major obstacles to the application of efficiency criteria to credit decisions. In particular, the absence of an extensive capital market and the highly antiquated state of much of the plant and equipment of Hungarian enterprises continue to make meaningful evaluation of the book value of fixed assets very difficult.

Privatization

The general acceleration of the Hungarian privatization process after 1989 has altered the ownership structure and competitive environment of the banking sector. By 1991, the Hungarian state's equity investment in the original five commercial banks had declined from majority ownership to about 40 percent of shares outstanding. This was the result not of the state's divestiture of its shares in the banks, but rather the expansion of their total equity capital by way of sales of new shares to non-state investors.[23] This means, among other things, that the state's aggregate stake in the banks has barely diminished. Thus, the central authorities are still caught in the dilemma described early, the tension between the state's objectives as economic policymaker and its proprietary interests as shareholder.

Meanwhile, the banks and the Hungarian state remain deadlocked over the loan portfolio problem. In early 1991, the authorities offered a 50 percent governmental guarantee against the banks' non-performing assets. The bank managers resisted, still insisting that they could not expect the shareholders to assume responsibility for imprudent decisions taken under the monobanking system.[24]

The continued failure of the banks and the state to resolve this issue has two important consequences for the banking system. First, the incentive structure guiding the lending policies of the Hungarian banks remains basically the same despite the diminution of the relative share of state ownership. Loan officers continue to face strong pressures to channel credit towards weak enterprises. Second, full-fledged privatization of the banks (i.e., actual state divestiture rather than mere expansion of capital base) cannot take place until the loan portfolio problem is resolved. The assets of the banks are too risky to attract large numbers of private investors.

The post-1989 period *has* seen an improvement in the general patterns of credit allocation in Hungary. But this is due not to a transformation of the credit policies of the Hungarian banks, but rather the appearance of new competitors in the financial sector. From the original five banks at the startup of the two-tiered system in 1987, by 1990 there were nearly thirty commercial banks and specialized financial institutions licensed for operation in Hungary. Eight of the banks are of mixed ownership, underscoring the increasingly visible role of foreign capital in the Hungarian economy. Moreover, the liberalization of the financial sector spurred the establishment of a score of insurance companies, brokerage houses, investment funds, and auditing firms, many of them wholly- or partly-owned by foreign investors.[25]

The new Western-owned and joint venture financial institutions enjoy considerable advantages over the Hungarian banks. First, they possess greater expertise and superior technical resources. Second, unlike the Hungarian banks, they are not saddled with large backlogs of dubious loans, and hence do not face any imperative to reallocate credit to sustain the debt-servicing capabilities of weak enterprises. However, their ability to reshape broader patterns of capital allocation in the economy remains limited, as some 80 percent of total credit still comes from the three largest Hungarian banks.[26]

In short, while the expansion of the political authority of the National Bank, modernization of the accounting system, and acceleration of the privatization program constitute important developments in the ongoing reform of the Hungarian banking system, the loan portfolio problem continues to serve as a drag on the general performance of the financial sector. The extent to which credit allocation has become more efficient over the past few years is chiefly attributable to the appearance of new entrants in the financial market, not the transformation of the behavior of the Hungarian banks themselves.

The Banks and the Hungarian Private Sector

Amidst the general liquidity squeeze engineered by the newly assertive National Bank, one sector of the Hungarian economy has enjoyed a sharp increase in its allocation of bank credit: the stock of credits raised by small private businesses and entrepreneurs nearly tripled between 1989 and 1990. This development is due in large part to the establishment by the National Bank of a special facility offering refinancing credits to the commercial banks on exceptionally favorable terms to finance loans earmarked for the emergent private sector. The purpose of the facility is to spur domestic capital formation and accelerate the broader program of privatization administered by Hungary's State Property Agency (SPA).[27]

But while the growth of private sector credit is impressive, in relative terms it still represents a very small percentage of total enterprise credit disbursed by the Hungarian banks, most of whose assets remain tied down in the state sector. This underscores again the constraints imposed by the loan portfolios inherited by the banks in 1987. The structure of those portfolios creates powerful disincentives for the banks to reallocate credit within the state sector from weak to strong enterprises. It also greatly limits their ability to shift capital from the state to the private sector, even in the presence of a highly attractive refinancing facility in the National Bank designed specifically for private sector lending.

These limitations on domestic capital formation outside of the state sector have important implications for the general trajectory of Hungary's privatization campaign. At least for the foreseeable future, foreign investors, and not local banks, will serve as the primary source of capital for the private sector. Foreign capital has, in fact, played the dominant role in the privatizations of large state enterprises undertaken by the SPA since 1990. Total foreign direct investment in Hungary has surpassed that of all of the other former socialist countries.[28] Thus Hungary, even with a still-limited domestic banking industry, seems very well placed to use its international financial ties to promote its private sector in ways which may be much less available elsewhere in the former socialist nations.

Notes

1. Arthur Z. Arnold, *Banks, Credit, and Money in Soviet Russia* (New York: Columbia University Press, 1937), 70–145; Maurice Dobb, *Soviet Economic Development* (New York: International Publishers, 1948), 366–382; George Garvy, *Money, Financial Flows and Credit in the Soviet Union* (Cambridge: Harvard University Press, 1977), 22–35.

2. Garvy, *Money*, 13–35, 76–77, 157–158; Paul Gregory and Robert Stuart, *Soviet Economic Structure and Performance* (New York: Harper & Row, 1981), 141; Gregory Grossman, ed., *Money and Plan* (Berkeley: University of California Press, 1968), 153–183; T.M. Podolski, *Socialist Banking and Monetary Control: The Experience of Poland* (Cambridge: Harvard University Press, 1973), 335–354; Adam Zwass, *Money, Banking, and Credit in the Soviet Union and Eastern Europe* (White Plains: M.E. Sharpe, 1979), 3–23.

3. Garvy, *Money*, 52–75; Gregory and Stuart, *Soviet Economic Structure*, 154; Zwass, *Money, Banking, and Credit*, 78–113.

4. Donald Hodgman, "Soviet Monetary Controls Through the Banking System," in *Readings on the Soviet Economy*, edited by Franklyn Holzman, 117–122 (Chicago: Rand McNally, 1962).

5. Zwass, *Money, Banking, and Credit*, 119–120.

6. Katherine Hsiao, *Money and Monetary Policy in Communist China* (New York: Columbia University Press, 1971), 225–253; Raymond Powell, "Recent Developments in Soviet Monetary Policy," in *Readings on the Soviet Economy*, 573–576; Zwass, *Money, Banking, and Credit*, 3–23, 65.

7. Aleksander Bajt, "Investment Cycles in European Socialist Economies: A Review Article," *Journal of Economic Literature* IX, no. 1 (March 1971): 53–63.

8. Tamas Bauer, "Investment Cycles in Planned Economies," *Acta Oeconomica*

21, no. 3 (1978): 243–260; Laura Tyson, "Investment Allocation: A Comparison of the Reform Experiences of Hungary and Yugoslavia," *Journal of Comparative Economics* 7 (1983): 288–303.

9. For accounts of Hungarian financial policy in the pre-1987 period, see Laszlo Antal and Gyorgy Suranyi, "The Prehistory of the Reform of Hungary's Banking System," *Acta Oeconomica* 38, no. 1–2 (1987): 35–48; Laszlo Asztalos, Lajos Bokros, and Gyorgy Suranyi, "Reform and Financial Institutional System in Hungary," *Acta Oeconomica* 32, no. 3–4 (1984): 251–268; I. Fenyovari, "On the Hungarian Financial System," *Acta Oeconomica* 25, no. 3–4 (1980): 277–290; Janos Kornai, *The Economics of Shortage*, Vol. B (Amsterdam: North Holland Publishing Company, 1980), 513–532.

10. Paul Marer, "Hungary's Balance of Payments Crisis and Response, 1978–84," in *Eastern European Economies: Slow Growth in the 1980s*, Vol. 3, Joint Economic Committee of the U.S. Congress (Washington: General Printing Office, 1986), 311–317.

11. Eva Varhegyi, "Sources of the Growth of Enterprises in Hungary," *Acta Oeconomica* 37, no. 3–4 (1986): 267–284.

12. Antal and Suranyi, "The Prehistory," 35–48; Asztalos, Bokros, and Suranyi, "Reform and Financial Institutional System," 251–268; Tamas Bacskai, "The Reorganization of the Banking System," *The New Hungarian Quarterly*, no. 107 (Autumn 1987): 127–136 ; Lajos Bokros, "Az Uzleti Viselkedes Kibontakozasanak Feltetlei Ketszinten Bankrendszerben" ("The Conditions of the Development of Businesslike Behavior in a Two-Tiered Banking System"), manuscript, 1986; Michael Friedlander, "Hungary's Banking Reform," *Wiener Institut Fur Internationale Wirtschaftsvergleiche* (December 1987): 1–6, 17–24.

13. Interviews, Hungarian Credit Bank, May, July, and August 1988; Ministry of Finance, June 1988. Assessments of intra-sectoral credit flows are based on unpublished data supplied to the author by the Ministry of Industry, August 1988.

14. Interviews, Budapest Bank, August 1988. Assessments of intra-sectoral credit flows are based on unpublished data supplied to the author by the Ministry of Industry, August 1988.

15. Dimitrije Dimitrijevic and George Macesich, *Money and Finance in Contemporary Yugoslavia* (New York: Praeger Publications, 1983), 9–55, 67–83, 100–162; Svetozar Pejovich, "The Banking System and the Investment Behavior of the Yugoslav Firm," in *Plan and Market: Economic Reform in Eastern Europe*, edited by Morris Bornstein, (New Haven: Yale University Press, 1973): 285–311.

16. Hungarian Credit Bank Ltd., *Annual Report, 1987*.

17. Laszlo Antal, "Conflicts of Financial Planning and Regulation in Hungary," *Acta Oeconomica* 30, no. 3–4 (1983): 341–368; T. Laky, "The Hidden Mechanisms of Recentralization in Hungary," *Acta Oeconomica* 24, no. 1–2 (1980): 95–109; A. Sipos and M. Tardos, "Economic Control and Structural Interdependence of Organizations in Hungary at the End of the Second Decade of Reform," *Acta Oeconomica* 37, no. 3–4 (1986): 241–265.

18. Interviews, Hungarian Credit Bank, May 1988; National Bank of Hungary, August 1988.

19. Interviews, Hungarian Council of Ministers, April 1988; National Bank

of Hungary, April 1988; Ministry of Finance, June and September 1988; Ministry of Industry, August 1988; Hungarian Credit Bank, May and July 1988; Budapest Bank, April, May, and August 1988.

20. Karoly Okolicsanyi, "New Hungarian Bank Laws Maintain Political Influence," *RFE/RL Research Report*, no. 21 (February 21, 1992): 43–45; Interviews, National Bank of Hungary, May 1991.

21. Interviews, Price Waterhouse Budapest, May 1991.

22. Hungarian Foreign Trade Bank Ltd., *Financial Statements*, 1989, 4–5.

23. Interviews, Hungarian Banking Association, May 1991.

24. Interviews, National Bank of Hungary, May 1991.

25. Gyorgy Kerekes, ed., *Hungarian Financial and Stock Exchange Almanac* 1990 (Budapest: Hungarian Television Enterprises, 1990), 403–408.

26. *Hungarian Financial Review* 2, no. 3 (February 1–14, 1991): 3.

27. National Bank of Hungary, *Quarterly Review*, no. 4 (1990): 15–16.

28. Hungary's reliance on foreign capital during the current phase of privatization contrasts sharply with the strategies pursued by other East European countries. Czechoslovakia and Poland, where public sensitivity to foreign capital penetration is somewhat higher than in Hungary, have opted for mass voucher programs designed to leapfrog the constraints imposed by shortages of domestic capital. Reunified Germany, which faces no such constraints, has utilized a gigantic state holding company, the *Treuhandanstalt*, to mobilize the vast stock of domestic capital for the rapid privatization of East German industry. See Michael Marrese, "Hungary Emphasizes Foreign Partners," *RFE/RL Research Report*, no. 17 (April 1992): 30–32; and David Bartlett, "The Political Economy of Privatization: Property Reform and Democracy in Hungary," *East European Politics and Societies* 6, no. 1 (Winter 1992): 81–91.

9

The Perils of Privatizing State Property: The Polish Case

Ben Slay[*]

Privatization, in the sense of transferring ownership of state property to private organizations or individuals, has been a key goal of all four of Poland's post-communist governments. Given that 8778 firms still belonged to the state in mid-1992,[1] realizing these goals requires the rapid sale of many state-owned firms.

Privatization's importance in Poland has been rivaled only by the controversy and difficulties it has encountered. Four distinct phases in the development of privatization in Poland can be identified, each of which is marked by a different approach to privatization on the part of the Polish government. All four phases share an important feature, however: none has been both a technically feasible and a politically viable method of significantly redrawing the property rights framework in Poland. While the privatization of state-owned shops, stores and small (and some medium-sized) firms proceeded fairly smoothly during 1990–1992, the transfer of larger enterprises from state to private ownership proceeded haltingly, especially in industry and agriculture. Indeed, as Chapter 2 describes, the rapid post-1989 growth in the share of private activity in Poland has resulted largely from the development of the indigenous private sector.

The "spontaneous privatization" episode of 1989–1990 can be regarded as the first phase of privatization in Poland. During this phase members of the Polish United Workers' Party (PUWP) *nomenklatura* expropriated state property in an attempt to broker their political elite status under socialism into economic elite status under capitalism.[2]

*The author would like to thank the Radio Free Europe/Radio Liberty Research Institute for the research materials upon which this chapter is based, as well as the Social Science Research Council and American Council of Learned Societies for research funding.

Although not necessarily illegal, these "insider" activities led to a public outcry and the development of competing programs for state-controlled privatization by the government of Prime Minister Tadeusz Mazowiecki (September 1989–December 1990). The second phase can be linked to the passage of privatization legislation in July 1990, which both sanctioned a wide variety of state-controlled "outsider" privatization techniques and created the Ministry of Ownership Transformation to implement them. The new Ministry attempted privatization according to the "British model," based upon open stock sales to the public, during the second half of 1990.

The slow pace of the public sales approach led the government of Prime Minister Jan Krzysztof Bielecki (January–December 1991) to adopt in February 1991 a "privatization offensive," in which the variety of privatization techniques authorized by the 1990 legislation were put into practice during the third phase of Poland's privatization efforts. However, the scaling back and postponement in October 1991 of the "mass privatization" program for privatizing 400 of Poland's largest industrial firms was a major setback for the privatization offensive, and left Poland's privatization strategy somewhat muddled. The fourth phase of reappraisal occurred during the first months of the government of Prime Minister Jan Olszewski (January–June 1992), but subsequently led to a return to the framework developed by the Bielecki government. This framework was continued by the government of Prime Minister Hanna Suchocka (July 1992–), but as of October 1992 it had been unable to accelerate the privatization process.

The First Phase: Spontaneous Privatization

The deregulation of private and state enterprises introduced by reform communist governments during 1987–1989 permitted state firms to issue and sell their own stock in an essentially unregulated manner. This allowed many state enterprises to transform themselves into corporations. Party-state officials controlled the composition and price of the stock offerings issued during these transformations, and used their position to become owners of what had previously been state enterprises. In effect, these officials were able to translate their political elite status under state socialism into economic elite status by becoming property owners in the unregulated capitalism that followed the collapse of the traditional structures during 1989–1990.

The forms which this "propertization of the *nomenklatura*" took in Poland were many and imaginative. The common theme was the creation of corporations enjoying a parasitic relationship with state enterprises.

The corporations would appropriate the most lucrative elements of the state firms' business (a new form of "cream skimming"), leaving the state firm (and ultimately the state budget) to bear the more costly and risky activities. In this way, profits were privatized while risk remained socialized. The state sector's capital stock could also be appropriated in this way. Managers would lease or sell (at low prices) state firms' physical assets to private firms (in which they were co-owners), which could then deploy the assets as desired. This could mean selling the assets to the highest bidder and pocketing the receipts.

Despite this element of corruption, it is difficult to condemn the spontaneous privatization of 1989–1990 out of hand. Not all conversions of state enterprises into private firms were cases of the "propertization of the *nomenklatura*" in the most undesirable sense of the phrase.[3] Some conversions were acquisitions of state firms by entrepreneurial managers, which involved a good deal of risk. Others took the form of issuing shares to employees and/or enterprise workers' councils, thus adding an element of worker ownership. Others served as vehicles for attracting foreign capital. The matter is further complicated by difficulties in assessing the value of enterprise assets and by opposition to any form of privatization from powerful interest groups, including workers' councils, which enjoyed unclear but important proprietary rights to state firms' assets as a result of reforms introduced during 1981–1982.[4] Finally, this spontaneous privatization wave did transfer state property to private actors who (eventually) should have incentives to act like "real" owners and either make good use of their new property themselves, or resell it to new owners (or hire managers) who can. Ultimately, this could increase the efficiency of capital allocation decisions. Moreover, criticism of spontaneous privatization is difficult to evaluate in the abstract, in the absence of comparison with the application of other privatization strategies.

Still, the fact that privatization became entangled with issues of privilege, the PUWP *nomenklatura*, and corruption did not bode well for the private sector's socio-political prospects. The public reaction evoked by these developments was ferociously negative, and weakened support for privatization, and private enterprise, in general. In economic terms, permitting a share of the state's wealth to pass into private hands via sweetheart deals could have important long-run implications for the state budget, since firms' non-taxable revenues cannot be used to finance public expenditures after privatization. Moreover, the absence of well-functioning markets for capital, other real assets, and corporate control implies that efficiency gains from this type of privatization are likely to be minimal (at least initially), since the new owners are unlikely to be subjected to effective market discipline and social control.

The Second Phase: Legislative Framework
and the "British Model"

The Ministry of Ownership Transformation was created in August 1990 in order to subject privatization to closer supervision by the new Solidarity government. In addition to formally creating the Ministry and authorizing a variety of privatization techniques, landmark privatization legislation also laid the foundation for the creation of a stock market. This legislation was the result of a political battle within the Mazowiecki government and between the government and the Sejm.[5] On the one hand, Privatization Plenipotentiary Krzysztof Lis favored public sales of stock to any and all buyers (subsequently known as the "British model"). This approach was thought to expedite the privatization process, to reduce inflationary pressures (via absorption of excess cash holdings), and to attract foreign capital. Opposition to this approach reflected the belief that open sales would lead to the propertization of wealthy members of the PUWP *nomenklatura*, the mafia, and foreigners at the expense of Polish citizens.

For similar reasons, support for programs that would lead to worker ownership of Polish factories was widespread. Proponents of these views were able to include in the legislation authorization for privatization vouchers and special privileges for workers buying stock in their firms, in order to facilitate the wide distribution of ownership across the population. Virtually all forms of privatization were thus authorized in the July 1990 legislation, with the understanding that the specifics would be determined by practice.

The Ministry of Ownership Transformation in September 1990 faced the daunting task of privatizing the bulk of some 8000 state enterprises, approximately 6000 of which formally belonged to the central authorities. The remaining 2000 belonged to the local authorities, 700–900 of which were classified as public utilities. Of the 6000 firms formally owned by the central authorities, 500 were classified as large industrial firms and 2500 as medium-sized or small industrial firms. The remaining 3000 were classified as construction, tourist, transportation, commercial and, "other" enterprises.[6]

The first step in the privatization process for large and medium-sized firms is their "commercialization" into state-owned corporations, which are then managed by independent boards of directors, rather than by central ministries or the local authorities (as is the case with other state enterprises). Central interference in managerial decisions is supposed to be reduced to a minimum, and worker participation in enterprise governance is limited to electing one-third of a supervisory council. (This contrasts with the larger role frequently played by workers' councils in state-owned firms.) The firm's value is also estimated at this stage.

Once fully commercialized, the firm's stock is then sold via auction, public offer, or agreements between the government and larger buyers. The Ministry is supposed to reduce its ownership position in commercialized state enterprises to below 50 percent within two years of commercialization. Unsold shares may be sold or otherwise "entrusted" to the banking system three months after the sale is announced. However, the sale of shares to other state-owned institutions is generally forbidden, in order to prevent the appearance of Hungarian-type cross ownership patterns among state institutions. Approximately 11 large firms were sold via public offer during 1990–1991, while 18 were sold to selected investors (including seven to Western multinationals like *Pepsi Cola, Gerber,* and *Phillips*) during 1991.

This approach is described as "large-scale" or "capital" privatization in Poland, because of the size of the firms being sold, and the emphasis on selling capital shares (stock), rather than whole firms or physical assets. Privatization can also occur through the sale or leasing of enterprise physical assets, through what is called "liquidation" privatization. State firms can in this way either be privatized in their entirety or through the piecemeal sale of plant and equipment. This contrasts with the large-scale privatization approach, in which ownership shares (stock) in privatized enterprises are sold (or given away). The liquidation approach has the advantage of relying upon markets that already exist,[7] unlike the large-scale privatization approach which must artificially conjure up "market values" for privatized firms in the absence of markets to perform the valuation. The disadvantage is that it may unnecessarily break up efficient management teams.

Privatization efforts under the Mazowiecki government focused primarily on selling medium-sized and large industrial firms via public sales. In practice, however, the British model proved incapable of quickly privatizing many large firms through open stock sales. This reflected a number of factors, including the technical difficulties the Ministry of Ownership Transformation faced in determining enterprise value in the absence of a well-functioning stock market.[8] The valuation problem was especially important for large industrial firms, where extensive synergies within integrated production complexes made the book value of an enterprise's assets a poor guide to determining its "market" worth. The lack of domestic capital,[9] combined with restrictions on foreign purchases of state enterprises (which were relaxed in July 1991), slowed the process down by reducing the demand for Polish assets.

By November 1990, some 15 months after the Solidarity government had come to power, only 20 of the 157 state enterprises that had been selected for large-scale privatization by the Ministry of Ownership Transformation had been commercialized. Moreover, only five state firms had actually been sold via public auction by January 1991. Though touted by the government as a great success, the sale of the first five firms was not without its problems. Although months were required to estimate these firms' value (which was determined to be some 500 billion zloty) and generally prepare them for privatization, the five firms when finally sold only yielded some 300 billion in revenues, 67 billion of which went for the costs incurred in administering the privatization of these firms.

This slow pace of privatization heightened uncertainty among managers and workers about the ultimate fate of their firms[10] and exacerbated tensions between the Ministry of Ownership Transformation and other central organs such as the Ministry of Industry and Trade. Criticism of the slow pace of privatization under the Mazowiecki government was an important element of Lech Walesa's "acceleration" theme during the November 1990 presidential campaign. Walesa also advocated the universal distribution of state property during the campaign, promising voters that they would each receive 100 million zloty (approximately $10,500) in privatization vouchers as their "share" of the state's wealth. Walesa's new government thus had an electoral mandate, as well as an economic rationale, for pursuing a more ambitious privatization program in 1991.

The Third Phase: The "Privatization Offensive"

The government of Prime Minister Jan Krzysztof Bielecki announced a "privatization offensive" in February 1991. Janusz Lewandowski, Bielecki's Minister of Ownership Transformation, promised an ambitious program featuring a wide variety of privatization techniques. As the co-author of one of Eastern Europe's first voucher-based privatization plans in 1988,[11] Lewandowski also advocated universal distribution as a way to turn Poland into a "society of capitalists."

Lewandowski's "mass privatization" program was formally announced in June 1991.[12] It envisioned the commercialization of 400 of the largest state-owned industrial firms (producing about 25 percent of industrial output, employing 12 percent of the industrial labor force) and the creation of five to twenty investment funds called "national property boards" which would take the form of state-owned joint stock companies. Shares in the property boards would be distributed free of charge to the public, with each of Poland's 28 million adults receiving a single share of stock in each property board. The boards would in turn receive 60 percent of the stock in the 400 firms. The property boards would become the firms' owners, while the boards themselves would be owned by Polish citizens. Directors of the property boards would be appointed by no less a figure than the president himself. Incentive systems and personnel matters in the management of the 400 enterprises would be determined by Western consulting and financial-management firms hired by the property boards. These "experts" were to help the property boards fulfill their mission of maximizing the value of the enterprises in their portfolio. Of the remaining 40 percent of the firms' stock, 10 percent would be given *gratis* to the firms' workers and 30 percent would remain state property.

Mass privatization was seen as a method for avoiding the problems the Ministry of Ownership Transformation faced in attempting to estimate enterprise value in the absence of a stock market. By playing the role of the institutional investors in Western capital markets, the property boards would reconcentrate the property rights that would otherwise be diluted among 28 million individuals. Creating the property boards would allow the government to avoid difficult decisions about which of the 400 firms would be owned by which of 28 million individuals. Western expertise would be engaged in the privatization process without "selling out" the country's wealth to foreigners. Finally, since shares in the property boards would be distributed free of charge, this approach would avoid the problem of Polish households' relative lack of wealth.

The mass privatization program met with immediate press and professional criticism and a hostile reception in parliament. Criticism focused on the program's implications for the state budget, the program's inability to keep property ownership "out of the wrong hands," and the economic and administrative infeasibility of this approach. The prospect of the government giving away 400 of its largest firms without financial compensation in a time of fiscal tensions seemed untenable even to the government's supporters. Critics also focused on the program's fairness claim by pointing out that the equal distribution of property board shares across the population did nothing to prevent the subsequent reselling of shares on secondary markets. This would presumably produce a reconcentration of property rights in the hands of wealthy Polish and foreign investors, many of whom (i.e., representatives of the PUWP *nomenklatura*, the mafia, etc.) would be the "wrong hands."

Critics of mass privatization also expressed fears that the national property boards would aggravate Poland's monopoly problem.[13] In addition to being able to exercise monopoly power on nascent capital markets by virtue of their large size and small numbers, the boards could seek to gain control over entire branches of production. Monopoly rents, after all, generally increase the market value of the firms receiving them. Such an outcome could prevent the development of competitive markets composed of autonomous private firms. Critics also claimed that, because of their size and importance as holders of industrial capital, property boards that chronically mismanaged their assets or that received an initial portfolio of unprofitable firms could pose a moral-hazard problem. Would the Polish government be willing to bankrupt an insolvent property board, thus putting at risk a large chunk of industrial capital as well as dozens of firms employing hundreds of thousands of workers? Not likely, given the difficulties governments everywhere face in resisting pressures to bail out large insolvent firms (not to mention the paternalistic legacy of state socialism). According to this view, the lack of a viable bankruptcy threat would further soften the (state-owned) property boards' budget constraints and reintroduce the inefficiencies associated with socialism.

Privatization via national property boards could thus be an artificial exercise that would create a new layer of neo-socialist bureaucracy rather than genuine private owners. The lack of a date when the funds would go out of existence contributed to these fears. Criticism also focused on the difficulties in devising effective incentive schemes for the foreign "experts" managing the property boards' assets, and on the costs of administering the program.

The economic, administrative and political weaknesses of the mass privatization program, combined with the sharpening recession and the run-up to October parliamentary elections, by late 1991 had made the program a political non-starter. Meanwhile, closer financial inspection of the 400 firms revealed that 170 were too close to insolvency to be "viable" candidates for mass privatization. Antitrust objections to other firms by the Anti-Monopoly Office whittled the list down further, so that by October 9, 1991 only 209 firms (producing about 7 percent of Poland's industrial output) remained from the original list of 400.

In light of these problems, Lewandowski's announcement on October 15, 1991 that the mass privatization program was being scaled back and postponed did not come as a surprise. Although the Olszewski and Suchocka governments subsequently made mass privatization a key element in their privatization strategy, neither was able to obtain parliamentary approval for the program. As of October 1992, it was unclear when and whether mass privatization would ever get off the ground.

The privatization offensive was not limited to the mass privatization program. In addition to the small and liquidation privatization programs discussed below, six firms were sold via public offerings during 1991; another 18 were sold to selected investors. The sectoral privatization program, as well as the "restructuring" privatization program based upon "business" and "managerial" contracts, were also developed during 1991. In keeping with the slogan "first restructure, then privatize," these programs grew in importance as the profitability of hundreds of firms deteriorated with the recession during the second half of 1991.

Under sectoral privatization, the feasibility of restructuring and privatizing entire branches is evaluated by (mostly Western) consulting firms, with one consulting firm assigned to "handle" an entire branch. The consulting firms then attempt to sell large chunks of stock in the firms belonging to that branch. In theory, a number of enterprises could be sold at once through this program. While both domestic and foreign buyers would be welcome, the program is obviously oriented towards foreign investors. However, while firms in some 16 branches of industry (including automobiles, banking and machine tools) were initially included in the program in September 1991, sectoral privatization subsequently proved unable to privatize entire sectors at one go as advertised. It also failed to serve as the mechanism for coordinating privatization and industrial policies which its proponents hoped it would become.

Like sectoral privatization, restructuring privatization linked privatization more directly to enterprise restructuring and industrial policy. The development of "business" and "managerial" contracts, as mechanisms for effecting this restructuring, began in late 1991. Both of these schemes were intended to involve Polish and/or foreign managers in the restructuring of firms slated for privatization. Managers were to "bid" for the right to manage commercialized enterprises by submitting competing business plans for the firms' reorganization and future development. The "winning" group (with the program for restructuring the firm deemed most promising) would make a "downpayment" equal to some percentage of the firm's book value; this collateral would be lost if the program is unsuccessful. The group would then be given a free hand in managing and restructuring the firm; the prerogatives of the workers' council would be dramatically reduced, for example. The managerial group would then obtain a significant share of the revenues accruing from the restructuring, either in the form of a capital gain when the stock was sold in the firm's privatization, or in the form of bonuses paid out of profits. The attraction for managers thus rested in the possibility of a large payoff with a relatively small investment, while the central authorities would be relieved of some of the burden of enterprise restructuring.

However, as of mid-1992, these programs had acquired only marginal significance, in part because managers were unwilling to take the risks they required. As of March 1992, no firms had yet been put on the "business contract" system, and the first managerial contracts were introduced into the *VIS* Tool-Making Kombinat (in Warsaw) and the *Syntex* apparel firm (in Lowicz) during January 1992. Once again, an innovative idea proved unable to make much of a dent in Poland's privatization challenge.

The Fourth Phase: Reconsideration and Reappraisal

Shortly after being formed in late December 1991, the Olszewski government signaled its intention to re-evaluate the privatization process. Instead of accelerating privatization within the existing framework, the new government seemed to want to find a new strategy that would impose some order (and greater social control) on what had become viewed as an overextended and confused privatization effort. Privatization was not the only aspect of the previous governments' economic program subject to reconsideration, however. The parliamentary coalition that created the Olszewski government was elected on the slogan of a *przelom* (break) with the policies of 1990–1991, which were thought to have contributed to the severity of the recession and the damage it wreaked upon Polish industry.[14]

The Olszewski government's efforts during the first months of 1992 focused on redrawing the administrative and legislative frameworks for privatization. A reorganization of the central administration was planned, in part to place privatization policy into a unified, integrated economic decisionmaking process. The Ministries of Ownership Transformation, Industry and Trade, Housing and Spatial Affairs and perhaps External Economic Relations were to be merged with the Central Planning Office, in order to create a Ministry of the Economy that would act as a "single decisionmaking center." According to its proponents, this reorganization would allow decisions about privatization to be better made in tandem with macroeconomic policy, industrial policy, and policies toward foreign trade and capital. Redrawing the legislative framework for privatization in turn was intended to resolve the reprivatization question, which had not been effectively addressed by the previous governments.

New legislation and administrative reform were seen as necessary to clarify the nature of state property and the state's ownership responsibilities. This reflected the belief that privatization can not succeed if the state does not act like a "real owner." The "state treasury" was to be that "single owner" necessary to improve the state sector's efficiency. While the Ministry for Ownership Transformation (or that section of the Economics Ministry responsible for privatization) would continue to determine the general framework of privatization policy, the State Treasury, acting as the owner of state property, would function as a commercial agency within that framework. Local divisions of the State Treasury would contract with private actors (similar to the managerial groups introduced under restructuring privatization) that would actually sell (or rent) state property. The local divisions of the State Treasury would themselves be structured as joint-stock companies, with up to 49 percent of the stock held privately. This would ensure that the State Treasury would function as a commercial agency, rather than as a bureaucracy.

By April 1992, however, plans for redrawing the administrative and legislative frameworks had been placed on the back burner, and emphasis began to return to programs begun in 1991. The role of liquidation privatization was slated to expand due to the deterioration of enterprise profitability linked to the recession. Thirty to forty firms were expected to be sold via public offer in 1992, and this was to provide the bulk of the six trillion zloty (approximately $440 million) in anticipated privatization revenues. Sectoral privatization was slated in some 400 firms from 30 industrial and agricultural branches. The privatization of state-owned banking and foreign trade enterprises was to begin in 1992 as well. With the exception of suspending the proposal to create the Ministry of the Economy, these programs were by and large continued in the second half of 1992 by Lewandowski, who returned to the position of Minister of Ownership Transformation in the Suchocka government.

Despite its problems, the mass privatization program was again emphasized by the Olszewski and Suchocka governments. Some 173 firms on the mass privatization "list" had been commercialized by March 1992, and as of October 1992 the list had expanded to 600 firms. Some lessons were learned from the difficulties encountered in 1991. In contrast to the original version, mass privatization in 1992 abandoned the free universal distribution of stock in the property boards (now renamed "national investment funds" in order to make them seem more like commercial organizations and less like state bureaucracies). Stock in these funds was to be sold at prices equal to 5 to 20 percent of either the stock's value or the average monthly wage. The selection of fund managers was to be depoliticized, with a qualifying commission composed of some twenty "financial specialists, economists, lawyers, and representatives of the state administration and private business" selecting Polish and foreign managers for the funds.[15] Steps were also taken to prevent the funds from becoming owners of entire branches of industry.

The Olszewski government's reappraisal of Poland's privatization strategy thus failed to produce a breakthrough. Moreover, the search for a new approach and the public reconsideration of some of the previous government's privatization decisions did slow the process down further, and added to the uncertainty and suspicion surrounding privatization. Lewandowski signalled his desire to accelerate the process upon his return to the Ministry of Ownership Transformation in July 1992, but quickly found himself enveloped by other events. These included strikes during July–August 1992 at a number of commercialized state enterprises (including the *Polska Miedz* copper complex and the FSO automobile factory),[16] as well as a report issued in September by the Supreme

Control Chamber (NIK) charging the Ministry of Ownership Transformation with numerous types of malfeasance during Lewandowski's tenure in 1991. As of October 1992, legislation authorizing the reprivatization and mass privatization programs had yet to be approved by the Sejm.

Unresolved Issues in Polish Privatization

Reprivatization

Reprivatization, concerning the restitution of (or compensation for) properties expropriated by the government during and after the Second World War to their former owners, has been the greatest weakness of Poland's privatization efforts.[17] In contrast to Czechoslovakia and Hungary, where the reprivatization question was legally addressed at an early stage in the privatization process, the issue continued to hang over Poland's privatization effort like a sword of Damocles in late 1992, some three years after the collapse of state socialism. Failure to resolve this issue cast a long shadow over other privatization programs, especially in such areas as housing and agriculture.

The reasons for this delay were both political and economic. Dispossessed owners (and their heirs) formed a powerful lobby aimed at reclaiming their lost properties, and have received a good deal of support from the general public and influential politicians, including Solidarity leader and then President Lech Wałesa. Demands have been made for compensation for the confiscation during and immediately after the Second World War of properties which, as a result of Poland's border changes sanctioned at Yalta, found themselves located in the (former) Soviet Union. In addition to considerations of justice, advocates have touted reprivatization as a quick method for expanding Poland's entrepreneurial community and/or middle class.

All four post-communist governments resisted these arguments, for a number of reasons. Returning state property that could otherwise be sold reduces the budgetary revenue privatization is expected to produce. Offering financial compensation to former owners further increases the budgetary burden. Perhaps most important is the fear that acknowledging the legitimacy of reprivatization claims could forestall other forms of privatization and create a bureaucratic morass. How can title be definitively proved to a piece of property that has undergone significant changes during 45 years? What should be done about state-financed modernization and expansion of facilities taken from private owners 45 years ago? What if the former owners were foreigners, or collaborated with the Nazis during World War II?

The sheer number of claims could be a large part of the problem. A representative of the Agricultural and Food Processing Ministry announced in April 1992 that some 17,000 restitution claims had been filed with the Ministry for confiscated land alone. Jerzy Grohman, President Walesa's privatization plenipotentiary during the Bielecki government, estimated that the total number of claims could reach 500,000. (Some 750,000 compensation claims were filed in Hungary in 1991, for example.) The costs of adjudicating this mess and compensating former owners could go as high as 250 trillion zloty (approximately $18.5 billion, which is equivalent to about 40% of Poland's gross foreign debt). And if other legal bases for claims are recognized, such as bonds issued by the pre-war Second Republic or the currencies in use in Poland during the second world war, the costs of reprivatization could rise to 400 trillion zloty (approximately $30 billion).

Faced with these dilemmas, the Mazowiecki and Bielecki governments tried to adjudicate restitution claims on the basis of pre-war legislation. Physical restitution was limited to properties whose expropriation was clearly illegal at the time of seizure, and whose return is not clouded by issues of property alteration or modernization. Cases of property alteration or modernization were to be resolved by privatization vouchers, although neither government was able to pass legislation authorizing and spelling out the details of this procedure. The Olszewski government placed greater emphasis upon restitution in kind, but its bill was rejected in parliament as well.

Privatization in Agriculture

Little progress was made in agricultural privatization prior to 1992, due both to opposition on the part of the 2000 state farms (cultivating approximately 15 percent of Poland's agricultural land) as well as official uncertainty about the best way to proceed. However, the Sejm approved legislation in October 1991 authorizing the privatization of the state farms and creating the Agricultural Property Agency which, beginning in 1992, acts as the equivalent of the Ministry of Ownership Transformation in supervising the transformation of agricultural property. In order to counter opposition from farm personnel, the farms' housing stock is to be separated from other properties and offered for sale to tenants, many of whom are retired farm employees, at preferential prices. The proceeds from property sales and rentals are to be used to finance agricultural restructuring.

The Agricultural Property Agency possesses sweeping powers. In addition to obtaining all the land in the state land fund, the Agency will assume the role of owner vis-à-vis all state farms by the end of 1993. Farms are either to be sold in their entirety, leased, or run by administrators appointed by the Agency on the basis of managerial contracts. The

Agency is authorized to emit bonds (which are to ultimately be repur-chased by the government, if necessary) in order to finance the restruc-turing and recapitalization of state farms, many of which were on the brink of bankruptcy in mid-1992. While sales of physical assets are autho-rized by the October 1991 legislation, the farms are by and large to main-tain their physical integrity; the "parcelization" of the state farms' land and capital stock is not anticipated.

Privatization via Foreign Capital

Poland's performance in attracting foreign capital since the PUWP lost power in August 1989 has been mixed at best. On the one hand, the num-ber of partly- and wholly-owned foreign firms in Poland has increased substantially since 1988. Some 1400 joint ventures applied for registration with the authorities from January 15, 1989 to March 31, 1990; some 1146 applications were approved. Some 2480 new joint ventures were regis-tered in 1990,[18] and the total number of joint ventures had risen to 7648 at the end of June 1992.

On the other hand, the value of the capital created through direct foreign investment at the end of 1991 was estimated at $800 million,[19] a paltry figure in comparison with Poland's pressing need for, as well as capacity to absorb, foreign capital. By way of comparison, Hungary, although a fraction of Poland's size, attracted $1.7 billion in direct foreign investment in 1991 alone, bringing its cumulative total up to some $3 bil-lion.[20] The joint venture between *Volkswagen* and the *Skoda* automobile works alone will ultimately account for an estimated $6.5 billion in direct and financial foreign investment in Czechoslovakia. According to West-ern press reports, Poland's $21 in per capita direct foreign investment in 1991 was 50 percent of the Czechoslovak level and only 10 percent of the Hungarian level.[21] The relatively small size of direct foreign investment in Poland is reflected in the small-scale nature of many projects. Only 0.5 percent of the projects exceeded $3 million in value in 1991, for example.[22]

This ambiguous record with joint ventures reflects in part the political instability that has characterized post-communist Poland. Four different post-communist governments have held power since August 1989; none has had a strong parliamentary base. Poland between mid-1989 and mid-1992 had five finance ministers, three central bank presidents, five minis-ters for external economic relations, and six ministers of industry. Despite important increases in Poland's external creditworthiness during 1990–1991, the disorder into which Poland's macroeconomic house has fallen since mid-1991 (during which time the budget deficit spiraled out of con-trol and aid from the IMF was suspended) has not helped Poland's stat-ure in the eyes of the international financial community.

Fears of foreign (and especially German) capital have imposed additional constraints on policies towards direct foreign investment. Although Poland's need for capital, technology and know-how is undeniable (and proximity to Germany affords Poland certain advantages in this regard) opening the door to direct foreign investment raises political questions about possible reductions in Polish sovereignty vis-à-vis Germany. The imperative of preventing Poland from becoming an economic appendage of Germany has been used as a justification for restrictions on foreign investment.[23] These include the (subsequently abolished) requirement in the July 1990 privatization legislation that foreign purchases of more than 10 percent of privatized state enterprises had to be approved by the central authorities. The Sejm in May 1992 passed legislation which would force foreigners to divest themselves of holdings in the most strategic of Poland's industries—casinos. And foreign firms and individuals must obtain permission from the Ministry of Internal Affairs in order to purchase land in Poland. Only 1100 hectares of Polish land passed into foreign ownership during 1990–1991. Restraints on land ownership are often cited as major obstacles in attracting greenfield investment.

Despite these restrictions, the trend towards liberalizing the regulatory environment for foreign capital that began with passage of joint venture legislation in 1986 accelerated after 1990. Poland's 1988 joint venture law (which was then quite liberal by East European standards) was further liberalized in June 1991. Among other things, this legislation removed restrictions imposed on foreign ownership in privatized firms by the July 1990 privatization laws, so that the restrictions applying to foreign stockholders are the same as those affecting Polish citizens or firms.[24] The 1991 legislation also abolished the minimum capital requirement ($50,000) for direct foreign investments, reduced the number of sectors for which direct foreign investment must receive official permission,[25] and authorized the yearly repatriation of zloty profits in foreign exchange purchased in Polish banks. (Foreign exchange can also be purchased when the joint venture or foreign firms is liquidated, or when foreigners sell stock in the company.) And tax holidays may be granted by the Minister of Finance if the size of the foreign investment exceeds 2 million ECU's (approximately $2.4 million), if the venture has an important technology-transfer component, or if it is located in an area of high unemployment.

These changes seem to have had a salutary effect in 1991, as the amount of direct foreign investment in that year approximately doubled. Important deals were consummated in steel, automobiles, food processing and telecommunications industries during 1991–1992. The June 1991 law and the agreement on Poland's associate membership in the European Community initialed in December 1991 could prove to be major stimuli for direct foreign investment in Poland. However, much still depends upon preventing further declines in macroeconomic and political stability.

Privatization in Poland: An Assessment

Privatization in Poland during 1990–1992 was characterized by the development of numerous innovative, often grandiose programs and the simultaneous failure of most of them to have much of an impact upon state enterprises. Instead, the decentralized, relatively straightforward liquidation-privatization and small privatization procedures have been the most successful programs, in terms of transferring state property to private hands. However, since both programs make extensive use of long-term leasing arrangements (rather than outright sales) questions have been raised about the desirability, authenticity and permanence of these solutions.[26]

In addition to providing a mechanism for bankrupting insolvent firms and reallocating their assets, liquidation served a convenient avenue for privatizing relatively healthy small and medium-sized firms as well. Of the 1055 firms slated for liquidation-privatization through February 1992, only 589 were classified as bankruptcies. Liquidation-privatization offers state firms the chance to correct the mistakes of previous central investment decisions by restructuring their capital stock. Perhaps most importantly, liquidation-privatization acquired a momentum of its own: approximately 20 requests for liquidation were arriving daily at the Ministry of Ownership Transformation during fall 1991. According to Poland's Central Planning Office, 80 percent of the state enterprises whose privatization had been authorized by the Ministry of Ownership Transformation between July 1990 and June 1991 took the liquidation route. Liquidation-privatization was initiated in 932 state firms during 1991, and in another 105 during the first two months of 1992.

The vast majority of the firms privatized through this method have been "insider" jobs, although outside investors play an important role in many cases. Assets in 354 of the 932 firms under liquidation in 1991 were in fact transferred to corporations owned mostly by the firms' workers; managerial buyouts (or leaseouts) comprised another important share of the total. This indicates that the managerial and worker-ownership conceptions rejected during the 1989–1990 political battle over spontaneous privatization may have proven stronger than the policies intended to prevent them.

On the other hand, out of the 1055 state enterprises in which liquidation-privatization proceedings were initiated through February 1992, significant asset sales took place in only 510 of them. Because of the relatively large scale upon which liquidation-privatization has been applied and the speed with which it has moved, the Ministry of Ownership Transformation has been unable to thoroughly monitor the use of state property transferred to the private sector. This has led to numerous allegations of abuse by the private firms leasing the property in question. According to some observers, liquidation-privatization allows insiders to "piratize" state enterprises' most profitable assets and activities, leaving the state holding the bag when the lease expires.

Small privatization—the sale or lease of state-owned housing, stores, shops and small firms to single individuals or small groups of private investors—is also regarded as a success. Approximately 35,000 state-owned and cooperative stores were transferred to private hands in 1990, some through leases, others through outright sales.[27] Lewandowski announced in September 1991 that 75 percent of retail trade was back in "private hands." However, progress with small privatization has been rather uneven. Local officials in some areas resist small privatization, and local governments often seem to prefer to lease state-owned shops and stores rather than sell them. The end result is that, as with privatization via liquidation, small-scale "privatization" often leaves property in state ownership. Poland's Central Planning Office announced in October 1991 that "there are *wojewodztwa* (counties) where not a single store has been sold."[28] Moreover, whereas leasing arrangements made under privatization through liquidation often break up state firms' assets, thus reducing the state's direct control over the properties in question, small privatization via leasing is more likely to leave the physical structures (and thus control) intact.

So while important progress was made in some areas, the failure to resolve the uncertainty surrounding mass privatization and reprivatization has left Poland's privatization program in a state of confusion. This is most apparent in reprivatization, which is unlikely to be resolved before 1994 (five years after the collapse of communism) at the earliest. Questions of timeliness also pertain to the mass privatization program, since, as of October 1992, the legislation needed to create the investment funds still had not been passed. Even with this legislation, however, the program is unlikely to really privatize any state enterprises prior to 1994, as the 1992–1993 period would be devoted to the creation and management of the investment funds.[29] This means that some firms on the mass privatization list could remain there in limbo for as long as three years before being entrusted to an investment fund. And even after the legislative framework has been created, effective managerial control over the investment funds and the firms in their portfolio is unlikely to develop quickly.

Moreover, because the general legal framework created by the July 1990 legislation did not impose a well-defined structure on the various privatization processes that developed during 1990–1991, the large number of state agencies that became involved in the process added to the confusion. According to Tomasz Gruszecki, the Olszewski government's Director of the Ministry of Ownership Transformation, more than sixty different central and local organs in 1992 could influence or impede privatization deals. And powerful trade union and workers' council officials within firms often acted as a brake upon entrepreneurial managers seeking to privatize their firms.[30] As of October 1992, these problems had yet to be resolved.

A final question concerns the Ministry of Ownership Transformation's ability to police the privatization process. Although the Ministry was created to prevent the abuses associated with spontaneous privatization during 1989–1990, few observers would maintain that the Ministry has been able to guarantee the integrity of the process. In effect, the Ministry has been so engrossed in designing and implementing privatization programs that it has been unable to supervise the privatization of numerous smaller firms. The harried local authorities have also been preoccupied with other matters, and have generally been unable to closely supervise the privatization of firms under their jurisdiction. Moreover, the difficulties in selling large firms either via foreign investment or mass privatization meant that more and more commercialized state enterprises had no prospects for immediate sale. Since these firms are directly subordinated to the Ministry of Ownership Transformation, ministerial officials in mid-1992 seemed to be progressively more engrossed with the problems of supervising the operation of these firms, rather than supervising the privatization process *per se.*

Obtaining official approval for privatization in many cases was thus a *pro forma* matter. According to accounts in the Polish press, this lack of close supervision led to a series of questionable practices. These included the routine bribing of officials conducting the sale of state property;[31] habitual undervaluation of the assets belonging to state enterprises (in order to sweeten the deal for the private firms or individuals acquiring the firm or its assets); placing ministerial or local officials (as well as members of parliament) on the board of directors of the new firms; and incestuous relationships between the local authorities and the consulting firms evaluating the net worth of enterprises to be privatized. Since enterprise managers and workers frequently became the privatized firms' new owners, there is frequently no one to look after the state's interests as the owner of state property.

The Ministry's inability to guarantee the integrity of the privatization process partially undermines its own *raison d'être.* Does it make sense to entrust privatization to a bureaucracy which slows the process down without really cleaning it up? If, on the other hand, some sort of bureaucratic control over the process is politically inevitable, the fact that the pace of privatization exceeds the Ministry's ability to control it may not necessarily be a bad thing.

In effect, the Polish privatization effort in late 1992 seemed to face two options: (1) state-controlled "outsider" privatization, which centralizes the process without guaranteeing its integrity; and (2) decentralized "insider" types of privatization that would benefit primarily enterprise managers and workers. While probably being a more corrupt form of privatization, the "insider" approach would probably occur more rapidly and in a less costly manner. If the second approach may be less feasible politically, the first approach has been unable to resolve the economic and political questions confronting it since it was introduced in 1990. The resulting slow pace may itself be the major threat to the privatization process.[32]

These unanswered questions show that creating industrial capitalism out of state enterprises is a very difficult task, and that promoting the development of the indigenous private sector may be the only mechanism for rapidly transforming ownership relations in the post-communist economy. The Polish experience can thus be used to support arguments advanced by Murrell, Ickes and Ryterman that large-scale privatization programs are not effective avenues for supporting the growth of the private sector.[33]

On the other hand, the successes of liquidation and small privatization indicate that decentralized programs promoting insider privatization can provide such a mechanism. This implies that privatization could be accelerated by breaking up the large industrial firms into smaller units that would be more amenable to small and liquidation privatization. The efficiency losses resulting from smaller production scales in these firms may be more than offset by the benefits of more rapid privatization. In fact, this process has been occurring in a more spontaneous form since 1989, as seen in the growth in the number of state enterprises and the progress with small and liquidation privatization. Despite the privatization of at least 1200 firms since 1990, the number of state enterprises increased by 10 percent (from 8000 to almost 8800) by mid-1992. This was because market forces forced many large state enterprises to spin off smaller production units that, once becoming autonomous firms in their own right, are more amenable to liquidation or, less frequently, small privatization. This implies that shifting the emphasis away from large-scale privatization towards demonopolization and decentralized privatization programs may be an effective method of accelerating the development of the private sector.

Notes

1. "Statystyka Polski," supplement to *Rzeczpospolita* (August 4, 1992): iv. This chapter makes extensive use of Polish press accounts which, for reasons of space, can not be cited here. Much of this literature is cited in Ben Slay, "Privatization in Poland: An Overview," *RFE/RL Research Report* 1, no. 17 (1992): 15–21; and "Poland: 'Mass Privatization' Unravels," *Report on Eastern Europe* 2, no. 44 (1991): 13–18.

2. Jadwiga Staniszkis, "'Political Capitalism' in Poland," *East European Politics and Societies* 5, no. 1 (Winter 1991): 127–141.

3. Anthony Levitas and Piotr Strzalkowski, "What Does 'uwlaszczenie nomenklatury' ('Propertisation of the *nomenklatura'*) Really Mean?," *Communist Economies* 2, no. 3 (1990): 413–416.

4. Jeffrey Sachs and David Lipton, "Privatization in Eastern Europe: The Case of Poland," *Brookings Papers on Economic Activity*, no. 2 (1990): 293–333.

5. For an excellent account of the economics and politics of this battle, see Janusz M. Dabrowski, Michal Federowicz and Anthony Levitas, "Polish State Enterprises and the Properties of Performance: Stabilization, Marketization, Privatization," manuscript, Center for International Affairs, Harvard University, May 1991.

6. Zbigniew M. Fallenbuchl, "Poland: The New Government and Privatization," *Report on Eastern Europe* 2, no. 12 (March 22, 1991), 11–12; and Ada Kostrz-Kostecka, "Co sie dzieje w gminie?" *Rzeczpospolita* (August 1, 1991). According to Fallenbuchl the local authorities in 1991 owned 700 public utilities; Kostrz-Kostecka put the figure at 900.

7. For example, under liquidation privatization a large shipping company could be privatized through the sale of its boats, planes and trucks—since markets for these goods function relatively well—rather than in its entirety. The latter would be a case of large privatization, and would face the obstacle of a lack of well-developed markets for the buying and selling of entire enterprises.

8. The Warsaw stock market re-opened on April 16, 1991, but is too small to have much of an impact on capital allocation. Weekly trading volume during the summer of 1991 rarely exceeded 4 billion zloty (approximately $360,000); as of March 1992, only eleven stocks were traded; and the market was only open two days per week. For more on the stock market, see Christopher Wellisz, "Warsaw's Bears and Bulls," *Report on Eastern Europe* 2, no. 34 (1991): 18–21.

9. According to various calculations, the savings of Polish households in 1991 were sufficient to purchase anywhere from two to fifteen percent of state enterprises, as measured by their book value. Even the high end of this range would be too small to purchase more than a small fraction of the firms to be privatized. For the two percent figure, see Tadeusz Kowalik, "The Costs of 'Shock Therapy': Economic Transition in Poland," *Dissent* (Fall 1991): 497–504. The 15 percent figure comes from "Survey: Business in Eastern Europe," *The Economist* (September 21, 1991): 15.

10. For more on workers' and managers' attitudes towards privatization, see Marek Kozak, "Social Support for Privatization in Poland," *Communist Economies and Economic Transformation* no. 2 (1991): 155–167.

11. Janusz Lewandowski & Jan Szomburg, "Uwlaszczenie jako fundament reformy spoleczno-gospodarczej," in *Propozycje przeksztalcen polskiej gospodarki,* 63–81 (Warsaw: Polish Economics Association: 1989).

12. For more on mass privatization in 1991, see Ben Slay, "Poland: 'Mass Privatization' Unravels."

13. For more on Poland's monopoly problem, see Ben Slay, "Monopoly and Marketization in Polish Industry," *Jahrbuch der Wirtschaft Osteuropas* 14, no. 1 (1990): 58–84, and Mark E. Schaffer, "State-Owned Enterprises in Poland: Taxation, Subsidization and Competition Policies" *European Economy* no. 43 (March 1990): 183–201.

14. Ben Slay, "The Rise and Fall of the Balcerowicz Plan," *RFE/RL Research Report* (January 31, 1992): 40–47.

15. A. Kostrz-Kostecka, "Powszechna prywatyzacja: Przed przetargiem," *Rzeczpospolita* (February 28, 1992).

16. For more on the strikes, see Anna Sabbat-Swidlicka, "Summer Strikes: First Test for New Polish Government," *RFE/RL Research Report* no. 34 (August 28, 1992).

17. Christopher Wellisz, "The Perils of Restitution," *Report on Eastern Europe* no. 32 (August 9, 1991): 1–5.

18. Patrice Dabrowski, "The Foreign Investment Boom," *Report on Eastern Europe* (July 26, 1991): 36.

19. Philippa Fletcher, "Investment Eludes East European Reform Pioneer," *Reuter* (April 22, 1992).

20. Nicolas Denton, "A Kiss of Life From Across the Border," *Financial Times* (April 21, 1992).

21. P. Fletcher, "Investment Eludes East European Reform Pioneer."

22. P. Dabrowski, "The Foreign Investment Boom."

23. Public-opinion surveys indicate that fear of foreign ownership is fairly widespread in Poland. According to a 1990 survey conducted by Warsaw's Center for Public Opinion Research, more than one-third of the respondents believed that only "some" purchases should be allowed. See Market Kozak, "Social Support for Privatization in Poland," *Communist Economies and Economic Transformation* no. 2 (1991): 155–167.

24. These restrictions pertain to the purchases of large bundles of stock in Polish firms. They include the requirement that the Anti-Monopoly Office and the Securities Commission must be informed about purchases of between 10 to 75 percent of the preferred stock in a corporation (as must a general meeting of the shareholders). Large shares of stock may only be purchased after a public announcement of the buyer's intention has been made (presumably this is meant to prevent insider trading).

25. Areas for which direct foreign investment remains subject to Polish approval include air and sea ports, real estate, some parts of the defense industry, wholesale trade of imported consumer goods, and legal services.

26. For a more general investigation of the disadvantages of leasing as a method of privatizing state firms, see Chapter 7.

27. Z.M. Fallenbuchl, "The New Government and Privatization," 14.

28. "Centralny Urzad Planowania: O prywatyzacji i zmianach strukturalnych w gospodarce," *Wspolnota* (October 5, 1991).

29. "Poland Gears Up For Mass Privatization," *PlanEcon Business Report* (February 19, 1992): 1–2.

30. Wojciech Bienkowski, "Poland's Bermuda Triangle," *RFE/RL Research Report* no. 17 (April 24, 1992): 22–24.

31. According to one account, the costs of becoming the owner of a (formerly) state-owned store in a choice location include bribes ranging from $10,000 to $50,000 in value. See "Ile, komu, za co?" *Kurier Polski* (October 28, 1991).

32. J. Sachs and D. Lipton, "Privatization."

33. See Peter Murrell, "Privatization Complicates the Fresh Start," *Orbis* (Summer 1992): 323–332; and Barry Ickes and Randi Ryterman, "Credit for Small Firms, Not Dinosaurs," *Orbis* (Summer 1992): 333–348.

Afterword: On the Future of Private Entrepreneurship in Former Command Economies

Perry L. Patterson

Based on the chapters in this book, it is possible to reach quite varied conclusions about the prospects for the private sectors of the former socialist countries. For those who remember what Soviet and East European socialism was like ten years ago, the evidence presented here summarizes a virtual revolution in cultural attitudes about the economy and the proper role of government intervention therein. Had the preceding chapters been written as late as, say, 1987, the degree of progress documented here would have seemed nothing less than phenomenal. Thus it is strange, in one sense, that this book is peppered with allusions to corruption, to the continuing role of the *nomenklatura*, to the defective functioning of the private sector, and the like.

It would seem that the standards we apply to the former socialist countries have changed almost as radically as have those economies themselves. This is probably due to more than generalized impatience in the West. More likely, it is the acceleration of desires in Eastern Europe and the former Soviet Union to become more and more integral parts of the world economic community which has brought ever-closer scrutiny of the emerging markets. If, for example, Russia is to receive International Monetary Fund credits for support of a convertible ruble, the international community (via its taxpayers) will insist on a full accounting of what is being done with the money. This form of openness is something to which few of the states of the region (with the possible exception of Poland, Hungary, and Yugoslavia) are accustomed. Yet, full access to world markets will require change that goes well beyond what has been accomplished to date. Thus, the contributors to this volume are quite justified in their suspicions about the current state of private markets and entrepreneurship in the region.

In Chapter 1 (p. 12), we raised a series of questions about the directions and prospects for the new private sectors of Eastern Europe and the former Soviet Union. The provisional answers which the authors of this volume provide are of the following sort:

1. The private sector has grown fastest to date in industries which have required the least capital input, and where ideological and technical concerns have been relatively minor. Thus, small labor-intensive firms have been much easier to create than those requiring large amounts of land or equipment, or requiring a difficult selloff or conversion to some form of joint-stock ownership. In addition, private firms with continued access to state resources have grown particularly rapidly, though not always with desirable social results.

2. State policies have had numerous negative impacts on the development of a healthy, growing, competitive private sector. These include, but are certainly not limited to: an unstable taxation and regulatory environment; a favoring of state-owned and large firms when granting credit; a failure to vigorously pursue anti-monopoly policies; and a refusal to make land and other state-owned property available for sale to private firms. However, it should be noted that private firms have often been subject to noticeably *less* regulation than the remaining state firms.

3. Those remaining state firms interact with the new private sector in complex ways. For both technical and financial reasons, it has proven difficult to mount massive privatization of the large state firms. Furthermore, such firms seem likely to drain off credit resources which might otherwise be available for the private sector. Thus, the large state firms are neither a major direct source of private enterprise formation nor a contributor to private-sector credit access. However, we also find state- and private-sector firms increasingly interdependent on each other, as insiders at state firms form small private working groups attached to the state firm, and as private firms gradually become both suppliers and customers to state firms. Thus, the relationship between the two sectors remains ambiguous.

Perhaps surprisingly, the authors of the preceding chapters would not be likely to agree if asked for a prediction regarding the near- or long-term prosperity of the former socialist countries. Some would cite the evidence above as an indication of the extreme reluctance of the state in

Eastern Europe to give up its direct control over the economy, and of the strong incentives for current bureaucrats to hold onto their lucrative decisionmaking authority. They would also cite opinion polls like those seen here, which indicate a continuing high degree of distrust of markets among the populations of the former socialist states. Thus the future would seem to be a pseudo-capitalism hobbled by a meddling state and run by corrupt insiders.

None of the analyses in this book predicts such an outcome, however. It is quite possible to interpret the current ill-defined state of the private sector as merely the inevitable but transient result of a process of radically shifting patterns of ownership and control within the former socialist states. That is, an environment in which the bulk of a nation's property is suddenly "up for grabs" will inevitably produce a lot of "grabbing," or lobbying, rent-seeking, bribe-taking, etc., until clear title to property is reestablished. Since the general direction of change is toward private ownership, even those owners who have received property unfairly may ultimately face the sorts of incentives faced by any private entrepreneur in the West. That is, their attention may ultimately turn to more productive directions than at present. One budding Russian capitalist, recently explaining his purported "sixty-man private security force," described his environment as "Chicago in the 1920s."[1] This does not sound very promising—until one remembers that a noticeably more prosperous and stable city arose in the Chicago of later decades.

Whatever the prospects for the Central and East European private sector, the richer nations of the world are going to be called upon repeatedly over the next decade to help repair the damages of pollution, of war, and of simple mismanagement throughout the former socialist nations. The debate, therefore, over how much help to provide, and in what form, has only just begun. While for the most part we do not seek to enter that debate here, we do hope that the discussion presented here will inform that debate, and contribute to a better understanding of the difficulties currently standing in the way of a truly flourishing private-sector future in the East.

Notes

1. Herman Sterligov, founder of *Alisa* network of commodity exchanges, cited in Paul Klebnikov, "A Market Grows in Russia," *Forbes* (June 8, 1992): 78–82.

About the Editor and Contributors

David L. Bartlett is assistant professor of Political Science at Vanderbilt University.

Evan Kraft is assistant professor of Economics at Salisbury State University.

Michael A. Murphy is assistant professor of Economics at Tufts University.

Perry L. Patterson is associate professor of Economics and lecturer in Russian at Wake Forest University.

Dennis A. Rondinelli is professor of International Business at the Kenan-Flagler Business School, University of North Carolina at Chapel Hill.

Ben Slay is assistant professor of Economics at Bates College.

Catherine Sokil-Milnikiewicz is assistant professor of Economics at Middlebury College.

John E. Tedstrom is research associate at the RAND Corporation.

Index